Advanced Information and Knowledge Processing

Series Editors
Professor Lakhmi Jain
Xindong Wu

Also in this series

Yannis Manolopoulos, Alexandros Nanopoulos,
Apostolos N. Papadopoulos and
Yannis Theodoridis

R-Trees: Theory and Applications

With 77 Figures

 Springer

Yannis Manolopoulos, PhD
Alexandros Nanopoulos, PhD
Apostolos N. Papadopoulos, PhD
Aristotle University of Thessaloniki, Greece

Yannis Theodoridis, PhD
University of Piraeus & Computer Technology Institute, Greece

British Library Cataloguing in Publication Data
A catalogue record for this book is available from the British Library

AI&KP ISSN 1610-3947

ISBN-10: 1-85233-977-2
ISBN-13: 978-1-84996-986-4   e-ISBN-13: 978-1-84628-293-5
Springer Science+Business Media
springeronline.com

34-543210   Printed on acid-free paper

Dedicated to our families.

Preface

Spatial data management has been an active area of intensive research for more than two decades. In order to support spatial objects in a database system several issues should be taken into consideration including spatial data models, indexing mechanisms, efficient query processing, and cost models. One of the most influential access methods in the area is the R-tree structure proposed by Guttman in 1984 as an effective and efficient solution to index rectangular objects in VLSI design applications. Since then several variations of the original structure have been proposed to provide more efficient access, handle objects in high-dimensional spaces, support concurrent accesses, support I/O and CPU parallelism, and support efficient bulk loading. It seems that due to the modern demanding applications and after academia paved the way, recently the industry has recognized the use and necessity of R-trees. The simplicity of the structure and its resemblance to the B-tree allowed developers to easily incorporate the structure into existing database management systems to support spatial query processing. In this book we provide an extensive survey of the R-tree evolution, studying the applicability of the structure and its variations to efficient query processing, accurate proposed cost models, and implementation issues like concurrency control and parallelism. Based on the observation that "space is everywhere", we anticipate that we are in the beginning of the era of the "ubiquitous R-tree" in an analogous manner as B-trees were considered 25 years ago.

Book Organization

The book contains nine chapters organized in four parts. We tried to keep each chapter self-contained to provide maximum reading flexibility.

The first part of the book contains some fundamental issues and is composed of three chapters. Chapter 1 is the introductory chapter. In this chapter we give a brief introduction to the area, present the basic notations and the corresponding descriptions, and present the original R-tree access method, which is the root of the family tree of access methods presented in the book. Chapter 2 is devoted to the description of the most promising dynamic variations of the R-tree. These methods support insertions, deletions, and updates and therefore can be effectively used in a dynamic environment. Static variations of the R-tree are given in Chapter 3. These variations are optimized taking into consideration that the dataset to be organized is given a priori.

The second part of the book is composed of two chapters and covers query processing techniques that have been proposed to operate with R-trees. Chapter 4 studies fundamental query types such as range queries, nearest-neighbor queries, and spatial join queries. Each method is studied in detail, and the corresponding algorithm is given in pseudo-code where appropriate. Chapter 5 explores more complex query types such as categorical range queries, multi-way spatial joins, closest-pair queries, incremental processing, and approximate query techniques. These queries are characterized by higher computation costs and greater complexity than the fundamental ones, and therefore are covered separately.

The adaptation of the R-tree to modern application domains is discussed in the third part, which comprises two chapters. Chapter 6 studies the application of R-tree-like access methods to spatiotemporal database systems. The fundamental characteristic of these systems is that they handle temporal information in addition to the spatial properties of objects. Chapter 7 discusses the use of R-trees in multimedia databases, data warehouses, and data mining tasks. The exploitation of the R-tree by the aforementioned domains has proven very promising to faster algorithms and query processing techniques, taking into consideration the complexity of objects and the computationally intensive operations required.

The last part of the book comprises two chapters. Chapter 8 studies query optimization issues for R-tree based query processing. Formulae are given for various query types that estimate the corresponding cost of the operation. These formulae are valuable for cost-based query optimization and selectivity estimation in modern database systems. Chapter 9 discusses some implementation issues regarding the R-tree access method. Many DBMS vendors have incorporated the R-tree as an indexing technique for non-traditional objects. Moreover, several research prototypes have implemented the R-tree to index spatial or multi-dimensional objects.

The Epilogue at the end of the book summarizes our work and gives some directions for future research in the area.

Intended Audience

We believe that this book (or parts of it) will be valuable to course instructors, undergraduate and postgraduate students studying access methods for advanced applications. Moreover, it will be a valuable companion to researchers and professionals working with access methods, because it presents in detail a broad range of concepts and techniques related to indexing, query processing, query optimization, and implementation. Finally, practitioners working in the development of access methods and database systems can use this book as a reference.

How to Study This Book

The order of presentation is the proposed reading order of the material. However, according to the reader's expertise in the area, it is possible to focus directly on the topic of interest by studying the corresponding chapters. Expert readers could skip the first part of the book, whereas non-experts are encouraged to start from the beginning. Evidently, if the reader wishes to study more details with respect to a specific topic, then the corresponding references should be consulted.

More precisely, undergraduate students can focus on Chapters 1 through 4 and Chapter 9 to grasp the main characteristics of the R-tree and related access methods, and to understand how query processing is performed in a spatial database system. Postgraduate students will find Chapters 5, 6, and 8 motivating for further research in the area, because efficientquery processing and optimization techniques are active research fields. Course instructors and researchers should study all the material to select parts of the book required for class presentation or further research in the area.

Acknowledgments

A significant number of the papers contributed by the authors of this effort were the outcome of research funded by the EU Chorochronos program.

We would like to thank the co-authors of our papers: P. Bozanis, S. Brakatsoulas, A. Corral, M. Egenhofer, C. Faloutsos, C. Gurret, Y. Karydis, N. Mamoulis, E. Nardelli, M. Nascimento, D. Papadias, D. Pfoser, G. Proietti, M. Ranganathan, P. Rigaux, J.R.O. Silva, M. Scholl, T. Sellis, E. Stefanakis, V. Vasaitis, M. Vassilakopoulos, and M. Vazirgiannis.

There are also several people who helped significantly in the preparation of this book. We take the opportunity to thank Antonio Corral for his contribution in approximate queries cost models for distance joins, and Elias Frentzos for his contribution in query optimization issues.

Finally, we would like to thank Catherine Drury and Michael Koy from Springer, for their great help and support toward the completion of this project. Their comments and suggestions were very helpful in improving the readability, organization, and overall view of the book.

We hope that this book will be a valuable reference to the expert reader and a motivating companion for the non-expert who whishes to study the theory and applications of the R-tree access method and its variations.

Yannis Manolopoulos, Thessaloniki, Greece
Alexandros Nanopoulos, Thessaloniki, Greece
Apostolos N. Papadopoulos, Thessaloniki, Greece
Yannis Theodoridis, Athens, Greece

Contents

Part II. QUERY PROCESSING ISSUES

Part III. R-TREES IN MODERN APPLICATIONS

Part IV. ADVANCED ISSUES

List of Figures

List of Tables

FUNDAMENTAL CONCEPTS

1. Introduction

The paper entitled "The ubiquitous B-tree" by Comer was published in *ACM Computing Surveys* in 1979 [49]. Actually, the keyword "B-tree" was standing as a generic term for a whole family of variations, namely the B*-tree, the B+-tree and several other variants [111]. The title of the paper might have seemed provocative at that time. However, it represented a big truth, which is still valid now, because all textbooks on databases or data structures devote a considerable number of pages to explain definitions, characteristics, and basic procedures for searches, inserts, and deletes on B-trees. Moreover, B+-trees are not just a theoretical notion. On the contrary, for years they have been the de facto standard access method in all prototype and commercial relational systems for typical transaction processing applications, although one could observe that some quite more elegant and efficient structures have appeared in the literature.

The 1980s were a period of wide acceptance of relational systems in the market, but at the same time it became apparent that the relational model was not adequate to host new emerging applications. Multimedia, CAD/CAM, geographical, medical and scientific applications are just some examples, in which the relational model had been proven to behave poorly. Thus, the object-oriented model and the object-relational model were proposed in the sequel. One of the reasons for the shortcoming of the relational systems was their inability to handle the new kinds of data with B-trees. More specifically, B-trees were designed to handle alphanumeric (i.e., one-dimensional) data, like integers, characters, and strings, where an ordering relation can be defined. A number of new B-tree variations have appeared in the literature to handle object-oriented data (see [25] for a comparative study). Mainly, these structures were aimed at hosting data of object hierarchies in a single structure. However, these efforts had limited applicability and could not cover the requirements of many new application areas.

In light of this evolution, entirely novel access methods were proposed, evaluated, compared, and established. One of these structures, the R-tree, was proposed by Guttman in 1984, aimed at handling geometrical data, such as points, line segments, surfaces, volumes, and hypervolumes in high-dimensional spaces [81]. R-trees were treated in the literature in much the same way as B-trees. In particular, many improving variations have been proposed for various instances and environments, several novel operations have been developed for them, and new cost models have been suggested.

It seems that due to modern demanding applications and after academia has paved the way, the industry recently recognized the use and necessity of R-trees. Thus, R-trees are adopted as an additional access method to handle multi-dimensional data. Based on the observation that "trees have grown everywhere" [212], we anticipate that we are in the beginning of the era of the "ubiquitous R-tree" in an analogous manner as B-trees were considered 25 years ago. Nowadays, spatial databases and geographical information systems have been established as a mature field, spatiotemporal databases and manipulation of moving points and trajectories are being studied extensively, and finally image and multimedia databases able to handle new kinds of data, such as images, voice, music, or video, are being designed and developed. An application in all these cases should rely on R-trees as a necessary tool for data storage and retrieval. R-tree applications cover a wide spectrum, from spatial and temporal to image and video (multimedia) databases. The initial application that motivated Guttman in his pioneering research was VLSI design (i.e., how to efficiently answer whether a space is already covered by a chip). Gradually, handling rectangles quickly found applications in geographical and, in general, spatial data, including GIS (buildings, rivers, cities, etc.), image or video/audio retrieval systems (similarity of objects in either original space or high-dimensional feature space), time series and chronological databases (time intervals are just 1D objects), and so on. Therefore, we argue that R-trees are found everywhere.

We begin the exploration of the R-tree world with Table 1.1, which shows all R-tree variations covered in this book. For each R-tree variation we give the author(s), the year of publication, and the corresponding reference number. In Table 1.2 we give the most important symbols and the corresponding descriptions used throughout the book. The next section presents the structure and basic characteristics of the original R-tree access method proposed in [81].

Table 1.1. Access methods covered in this book, ordered by year of publication.

Year	Access Method	Authors and References
1984	R-tree	Guttman [81]
1985	Packed R-tree	Roussopoulos, Leifker [199]
1987	R$^+$-tree	Sellis, Roussopoloulos, Faloutsos [211]
1989	Cell-tree	Guenther [77]
1990	P-tree	Jagadish, [96] (and 1993 Schiwietz [206])
1990	R*-tree	Beckmann, Kriegel, Schneider, Seeger [19]
1990	RT-tree	Xu, Han, Lu [249]
1990	Sphere-tree	Oosterom [164]
1992	Independent R-trees	Kamel, Faloutsos [103]
1992	MX R-tree	Kamel, Faloutsos [103]
1992	Supernode R-tree	Kamel, Faloutsos [103]
1993	Hilbert Packed R-tree	Kamel, Faloutsos [104]

Table 1.1. Access methods covered in this book, ordered by year of publication (continued).

Year	Access Method	Authors and References
1994	Hilbert R-tree	Kamel, Faloutsos [105]
1994	R-link	Ng, Kameda [161]
1994	TV-tree	Lin, Jagadish, Faloutsos [138]
1996	QR-tree	Manolopoulos, Nardelli, Papadopoulos, Proietti [146]
1996	SS-tree	White, Jain [245]
1996	VAMSplit R-tree	White, Jain [244]
1996	X-tree	Berchtold, Keim, Kriegel [24]
1996	3D R-tree	Theodoridis, Vazirgiannis, Sellis [238]
1997	Cubtree	Roussopoulos, Kotidis [198]
1997	Linear Node Splitting	Ang, Tan [11]
1997	S-tree	Aggrawal, Wolf, Wu, Epelman [5]
1997	SR-tree	Katayama, Satoh [108]
1997	STR R-tree	Leutenegger, Edgington, Lopez [134]
1998	Bitemporal R-tree	Kumar, Tsotras, Faloutsos [125]
1998	HR-tree	Nascimento, Silva [158, 159]
1998	Optimal Node Splitting	Garcia, Lopez, Leutenegger [71]
1998	R_a^*-tree	Juergens, Lenz [102]
1998	STLT	Chen, Choubey, Rundensteiner [42]
1998	TGS	Garcia, Lopez, Leutenegger [70]
1999	GBI	Choubey, Chen, Rundensteiner [47]
1999	R^{ST}-tree	Saltenis, Jensen [201]
1999	2+3 R-tree	Nascimento, Silva, Theodoridis [159]
2000	Branch Grafting	Schrek, Chen [208]
2000	Bitmap R-tree	Ang, Tan [12]
2000	TB-tree	Pfoser, Jensen, Theodoridis [189]
2000	TPR-tree	Saltenis, Jensen, Leutenegger, Lopez [202]
2001	aR-tree	Papadias, Kanlis, Zhang, Tao [170]
2001	Box-tree	Agarwal, deBerg, Gudmundsson, Hammar, Haverkort [4]
2001	Compact R-tree	Huang, Lin, Lin [93]
2001	CR-tree	Kim, Cha, Kwon [110]
2001	Efficient HR-tree	Tao, Papadias [222]
2001	MV3R-tree	Tao, Papadias [223]
2001	PPR-tree	Kollios, Tsotras, Gunopulos, Delis, Hadjieleftheriou [113]
2001	RS-tree	Park, Heu, Kim [184]
2001	SOM-based R-tree	Oh, Feng, Kaneko, Makinouchi [162]
2001	STAR-tree	Procopiuc, Agarwal, Har-Peled, [192]
2002	aP-tree	Tao, Papadias, Zhang, [228]
2002	Buffer R-tree	Arge, Hinrichs, Vahrenhold, Vitter, [16]
2002	cR-tree	Brakatsoulas, Pfoser, Theodoridis, [32]
2002	DR-tree	Lee, Chung, [133]
2002	HMM R-tree	Jin, Jagadish, [100]
2002	Lazy Update R-tree	Kwon, Lee, Lee, [127]
2002	Low Stabbing Number	deBerg, Hammar, Overmars, Gudmundsson, [56]
2002	VCI R-tree	Prabhakar, Xia, Kalashnikov, Aref, Hambrusch, [191]
2003	FNR-tree	Frentzos, [67]
2003	LR-tree	Bozanis, Nanopoulos, Manolopoulos, [31]
2003	OMT R-tree	Lee, Lee, [131]
2003	Partitioned R-tree	Bozanis, Nanopoulos, Manolopoulos, [31]
2003	Q+R-tree	Xia, Prabhakar, [248]
2003	Seeded Clustering	Lee, Moon, Lee, [132]
2003	SETI	Chakka, Everspaugh, Patel, [38]
2003	TPR*-tree	Tao, Papadias, Sun, [227]
2003	TR-tree	Park, Lee, [185]
2004	Merging R-trees	Vasatitis, Nanopoulos, Bozanis, [240]
2004	MON-tree	Almeida, Guting, [7]
2004	PR-tree	Arge, deBerg, Haverkort, Yi, [15]
2004	R^{PPF}-tree	Pelanis, Saltenis, Jensen, [188]
2004	VMAT	Gorawski, Malczok, [73, 74]

Table 1.2. Basic notation used throughout the study, listed in alphabetical order.

Symbol	Description
$\mathcal{B}$	set of buckets
B_i	a bucket
b	bucket capacity in bytes
c	R-tree leaf node capacity
C_{MJJ}	cost of a multi-way spatial join query
C_{NN}	cost of a nearest-neighbor query
C_{SJ}	cost of a pair-wise join query
C_W	cost of a window query
Den	density of dataset
d	dataset dimensionality
$\mathcal{E}$	set of node entries
e, E	R-tree node entry
$e.mbr, E.mbr$	R-tree node entry MBR
f	R-tree fanout (non-leaf node capacity)
FD_0	Hausdorff fractal dimension
FD_2	correlation fractal dimension
H	Hilbert value
h	R-tree height
k	number of nearest neighbors
L	R-tree leaf node
M	maximum number of entries in an R-tree node
m	minimum number of entries in an R-tree node
N	number of data objects (dataset cardinality)
n	total number of nodes
n_l	number of leaf nodes
o, O	data object
$o.mbr, O.mbr$	object minimum bounding rectangle (MBR)
oid	object identifier
ptr	pointer to a node
q, Q	query object (point/rectangle/polygon)
$q.mbr, Q.mbr$	query object MBR
r	data object (point/rectangle/polygon)
RN	R-tree node
$RN.mbr$	R-tree node MBR
RN_l	R-tree leaf node
$RN.type$	type of node (leaf or internal)
$\mathcal{RS}$	set of data rectangles
σ	selectivity of a spatial query
$\sigma(k)$	index selectivity for k-CP query
T	a tree
t_{end}	interval ending time
t_{start}	interval starting time

1.1 The Original R-tree

Although, nowadays the original R-tree [81] is being described in many standard textbooks and monographs on databases [130, 147, 203, 204], we briefly recall its basic properties. R-trees are hierarchical data structures based on B$^+$-trees. They are used for the dynamic organization of a set of d-dimensional geometric objects representing them by the minimum bounding d-dimensional rectangles (for simplicity, MBRs in the sequel). Each node of the R-tree corresponds to the MBR that bounds its children. The leaves of the tree contain pointers to the database objects instead of pointers to children nodes. The nodes are implemented as disk pages.

It must be noted that the MBRs that surround different nodes may overlap each other. Besides, an MBR can be included (in the geometrical sense) in many nodes, but it can be associated to only one of them. This means that a spatial search may visit many nodes before confirming the existence of a given MBR. Also, it is easy to see that the representation of geometric objects through their MBRs may result in false alarms. To resolve false alarms, the candidate objects must be examined. For instance, Figure 1.1 illustrates the case where two polygons do not intersect each other, but their MBRs do. Therefore, the R-tree plays the role of a filtering mechanism to reduce the costly direct examination of geometric objects.

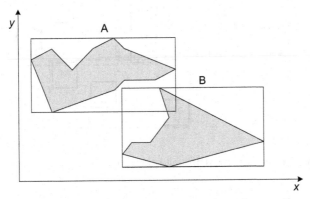

Fig. 1.1. An example of intersecting MBRs, where the polygons do not intersect.

An R-tree of order (m, M) has the following characteristics:

- Each leaf node (unless it is the root) can host up to M entries, whereas the minimum allowed number of entries is $m \leq M/2$. Each entry is of the form (mbr, oid), such that mbr is the MBR that spatially contains the object and oid is the object's identifier.
- The number of entries that each internal node can store is again between $m \leq M/2$ and M. Each entry is of the form (mbr, p), where p is a pointer to a child of the node and mbr is the MBR that spatially contains the MBRs contained in this child.

– The minimum allowed number of entries in the root node is 2, unless it is a
  leaf (in this case, it may contain zero or a single entry).
– All leaves of the R-tree are at the same level.

From the definition of the R-tree, it follows that it is a height-balanced tree.
As mentioned, it comprises a generalization of the B^+-tree structure for many
dimensions. R-trees are dynamic data structures, i.e., global reorganization is
not required to handle insertions or deletions.

Figure 1.2 shows a set of the MBRs of some data geometric objects (not
shown). These MBRs are $D, E, F, G, H, I, J, K, L, M$, and N, which will be
stored at the leaf level of the R-tree. The same figure demonstrates the three
MBRs $(A, B,$ and $C)$ that organize the aforementioned rectangles into an internal node of the R-tree. Assuming that $M = 4$ and $m = 2$, Figure 1.3 depicts
the corresponding MBR. It is evident that several R-trees can represent the
same set of data rectangles. Each time, the resulting R-tree is determined by
the insertion (and/or deletion) order of its entries.

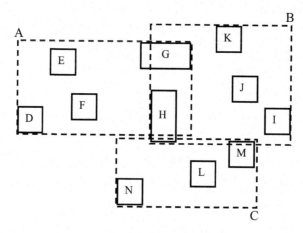

Fig. 1.2. An example of data MBRs and their MBRs.

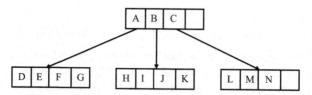

Fig. 1.3. The corresponding R-tree.

Let an R-tree store N data rectangles. In this case the maximum value for
its height h is:

$$h_{\max} = \lceil \log_m N \rceil - 1 \qquad (1.1)$$

The maximum number of nodes can be derived by summing the maximum possible number of nodes per level. This number comes up when all nodes contain the minimum allowed number of entries, i.e., m. Therefore, it results that the maximum number of nodes in an R-tree is equal to:

$$\sum_{i=1}^{h_{\max}} \lceil N/m^i \rceil = \lceil N/m \rceil + \lceil N/m^2 \rceil + \ldots + 1$$

Given a rectangle, Q, we can form the following query: find all data rectangles that are intersected by Q. This is denoted as a range (or window) query. The algorithm that processes range queries in an R-tree is given in Figure 1.4. For a node entry $E, E.mbr$ denotes the corresponding MBR and $E.p$ the corresponding pointer to the next level. If the node is a leaf, then $E.p$ denotes the corresponding object identifier (*oid*).

Algorithm RangeSearch(TypeNode RN**, TypeRegion** Q**)**
/* Finds all rectangles that are stored in an R-tree with root node RN, which are intersected by a query rectangle Q. Answers are stored in the set $\mathcal{A}$ */

1.   **if** RN is not a leaf node
2.   examine each entry e of RN to find those $e.mbr$ that intersect Q
3.   **foreach** such entry e call RangeSearch($e.ptr$,Q)
4.   **else** // RN is a leaf node
5.   examine all entries e and find those for which $e.mbr$ intersects Q
6.   add these entries to the answer set $\mathcal{A}$
7.   **endif**

Fig. 1.4. The R-tree range search algorithm.

We note that the rectangles that are found by range searching constitute the candidates of the filtering step. The actual geometric objects intersected by the query rectangle have to be found in a refinement step by retrieving the objects of the candidate rectangles and testing their intersection.

Insertions in an R-tree are handled similarly to insertions in a B$^+$-tree. In particular, the R-tree is traversed to locate an appropriate leaf to accommodate the new entry. The entry is inserted in the found leaf and, then all nodes within the path from the root to that leaf are updated accordingly. In case the found leaf cannot accommodate the new entry because it is full (it already contains M entries), then it is split into two nodes. Splitting in R-trees is different from that of the B$^+$- tree, because it considers different criteria. The algorithm for inserting a new data rectangle in an R-tree is presented in Figure 1.5.

The aforementioned insertion algorithm uses the so-called *linear split* algorithm (it has linear time complexity). The objective of a split algorithm is to minimize the probability of invoking both created nodes (L_1 and L_2) for

---

Algorithm Insert(TypeEntry E, TypeNode RN)
/* Inserts a new entry E in an R-tree with root node RN */

1. Traverse the tree from root RN to the appropriate leaf. At each level, select the node, L, whose MBR will require the minimum area enlargement to cover $E.mbr$
2. In case of ties, select the node whose MBR has the minimum area
3. **if** the selected leaf L can accommodate E
4.   Insert E into L
5.   Update all MBRs in the path from the root to L, so that all of them cover $E.mbr$
6. **else** // L is already full
7.   Let $\mathcal{E}$ be the set consisting of all L's entries and the new entry E
         Select as seeds two entries $e_1, e_2 \in \mathcal{E}$, where the distance between e_1 and e_2 is the maximum among all other pairs of entries from $\mathcal{E}$
         Form two nodes, L_1 and L_2, where the first contains e_1 and the second e_2
8.   Examine the remaining members of $\mathcal{E}$ one by one and assign them to L_1 or L_2, depending on which of the MBRs of these nodes will require the minimum area enlargement so as to cover this entry
9.   **if** a tie occurs
10.   Assign the entry to the node whose MBR has the smaller area
11.   **endif**
12.   **if** a tie occurs again
13.   Assign the entry to the node that contains the smaller number of entries
14.   **endif**
15.   **if** during the assignment of entries, there remain λ entries to be assigned and the one node contains $m - \lambda$ entries
16.   Assign all the remaining entries to this node without considering the aforementioned criteria
             /* so that the node will contain at least m entries */
17.   **endif**
18.   Update the MBRs of nodes that are in the path from root to L, so as to cover L_1 and accommodate L_2
19.   Perform splits at the upper levels if necessary
20.   In case the root has to be split, create a new root
21.   Increase the height of the tree by one
22. **endif**

Fig. 1.5. The R-tree insertion algorithm.

the same query. The linear split algorithm tries to achieve this objective by minimizing the total area of the two created nodes. Examples of bad and good splits are given in Figure 1.6. In the left part of the figure, the split is bad, because the MBRs of the resulting nodes have much larger area than that depicted in the right part of the figure.

The linear split algorithm, however, is one of the three alternatives to handle splits that were proposed by Guttman. The other two are of quadratic and exponential complexity. These three alternatives are summarized as follows:

Linear Split. Choose two objects as seeds for the two nodes, where these objects are as far apart as possible. Then consider each remaining object in a

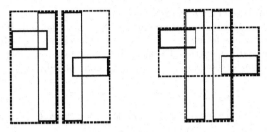

Fig. 1.6. Left: bad split; Right: good split.

random order and assign it to the node requiring the smallest enlargement of its respective MBR.

Quadratic Split. Choose two objects as seeds for the two nodes, where these objects if put together create as much dead space as possible (*dead space* is the space that remains from the MBR if the areas of the two objects are ignored). Then, until there are no remaining objects, insert the object for which the difference of dead space if assigned to each of the two nodes is maximized in the node that requires less enlargement of its respective MBR.

Exponential Split. All possible groupings are exhaustively tested and the best is chosen with respect to the minimization of the MBR enlargement.

Guttman suggested using the quadratic algorithm as a good compromise to achieve reasonable retrieval performance.

Algorithm Delete(TypeEntry E, TypeNode RN)
/* Deletes an entry E from an R-tree with root node RN */

1. **if** RN is a leaf node
2.   search all entries of RN to find $E.mbr$
3. **else** // RN is an internal node
4.   Find all entries of RN that cover $E.mbr$
5.   Follow the corresponding subtrees until the leaf L that contains E is found
6.   Remove E from L
7. **endif**
8. Call algorithm **CondenseTree(L)** /* Figure 1.8 */
9. **if** the root has only one child /* and it is not a leaf */
10.   Remove the root
11.   Set as new root its only child
12. **endif**

Fig. 1.7. The R-tree deletion algorithm.

Regarding the deletion of an entry from an R-tree, it is performed with the algorithm given in Figure 1.7. We note that the handling of an underflowing node (a node with fewer than m entries) is different in the R-tree, compared

---

Algorithm CondenseTree(TypeNode L)
/* Given is the leaf L from which an entry E has been deleted. If after
the deletion of E, L has fewer than m entries, then remove entirely
leaf L and reinsert all its entries. Updates are propagated upwards and
the MBRs in the path from root to L are modified (possibly become smaller) */

1. Set $X = L$
2. Let $\mathcal{N}$ be the set of nodes that are going to be removed from
    the tree (initially, $\mathcal{N}$ is empty)
3. **while** X is not the root
4.   Let $Parent_X$ be the father node of X
5.   Let E_X be the entry of $Parent_X$ that corresponds to X
6.   **if** X contains less than m entries
7.   Remove E_X from $Parent_X$
8.   Insert X into $\mathcal{N}$
9.   **endif**
10.   **if** X has not been removed
11.   Adjust its corresponding MBR $E_X.mbr$, so as to enclose
            all rectangles in X /* $E_X.mbr$ may become smaller */
12.   **endif**
13.   Set $X = Parent_X$
14. **endwhile**
15. Reinsert all the entries of nodes that are in the set $\mathcal{N}$

Fig. 1.8. The R-tree condense algorithm.

with the case of B^+-tree. In the latter, an underflowing case is handled by merging two sibling nodes. Since B^+-trees index one-dimensional data, two sibling nodes will contain consecutive entries. However, for multi-dimensional data, this property does not hold. Although one still may consider promising the merging of two R-tree nodes that are stored at the same level, reinsertion is more appealing for the following reasons:

– Reinsertion achieves the same result as merging. Additionally, the algorithm for insertion is used. Also, as the number of disk accesses during the deletion operation is crucial for its performance, we have to notice that the pages required during reinsertion are available in the buffer memory, because they were retrieved during the searching of the deleted entry.
– As described, the Insert algorithm tries to maintain the good quality of the tree during the query operations. Therefore, it sounds reasonable to use reinsertion, because the quality of the tree may decrease after several deletions.

In all R-tree variants that have appeared in the literature, tree traversals for any kind of operations are executed in exactly the same way as in the original R-tree. Basically, the variations of R-trees differ in how they perform splits during insertion by considering different minimization criteria instead of the sum of the areas of the two resulting nodes.

1.2 Summary

The original R-tree structure proposed by Guttman in [81] aimed at efficient management of large collections of two-dimensional rectangles in VLSI applications. The R-tree is a dynamic access method that organizes the data objects by means of a hierarchical organization of rectangles. The structure supports insertions, deletions, and queries and uses several heuristics to minimize the overlapping of MBRs and reduce their size. These two properties are fundamental to efficient query processing, because the performance of a query is analogous to the number of node accesses required to determine the answer.

Now, R-trees are found everywhere. Several modifications to the original structure have been proposed to either improve its performance or adapt the structure in a different application domain. Based on this fact, the next two chapters are devoted to the presentation and annotation of R-tree variations. The number of the R-tree variants is quite large, so we examine them in several subsections, having in mind the special characteristics of the assumed environment or application. Chapters 4 and 5 focus on query processing issues by considering new types of queries, such as topological, directional, categorical, and distance-based. Chapters 6 and 7 present the use of R-tree variations in advanced applications such as multimedia databases, data warehousing, and data mining. Query optimization issues are covered Chapter 8. Analytical cost models and histogram-based techniques are described. Finally, Chapter 9 describes implementation issues concerning R-trees, such as parallelism and concurrency control, and summarizes what is known from the literature about prototype and commercial systems that have implemented them. The Epilogue concludes the work and gives some directions for further investigation.

2. Dynamic Versions of R-trees

The survey by Gaede and Guenther [69] annotates a vast list of citations related to multi-dimensional access methods and, in particular, refers to R-trees to a significant extent. In this chapter, we are further focusing on the family of R-trees by enlightening the similarities and differences, advantages and disadvantages of the variations in a more exhaustive manner. As the number of variants that have appeared in the literature is large, we group them according to the special characteristics of the assumed environment or application, and we examine the members of each group.

In this chapter, we present dynamic versions of the R-tree, where the objects are inserted on a one-by-one basis, as opposed to the case where a special packing technique can be applied to insert an a priori known static set of objects into the structure by optimizing the storage overhead and the retrieval performance. The latter case will be examined in the next chapter. In simple words, here we focus on the way dynamic insertions and splits are performed in assorted R-tree variants.

2.1 The R$^+$-tree

The original R-tree has two important disadvantages that motivated the study of more efficient variations:

1. The execution of a point location query in an R-tree may lead to the investigation of several paths from the root to the leaf level. This characteristic may lead to performance deterioration, specifically when the overlap of the MBRs is significant.
2. A few large rectangles may increase the degree of overlap significantly, leading to performance degradation during range query execution, due to empty space.

R$^+$-trees were proposed as a structure that avoids visiting multiple paths during point location queries, and thus the retrieval performance could be improved [211, 220]. Moreover, MBR overlapping of internal modes is avoided. This is achieved by using the clipping technique. In simple words, R$^+$-trees do not allow overlapping of MBRs at the same tree level. In turn, to achieve this, inserted objects have to be divided in two or more MBRs, which means that a specific object's entries may be duplicated and redundantly stored in several nodes.

Figure 2.1 demonstrates an R$^+$-tree example. Although the structure looks similar to that of the R-tree, notice that object d is stored in two leaf nodes B and C. Also, notice that due to clipping no overlap exists between nodes at the same level.

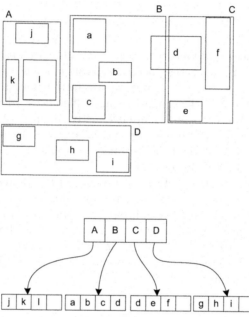

Fig. 2.1. An R$^+$-tree example.

The algorithm for range query processing is similar to the one used for R-trees. The only difference is that duplicate elimination is necessary to avoid reporting an object more than once. However, insertion, deletion, and node splitting algorithms are different due to the clipping technique applied. In order to insert a new entry E, the insertion algorithm starts from the root and determines the MBRs that intersect $E.mbr$. Then $E.mbr$ is clipped and the procedure is recursively applied for the corresponding subtrees. The insertion algorithm is given in Figure 2.2.

The fact that multiple copies of an object's MBR may be stored in several leaf nodes has a direct impact on the deletion algorithm. All copies of an object's MBR must be removed from the corresponding leaf nodes. The deletion algorithm is illustrated in Figure 2.3.

Evidently, an increased number of deletions may reduce storage utilization significantly. Therefore, appropriate reorganization must be performed to handle underutilized tree nodes. The CondenseTree algorithm, already illustrated in Figure 1.8 can be used for this purpose.

Algorithm Insert(TypeEntry E, TypeNode RN)
/* Inserts a new entry E in the R$^+$-tree rooted at node RN */

1. **if** RN is not a leaf node
2.   **foreach** entry e of RN
3.   **if** $e.mbr$ overlaps with $E.mbr$
4.   Call **Insert**$(E, e.ptr)$
5.   **endif**
6.   **endfor**
7. **else** // RN is a leaf node
8.   **if** there is available space in RN
9.   Add E to RN
10.   **else**
11.   Call **SplitNode**(RN)
12.   Perform appropriate tree reorganization to reflect changes
13.   **endif**
14. **endif**

Fig. 2.2. The R$^+$-tree insertion algorithm.

Algorithm Delete(TypeEntry E, TypeNode RN)
/* Deletes an existing entry E from the R$^+$-tree rooted at node RN */

1. **if** RN is not a leaf node
2.   **foreach** entry e of RN
3.   **if** $e.mbr$ overlaps with $E.mbr$
4.   Call **Delete** $(E,e.ptr)$
5.   Calculate the new MBR of the node
6.   Adjust the MBR of the parent node accordingly
7.   **endif**
8.   **endfor**
9. **else** // RN is a leaf node
10.   Remove E from RN.
11.   Adjust the MBR of the parent node accordingly
12. **endif**

Fig. 2.3. The R$^+$-tree deletion algorithm.

During the execution of the insertion algorithm a node may become full, and therefore no more entries can be stored in it. To handle this situation, a node splitting mechanism is required as in the R-tree case. The main difference between the R$^+$-tree splitting algorithm and that of the R-tree is that downward propagation may be necessary, in addition to the upward propagation. Recall that in the R-tree case, upward propagation is sufficient to guarantee the structure's integrity.

Therefore, this redundancy works in the opposite direction of decreasing the retrieval performance in case of window queries. At the same time, another side effect of clipping is that during insertions, an MBR augmentation may lead to a series of update operations in a chain reaction type. Also, under certain circumstances, the structure may lead to a deadlock, as, for example, when a split has to take place at a node with $M+1$ rectangles, where every rectangle encloses a smaller one.

2.2 The R*-tree

R*-trees [19] were proposed in 1990 but are still very well received and widely accepted in the literature as a prevailing performance-wise structure that is often used as a basis for performance comparisons. As already discussed, the R-tree is based solely on the area minimization of each MBR. On the other hand, the R*-tree goes beyond this criterion and examines several others, which intuitively are expected to improve the performance during query processing. The criteria considered by the R*-tree are the following:

Minimization of the area covered by each MBR. This criterion aims at minimizing the dead space (area covered by MBRs but not by the enclosed rectangles), to reduce the number of paths pursued during query processing. This is the single criterion that is also examined by the R-tree.

Minimization of overlap between MBRs. Since the larger the overlapping, the larger is the expected number of paths followed for a query, this criterion has the same objective as the previous one.

Minimization of MBR margins (perimeters). This criterion aims at shaping more quadratic rectangles, to improve the performance of queries that have a large quadratic shape. Moreover, since quadratic objects are packed more easily, the corresponding MBRs at upper levels are expected to be smaller (i.e., area minimization is achieved indirectly).

Maximization of storage utilization. When utilization is low, more nodes tend to be invoked during query processing. This holds especially for larger queries, where a significant portion of the entries satisfies the query. Moreover, the tree height increases with decreasing node utilization.

The R*-tree follows an engineering approach to find the best possible combinations of the aforementioned criteria. This approach is necessary, because the criteria can become contradictory. For instance, to keep both the area and overlap low, the lower allowed number of entries within a node can be reduced. Therefore, storage utilization may be impacted. Also, by minimizing the margins so as to have more quadratic shapes, the node overlapping may be increased.

For the insertion of a new entry, we have to decide which branch to follow, at each level of the tree. This algorithm is called ChooseSubtree. For instance, we consider the R*-tree depicted in Figure 2.4. If we want to insert data rectangle r, ChooseSubtree commences from the root level, where it chooses the entry whose MBR needs the least area enlargement to cover r. The required node is N_5 (for which no enlargement is needed at all). Notice that the examined criterion is *area minimization*. For the leaf nodes, ChooseSubtree considers the *overlapping minimization* criterion, because experimental results in [19] indicate that this criterion performs slightly better than others. Therefore, for the subtree rooted at N_5, ChooseSubtree selects the entry whose MBR enlargement leads to the smallest overlap increase among the sibling entries in the node, that is, node N_1.

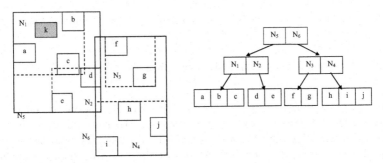

Fig. 2.4. An R*-tree example.

In case ChooseSubtree selects a leaf that cannot accommodate the new entry (i.e., it already has the maximum number of entries), the R*-tree does not immediately resort to node splitting. Instead, it finds a fraction of the entries from the overflowed node and reinserts them. The set of entries to be reinserted are those whose centroid distances from node centroid are among the largest 30% (i.e., this is a heuristic to detect and discard the furthest entries). In the example of Figure 2.4, assume that N_1 is overflowed. In this case, entry b is selected for reinsertion, as its centroid is the farthest from the centroid of N_1.

The reinsertion algorithm achieves a kind of tree rebalancing and significantly improves performance during query processing. However, reinsertion is a costly operation. Therefore, only one application of reinsertion is permitted for each level of the tree. When overflow cannot be handled by reinsertion, node splitting is performed; the Split algorithm consists of two steps. The first step decides a split axis among all dimensions. The split axis is the one with the smallest overall perimeter; it works by sorting all the entries by the coordinates of their left boundaries. Then it considers every division of the sorted list that ensures that each node is at least 40% full. Assume that we have to split the node depicted in Figure 2.5 (we assume that a node can have a single entry, which corresponds to 33% utilization). The 1-3 division (Figure 2.5a), allocates the first entry into N and the other 3 entries into N'. The algorithm computes the perimeters of N and N' and performs the same computation for the other (2-2, 3-1) divisions. A second pass repeats this process with respect to the MBRs' right boundaries. Finally, the overall perimeter on the x-axis equals the sum of all the perimeters obtained from the two passes.

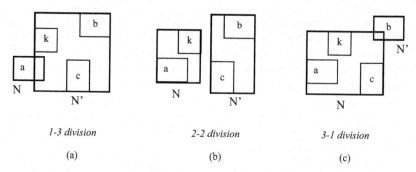

1-3 division   *2-2 division*   *3-1 division*

(a)   (b)   (c)

Fig. 2.5. An example of examined divisions, when split axis is x.

When the split axis is selected, the split algorithm sorts the entries (according to their lower or upper boundaries) on the selected dimension, and again, examines all possible divisions. The final division is the one that has the minimum overlap between the MBRs of the resulting nodes. Continuing the previous example, assume that the split axis is x. Then, among the possible divisions 2-2 incurs zero overlap (between N and N') and thus becomes the final splitting. The cost of the split algorithm of the R*-tree is computed as follows. Let M and m be the maximum and minimum allowed number of entries, respectively. The entries are sorted twice, with cost $O(M \log M)$. For each axis, the margin of $2 \times 2 \times (M - 2m + 2)$ rectangles and the overlap of $2 \times (M - 2m + 2)$ divisions is calculated.

Finally, we notice that the R*-tree does not use any specialized deletion algorithm. Instead, deletion in the R*-tree is performed with the deletion algorithm of the original R-tree.

2.3 The Hilbert R-tree

The Hilbert R-tree [105] is a hybrid structure based on the R-tree and the B$^+$-tree. Actually, it is a B$^+$-tree with geometrical objects being characterized by the Hilbert value of their centroid. The structure is based on the Hilbert space-filling curve . It has been shown in [97, 152] that the Hilbert space-filling curve preserves well the proximity of spatial objects. Figure 2.6 illustrates three space-filling curves.

Entries of internal tree nodes are augmented by the largest Hilbert value of their descendants. Therefore, an entry e of an internal node is a triplet (mbr, H, p) where mbr is the MBR that encloses all the objects in the corresponding subtree, H is the maximum Hilbert value of the subtree, and p is the pointer to the next level. Entries in leaf nodes are exactly the same as in R-trees, R$^+$-trees, and R*-trees and are of the form (mbr, oid), where mbr is the MBR of the object and oid the corresponding object identifier.

The algorithm for range query processing is the same as that of the R-tree and the R*-tree. Staring from the root, it descents the tree by checking if the

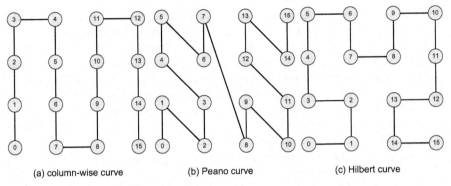

(a) column-wise curve   (b) Peano curve   (c) Hilbert curve

Fig. 2.6. Three space-filling curves.

query rectangle intersects with the MBRs of the accessed nodes. When a leaf is reached, all relevant objects are reported. However, insertion in a Hilbert R-tree differs significantly from that of other variants. In order to insert a new entry E, the Hilbert value H of its rectangle centroid is calculated. Then, H is used as a key that guides the insertion process. At each node, the Hilbert values of the alternative subtrees are checked and the smallest one that is larger than H is selected. The details of the insertion algorithm are given in Figure 2.7.

Algorithm Insert(TypeEntry E, TypeNode RN)
/* Inserts a new entry E in the Hilbert R-tree rooted at node RN */

1. **if** RN is not a leaf node
2.   Among the entries of the node select the entry e
        that has the smallest H value and is larger than the Hilbert value
        of the new object
3.   Call **Insert**(E, $e.ptr$)
4.   Adjust MBR of parent
5. **else** // RN is a leaf node
6.   **if** there is available space in RN
7.   Add E to RN in a position respecting the Hilbert order
8.   **else**
9.   Call **HandleOverflow**(E,RN)
10.   Propagate changes upwards
11.   **endif**
12. **endif**

Fig. 2.7. The Hilbert R-tree insertion algorithm.

An important characteristic of the Hilbert R-tree that is missing from other variants is that there exists an order of the nodes at each tree level, respecting the Hilbert order of the MBRs. This order allows defining siblings for each tree node, as in the case of the B$^+$-tree. The existence of siblings enables the delay of a node split when this node overflows. Instead of splitting a node immediately after its capacity has been exceeded, we try to store some entries in sibling nodes. A split takes place only if all siblings are also full. This unique property of the Hilbert R-tree helps considerably in storage utilization increase, and avoids unnecessary split operations. The decision to perform a split is controlled by the HandleOverflow algorithm, which is illustrated in Figure 2.8. In the case of a split, a new node is returned by the algorithm.

Algorithm HandleOverflow(TypeEntry E, TypeNode RN)
/* Takes care of the overflowing node RN upon insertion of E.
Returns a new node NN in the case of a split, and NULL otherwise */

1. Let $\mathcal{E}$ denote the set of entries of node RN and its s-1 sibling nodes
2. Set $\mathcal{E} = \mathcal{E} \cup E$
3. **if** there exists a node among the s-1 siblings that is not full
4.   Distribute all entries in $\mathcal{E}$ among the s nodes
        respecting the Hilbert ordering
5.   Return **NULL**
6. **else** // all s-1 siblings are full
7.   Create a new node NN
8.   Distribute all entries in $\mathcal{E}$ among the s+1 nodes
9.   Return the new node NN
10. **endif**

Fig. 2.8. The Hilbert R-tree overflow handling algorithm.

A split takes place only if all s siblings are full, and thus s+1 nodes are produced. This heuristic is similar to that applied in B*-trees, where redistribution and 2-to-3 splits are performed during node overflows [111].

It is evident that the Hilbert R-tree acts like a B$^+$-tree for insertions and like an R-tree for queries. According to the authors' experimentation in [105], Hilbert R-trees were proven to be the best dynamic version of R-trees as of the time of publication. However, this variant is vulnerable performance-wise to large objects. Moreover, by increasing the space dimensionality, proximity is not preserved adequately by the Hilbert curve, leading to increased overlap of MBRs in internal tree nodes.

2.4 Linear Node Splitting

Ang and Tan in [11] have proposed a linear algorithm to distribute the objects of an overflowing node in two sets. The primary criterion of this algorithm is to distribute the objects between the two nodes as evenly as possible, whereas the second criterion is the minimization of the overlapping between them. Finally, the third criterion is the minimization of the total coverage.

In order to minimize overlapping, all rectangles within an overflowed node are tried to be pushed as far apart as possible to the boundary of the overflowed node's MBR. Let each rectangle be denoted as (xl, yl, xh, yh), whereas the MBR of an overflowed node N is denoted $R_N = (L, B, R, T)$. The algorithm in [11] uses four lists, denoted $LIST_L$, $LIST_B$, $LIST_R$, $LIST_T$, which store the rectangles of N that are nearer to the corresponding border than to its opposite (borders are considered in pairs: left-right, bottom-top). The algorithm is given in Figure 2.9.

Algorithm NewLinear(TypeNode N)

1.   Set $LIST_L \leftarrow LIST_R \leftarrow LIST_B \leftarrow LIST_T \leftarrow \emptyset$
2.   **foreach** rectangle $S = (xl, yl, xh, yh)$ in N with $R_N = (L, B, R, T)$
3.   **if** $xl - L < R - xh$
4. $LIST_L \leftarrow LIST_L \cup S$
5.   **else**
6. $LIST_R \leftarrow LIST_R \cup S$
7.   **endif**
8.   **if** $xy - B < T - yh$
9. $LIST_B \leftarrow LIST_B \cup S$
10.   **else**
11. $LIST_T \leftarrow LIST_T \cup S$
12.   **endif**
13. **endfor**
14. **if** $\max(|LIST_L|, |LIST_R|) < \max(|LIST_B|, |LIST_T|)$
15.   Split the node along the x direction
16. **else if** $\max(|LIST_L|, |LIST_R|) > \max(|LIST_B|, |LIST_T|)$
17.   Split the node along the y direction
18. **else** //tie break
19.   **if** overlap($LIST_L$, $LIST_R$) < overlap($LIST_B$, $LIST_T$)
20.   Split the node along the x direction
21.   **else if** overlap($LIST_L$, $LIST_R$) > overlap($LIST_B$, $LIST_T$)
22.   Split the node along the y direction
23.   **else**
24.   Split the node along the direction with smallest total coverage
25.   **endif**
26. **endif**

Fig. 2.9. The Linear Node Split algorithm.

It is easy to notice that each rectangle in N will participate either in $LIST_L$ or $LIST_R$. The same applies for $LIST_B$ or $LIST_T$. The decision to carry the split along the horizontal or vertical axis depends on the distribution of the rectangles (the corresponding lines in the code are the ones that compare the maxima among sizes of the lists). In case of a tie, the algorithm resorts to the minimum overlapping criterion.

As mentioned in [11], the algorithm may have a disadvantage in the case that most rectangles in node N (the one to be split) form a cluster, whereas a few others are outliers. This is because then the sizes of the lists will be highly skewed. As a solution, Ang and Tan proposed reinsertion of outliers.

Experiments using this algorithm have shown that it results in R-trees with better characteristics and better performance for window queries in comparison with the quadratic algorithm of the original R-tree.

2.5 Optimal Node Splitting

As has been described in Section 2.1, three node splitting algorithms were proposed by Guttman to handle a node overflow. The three algorithms have linear, quadratic, and exponential complexity, respectively. Among them, the exponential algorithm achieves the optimal bipartitioning of the rectangles, at the expense of increased splitting cost. On the other hand, the linear algorithm is more time efficient but fails to determine an optimal rectangle bipartition. Therefore, the best compromise between efficiency and bipartition optimality is the quadratic algorithm.

Garcia, Lopez, and Leutenegger elaborated the optimal exponential algorithm of Guttman and reached a new optimal polynomial algorithm $O(n^d)$, where d is the space dimensionality and $n = M + 1$ is the number of entries of the node that overflows [71]. For n rectangles the number of possible bipartitions is exponential in n. Each bipartition is characterized by a pair of MBRs, one for each set of rectangles in each partition. The key issue, however, is that a large number of candidate bipartitions share the same pair of MBRs. This happens when we exchange rectangles that do not participate in the formulation of the MBRs. The authors show that if the cost function used depends only on the characteristics of the MBRs, then the number of different MBR pairs is polynomial. Therefore, the number of different bipartitions that must be evaluated to minimize the cost function can be determined in polynomial time.

The proposed optimal node splitting algorithm investigates each of the $O(n^2)$ pairs of MBRs and selects the one that minimizes the cost function. Then each one of the rectangles is assigned to the MBR that it is enclosed by. Rectangles that lie at the intersection of the two MBRs are assigned to one of them according to a selected criterion.

In the same paper, the authors give another insertion heuristic, which is called *sibling-shift*. In particular, the objects of an overflowing node are optimally separated in two sets. Then one set is stored in the specific node, whereas the other set is inserted in a sibling node that will depict the minimum increase of an objective function (e.g., expected number of disk accesses). If the latter node can accommodate the specific set, then the algorithm terminates. Otherwise, in a recursive manner the latter node is split. Finally, the process terminates when either a sibling absorbs the insertion or this is not possible, in which case a new node is created to store the pending set. The authors reported that the combined use of the optimal partitioning algorithm and the sibling-shift policy improved the index quality (i.e., node utilization) and the retrieval performance in comparison to the Hilbert R-trees, at the cost of increased insertion time. This has been demonstrated by an extensive experimental evaluation with real-life datasets.

2.6 Branch Grafting

More recently, in [208] an insertion heuristic was proposed to improve the shape of the R-tree so that the tree achieves a more elegant shape, with a smaller number of nodes and better storage utilization. In particular, this technique considers how to redistribute data among neighboring nodes, so as to reduce the total number of created nodes. The approach of branch grafting is motivated by the following observation. If, in the case of node overflow, we examined all other nodes to see if there is another node (at the same level) able to accommodate one of the overflowed node's rectangles, the split could be prevented. Evidently, in this case, a split is performed only when all nodes are completely full. Since the aforementioned procedure is clearly prohibitive as it would dramatically increase the insertion cost, the branch grafting method focuses only on the neighboring nodes to redistribute an entry from the overflowed node. Actually, the term *grafting* refers to the operation of moving a leaf or internal node (along with the corresponding subtree) from one part of the tree to another.

The objectives of branch grafting are to achieve better-shaped R-trees and to reduce the total number of nodes. Both these factors can improve performance during query processing. To illustrate these issues, the following example is given in [208]. Assume that we are inserting eight rectangles (with the order given by their numbering), which are depicted in Figure 2.10. Let the maximum (minimum) number of entries within a node be equal to 4 (2). Therefore, the required result is shown in Figure 2.10(a), because they clearly form two separate groups. However, by using theR-tree insertion algorithm, which invokes splitting after each overflow, the result in Figure 2.10(b) would be produced.

Using the branch and grafting method, the split after the insertion of rectangle H can be avoided. Figure 2.11(a) illustrates the resulted R-tree after the insertion of the first seven rectangles (i.e., A to G). When rectangle H has to be inserted, the branch grafting method finds out that rectangle 3 is covered by node R_1, which has room for one extra rectangle. Therefore, rectangle C is moved from node R_2 to node R_1, and rectangle H can be inserted in R_2 without causing an overflow. The resulted R-tree is depicted in Figure 2.11(b).

In summary, in case of node overflow, the branch grafting algorithm first examines the parent node, to find the MBRs that overlap the MBR of the overflowed node. Next, individual records in the overflowed are examined to see if they can be moved to the nodes corresponding to the previously found overlapping MBRs. Records are moved only if the resulting area of coverage for

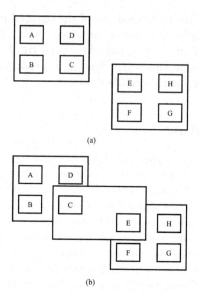

(a)

(b)

Fig. 2.10. Branch grafting technique: (a) Optimal result after inserting 8 rectangles; (b) actual result produced after two R-tree splits.

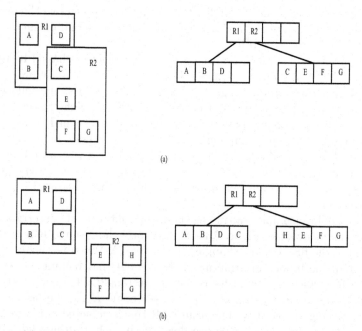

(a)

(b)

Fig. 2.11. (a) Resulted R-tree after the first 7 insertions (rectangles A to G); (b) result of branch grafting after inserting the rectangle H.

the involved nodes does not have to be increased after the moving of records. In the case that no movement is possible, a normal node split takes place.

In general, the approach of branch grafting has some similarities with the forced reinsertion, which is followed by the R*-tree. Nevertheless, as mentioned in [208], branch grafting is not expected to outperform forced reinsertion during query performance. However, one may expect that, because branch grafting tries to locally handle the overflow, the overhead to the insertion time will be smaller than that of forced reinsertion. In [208], however, the comparison considers only various storage utilization parameters, not query processing performance.

2.7 Compact R-trees

Huang et al. proposed Compact R-trees, a dynamic R-tree version with optimal space overhead [93]. The motivation behind the proposed approach is that R-trees, R^+-trees, and R*-trees suffer from the storage utilization problem, which is around 70% in the average case. Therefore, the authors improve the insertion mechanism of R-trees to a more compact R-tree structure, with no penalty on performance during queries.

The heuristics applied are simple, meaning that no complex operations are required to significantly improve storage utilization. Among the $M+1$ entries of an overflowing node during insertions, a set of M entries is selected to remain in this node, under the constraint that the resulting MBR is the minimum possible. Then the remaining entry is inserted to a sibling that:

− has available space, and
− whose MBR is enlarged as little as possible.

Thus, a split takes place only if there is no available space in any of the sibling nodes.

Performance evaluation results reported in [93] have shown that the storage utilization of the new heuristic is between 97% and 99%, which is a great improvement. A direct impact of the storage utilization improvement is the fact that fewer tree nodes are required to index a given dataset. Moreover, less time is required to build the tree by individual insertions, because of the reduced number of split operations required. Finally, caching is improved because the buffer associated with the tree requires less space to accommodate tree nodes. It has been observed that the query performance of window queries is similar to that of Guttman's R-tree.

2.8 cR-trees

Motivated by the analogy between separating of R-tree node entries during the split procedure on the one hand and clustering of spatial objects on the other hand, Brakatsoulas et al. [32] have altered the assumption that an R-tree overflowing node has to necessarily be split in exactly two nodes. In particular, using the k-means clustering algorithm as a working example, they implemented a novel splitting procedure that results in up to k nodes ($k \geq 2$ being a parameter).

In fact, R-trees and their variations (R*-trees, etc.) have used heuristic techniques to provide an efficient splitting of $M+1$ entries of a node that overflows into two groups (minimization of area enlargement, minimization of overlap enlargement, combinations, etc.). On the other hand, Brakatsoulas et al. observed that node splitting is an optimization problem that takes a local decision according to the objective that the probability of simultaneous access to the resulting nodes after split is minimized during a query operation. Indeed, clustering maximizes the similarity of spatial objects within each cluster (intracluster similarity) and minimizes the similarity of spatial objects across clusters (intercluster similarity). The probability of accessing two node rectangles during a selection operation (hence, the probability of traversing two subtrees) is proportional to their similarity. Therefore, node splitting should (a) assign objects with high probability of simultaneous access to the same node and (b) assign objects with low probability of simultaneous access to different nodes. Taking this into account, the authors considered the R-tree node splitting procedure as a typical clustering problem of finding the "optimal" k clusters of $n = M + 1$ entries ($k \geq 2$).

The well-known k-means clustering algorithm was chosen to demonstrate the efficiency of the cR-tree. According to the authors of the paper, the choice was based on the efficiency of the k-means algorithm (O(kn) time complexity and O($n + k$) space complexity, analogous to the R-tree Linear split algorithm) and its order independence (unlike Guttman's linear split algorithm). However, a disadvantage of the chosen algorithm is the fact that it requires k to be given as input. Apparently, the "optimal" number of nodes after splitting is not known in advance. To overcome it, the authors adopted an incremental approach: starting from $k=2$ and increasing k by one each time, they compared the clustering quality of two different clusterings Cluster($M + 1, k$) and Cluster($M + 1, k + 1$) using average silhouette width, a clustering quality measure originally proposed by Kaufman and Rousseeuw [109]. In practice, the

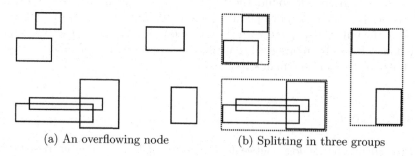

(a) An overflowing node   (b) Splitting in three groups

Fig. 2.12. Splitting an R-tree node in more than two nodes.

theoretical limit of $k_{max} = M + 1$ was bounded to $k_{max} = 5$ as a safe choice. An example is illustrated in Figure 2.12, where the entries of an overflowing node are distributed in three groups.

The empirical studies provided in the paper illustrate that the cR-tree query performance was competitive with the R*-tree and was much better than that of the R-tree. Considering index construction time, the cR-tree was shown to be at the efficiency level of the R-tree and much faster than the R*-tree.

2.9 Deviating Variations

Apart from the aforementioned R-tree variations, a number of interesting extensions and adaptations have been proposed that in some sense deviate drastically from the original idea of R-trees. Among other efforts, we note the following research works.

The Sphere-tree by Oosterom uses minimum bounding spheres instead of MBRs [164], whereas the Cell-tree by Guenther uses minimum bounding polygons designed to accommodate arbitrary shape objects [77]. The Cell-tree is a clipping-based structure and, thus, a variant has been proposed to overcome the disadvantages of clipping. The latter variant uses "oversize shelves", i.e., special nodes attached to internal ones, which contain objects that normally should cause considerable splits [78, 79].

Similarly to Cell-trees, Jagadish and Schiwietz proposed independently the structure of Polyhedral trees or P-trees, which use minimum bounding polygons instead of MBRs [96, 206].

The QR-tree proposed in [146] is a hybrid access method composed of a Quadtree [203] and a forest of R-trees. The Quadtree is used to decompose the data space into quadrants. An R-tree is associated with each quadrant, and it is used to index the objects' MBRs that intersect the corresponding quadrant. Performance evaluation results show that for several cases the method performs better than the R-tree. However, large objects intersect many quadrants and therefore the storage requirements may become high due to replication.

The S-tree by Aggarwal et al. relaxes the rule that the R-tree is a balanced structure and may have leaves at different tree levels [5]. However, S-trees are static structures in the sense that they demand the data to be known in advance.

A number of recent research efforts shares a common idea: to couple the R-tree with an auxiliary structure, thus sacrificing space for the performance. Ang and Tan proposed the Bitmap R-tree [12], where each node contains bitmap descriptions of the internal and external object regions except the MBRs of the objects. Thus, the extra space demand is paid off by savings in retrieval performance due to better tree pruning. The same trade-off holds for the RS-tree, which is proposed by Park et al. [184] and connects an R*-tree with a signature tree with a one-to-one node correspondence. Lastly, Lee and Chung [133] developed the DR-tree, which is a main memory structure for multi-dimensional objects. They couple the R*-tree with this structure to improve the spatial query performance.

Bozanis et al. have partitioned the R-tree in a number of smaller R-trees [31], along the lines of the binomial queues that are an efficient variation of heaps.

Agarwal et al. [4] proposed the Box-tree, that is, a bounding-volume hierarchy that uses axis-aligned boxes as bounding volumes. They provide worst-case lower bounds on query complexity, showing that Box-trees are close to optimal, and they present algorithms to convert Box-trees to R-trees, resulting in R-trees with (almost) optimal query complexity.

Recently, the optimization of data structures for cache effectiveness has attracted significant attention, and methods to exploit processors' caches have been proposed to reduce the latency that incurs by slow main memory speeds. Regular R-trees have large node size, which leads to poor cache performance. Kim et al. [110] proposed the CR-tree to optimize R-trees in main memory environments to reduce cache misses. Nodes of main memory structures are small and the tree heights are usually large. In the CR-tree, MBR keys are compressed to reduce the height of the tree. However, when transferred to a disk environment, CR-trees do not perform well. TR-trees (Two-way optimized R-trees) have been proposed by Park and Lee [185] to optimize R-trees for both cases, i.e., TR-trees are cache- and disk-optimized. In a TR-tree, each disk page maintains an R-tree-like structure. Pointers to in-page nodes are stored with fewer cost. Optimization is achieved by analytical evaluation of the cache latency cost of searching through the TR-tree, taking into account the prefetching ability of today's CPUs.

2.9.1 PR-trees

The Priority R-tree (PR-Rtree for short) has been proposed in [15] and is a provably asymptotically optimal variation of the R-tree. The term *priority* in the name of PR-tree stems from the fact that its bulk-loading algorithm utilizes the "priority rectangles".

Before describing PR-trees, Arge et al. [15] introduce pseudo-PR-trees. In a pseudo-PR-tree, each internal node v contains the MBRs of its children nodes v_c. In contrast to regular R-tree, the leaves of the pseudo-PR-tree may be stored at different levels. Also, internal nodes have degree equal to six (i.e., the maximum number of entries is six). More formally, let S be a set of N rectangles, i.e., $S = r_1, \ldots, r_N$. Each r_i is of the form $(x_{\min}(r_i), y_{\min}(r_i)), (x_{\max}(r_i), y_{\max}(r_i))$. Similar to Hilbert R-tree, each rectangle is mapped to a 4D point, i.e., a mapping of $r_i^* = (x_{\min}(R_i), y_{\min}(R_i), x_{\max}(R_i), y_{\max}(R_i))$. Let S^* be the set of N resulting 4D points. A pseudo-PR-tree T_S on S is defined recursively [15]: if S contains fewer than c rectangles (c is the maximum number of rectangles that can fit in a disk page), then T_S consists of a single leaf. Otherwise, T_S consists of a node v

with six children, the four so-called priority leaves and two recursive pseudo-PR-trees. For the two recursive pseudo-PR-trees, v stores the corresponding MBRs. Regarding the construction of the priority leaves: the first such leaf is denoted as $v_p^{x\min}$ and contains the c rectangles in S with minimal $x_{\min}$-coordinates. Analogously, the three other leaves are defined, i.e., $v_p^{y\min}, v_p^{x\max}$, and $v_p^{y\max}$. Therefore, the priority leaves store the information on the maximum/minimum of the values of coordinates. Let S_r be equal to the set that results from S by removing the aforementioned rectangles that correspond to priority leaves. S_r is divided into two sets $S_<$ and $S_>$ of approximately the same size. The same definition is applied recursively for the two pseudo-PR-trees $S_<$ and $S_>$. The division is done by using in a round-robin fashion the $x_{\min}, y_{\min}, x_{\max}$, or $y_{\max}$ coordinate (a procedure that is analogous to that of building a 4D k-d-tree on S_r^*).

The following is proven in [15]: a range query on a pseudo-PR-tree on N rectangles has I/O cost $O(\sqrt{N/c} + A/c)$, in the worst case, where A is the number of rectangles that satisfy the range query. Also, a pseudo-PR-tree can be bulk-loaded with N rectangles in the plane with worst-case I/O cost equal to $O(\frac{N}{c} \log_{M/c} \frac{N}{c})$.

A PR-tree is a height-balanced tree, i.e., all its leaves are at the same level and in each node c entries are stored. To derive a PR-tree from a pseudo-PR-tree, the PR-tree has to be built into stages, in a bottom-up fashion. First, the leaves V_0 are created and the construction proceeds to the root node. At stage i, first the pseudo-PR-tree T_{S_i} is constructed from the rectangles S_i of this level. The nodes of level i in the PR-tree consist of all the leaves of T_{S_i}, i.e., the internal nodes are discarded. For a PR-tree indexing N rectangles, it is shown in [15] that a range query has I/O cost $O(\sqrt{N/c} + A/c)$, in the worst case, whereas the PR-tree can be bulk-loaded with N rectangles in the plane with worst-case I/O cost equal to $O(\frac{N}{c} \log_{M/c} \frac{N}{c})$. For the case of d-dimensional rectangles, it is shown that the worst-case I/O cost for the range query is $O((N/c)^{1-1/d} + A/c)$. Therefore, a PR-tree provides a worst-case optimality, because any other R-tree variant may require (in the worst case) the retrieval of leaves, even for queries that are not satisfied by any rectangle.

In addition to its worst-case analysis, the PR-tree has been examined experimentally. In summary, the bulk-loading of a PR-tree is slower than the bulk-loading of a packed 4D Hilbert tree. However, regarding query performance, for nicely distributed real data, PR-trees perform similar to existing R-tree variants. In contrast, with extreme data (very skewed data, which contain rectangles with high differences in aspect ratios), PR-trees outperform all other variants, due to their guaranteed worst-case performance.

2.9.2 LR-trees

The LR-tree [31] is an index structure based on the *logarithmic dynamization* method. LR-trees are based on decomposability. A searching problem is called *decomposable* if one can partition the input set into a set of disjoint subsets, perform the query on each subset independently, and then easily compose the partial answers. The most useful geometric searching problems, like range searching, nearest-neighbor searching, or spatial join, as we will see, are in fact decomposable.

LR-trees consist of a number of component substructures, called *blocks*. Each block is organized as a *weak R-tree*, termed wR-tree, i.e., a semidynamic, deletions-only R-tree version. Whenever an insertion operation must be served, a set of blocks are chosen for reconstruction. On the other hand, deletions are handled locally by the block structure that accommodates the involved object. Due to the algorithms for block construction, LR-trees achieve good tightness that provides improved performance during search queries. At the same time, LR-trees maintain the efficiency of dynamic indexes during update operations.

A wR-tree on a set S of items is defined as an R-tree, which either is a legitimate created instance on only the members of S (i.e., it does not violate any of the properties of the R-tree) or is constructed from a legitimate instance on members of a set $S' \supset S$ by deleting each $x \in S' - S$ from the leaves so that: firstly, all MBRs of the structure are correctly calculated, and, secondly, the tree nodes are allowed to be underutilized (i.e., they may store fewer than m entries). The approach of wR-trees is completely opposite to the time-consuming treatment adopted by R*-trees, according to which, to strictly maintain the utilization, all underflowing nodes on the search path are deleted, and the resultant "orphaned" entries are compulsorily reinserted to the tree level that they belong.[1]

An LR-tree on a set S of N items is defined as a collection $\mathcal{C} = \{T_0, T_1, \ldots\}$ of wR-trees on a partition $V = \{V_0, V_1, \ldots\}$ of S into disjoint subsets (blocks), such that:

1. there is a "one-to-one" correspondence $V_j \leftrightarrow T_j$ between the subsets (blocks) and the elements accommodated in the trees;
2. $\left(B^{j-1} < |V_j| \le B^{j+1}\right) \vee (|V_j| = 0)$, for some constant $B \ge 2$, which is called "base"; and
3. $|\mathcal{C}| = O(\log_B n)$.

An insertion into an LR-tree can be served by finding the first wR-tree T_j that can accommodate its own items, the items of all wR-trees to its left and the new item, then destroying all wR-trees T_k, where $k \le j$, and finally bulk-loading a new index T_j, which stores the items in the discarded structures and the new element. This procedure is exemplified in Figure 2.13, for base $B = 2$ and node capacity $c = 4$: the LR-tree of Figure 2.13(a) accommodates 11 items. Since the binary representation of 11 is 1011, items are partitioned into three blocks, namely V_0, V_1 and V_3. Each block V_i is stored into wR-tree T_i. When the item L is inserted (Figure 2.13(b)), the cardinality of the collection becomes 12, which equals 1100 in the binary enumeration system. So the first blocks V_0, V_1 must be destroyed and replaced by a single block V_3, consisting

---

[1] It is important to note that B+-trees follow a similar behavior in industrial applications, i.e., they do not perform node merging but only free nodes when they are completely empty.

of the elements of the set $V_0 \cup V_1 \cup \{L\}$. That change is reflected to the LR-tree, by replacing the wR-trees T_0 and T_1 by a single one T_3.

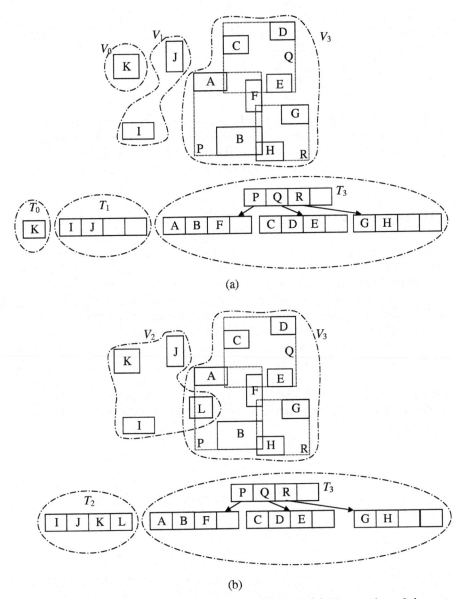

Fig. 2.13. Insertion of item L in an LR-tree with $B=2$. (a) The number of elements before insertion equals $11=1011_2$, so there are the blocks V_0, V_1, V_3 implemented as wR-trees T_0, T_1, T_3, respectively, (b) after insertion we have $12=1100_2$ items and therefore destruction of trees T_0, T_1 and replacement by a single tree T_2.

Algorithm RangeSearch(TypeRect Q**, TypeArray** *Root***)**
/* Root contains the root nodes of subtrees of LR-tree */

1. $QS = \{\text{Root}[i] \mid \text{Root}[i] \cap Q \neq \emptyset\}$
2. $Answer = \bigcup_{T \in QS} \text{RSEARCH}(T,Q)$
3.   **return** *Answer*

Fig. 2.14. The LR-tree range search algorithm.

A range query with query rectangle Q seeks for all items whose MBRs share with Q common point(s). In LR-tree, this operation is treated by querying the individual wR-trees and concatenating the partial results trivially in $O(1)$ time. The range search algorithm for a wR-tree T is given in Figure 2.14.

2.10 Summary

Evidently, the original R-tree, proposed by Guttman, has influenced all the forthcoming variations of dynamic R-tree structures. The R*-tree followed an engineering approach and evaluated several factors that affect the performance of the R-tree. For this reason, it is considered the most robust variant and has found numerous applications, in both research and commercial systems. However, the empirical study in [105] has shown that the Hilbert R-tree can perform better than the other variants in some cases. It is worth mentioning that the PR-tree, although a variant that deviates from other existing ones, is the first approach that offers guaranteed worst-case performance and overcomes the degenerated cases when almost the entire tree has to be traversed. Therefore, despite its more complex building algorithm, it has to be considered the best variant reported so far.

3. Static Versions of R-trees

There are common applications that use static data. For instance, insertions and deletions in census, cartographic and environmental databases are rare or even not performed at all. For such applications, special attention should be paid to construct an optimal structure with regard to some tree characteristics, such as storage overhead minimization, storage utilization maximization, minimization of overlap or coverage between tree nodes, or combinations of these. Therefore, it is anticipated that query processing performance will be improved. These methods are well known in the literature as *packing* or *bulk loading*. Thus, we next examine such methods that require the data to be known in advance.

3.1 The Packed R-tree

The first packing algorithm was proposed by Roussopoulos and Leifker in 1985, soon after the proposal of the original R-tree [199]. Let the dataset contain N rectangles and each page can store up to c rectangles. The approach of [199] is summarized as follows:

1. Sort the rectangles in the dataset according to the x-coordinate of their center (equivalently, the x-coordinate of the lower-left corner can be used).
2. Pack the rectangles of the dataset into $\lfloor N/n \rfloor$ consecutive groups of c rectangles in each (except the last one, which can have from 1 to c rectangles).
3. Find the MBR of each group created in the previous step and associate along with each MBR the pointer to the page that stores the corresponding group.
4. Recursively pack the computed MBRs into nodes using steps 1-3. The recursion continues until a single root node is created.

No experimental work is presented for this first effort, to compare the performance of this method compared to that of the original R-tree. However, based on this simple inspiration a significant number of efforts have since been proposed in the literature.

3.2 The Hilbert Packed R-tree

The Hilbert packed R-tree [104] resembles its dynamic counterpart Hilbert R-tree, because it utilizes the concept of the Hilbert space-filling curve. The Hilbert packed R-tree has been proposed by Kamel and Faloutsos for building a static R-tree with near 100% storage utilization. The tree is constructed in a bottom-up manner, starting from the leaf level and finishing at the root. A number of different heuristics have been studied by the authors and the one that depends on the Hilbert values of the rectangles' centroids has proven the most efficient with respect to query processing costs. The basic steps of the packing algorithm are illustrated in Figure 3.1.

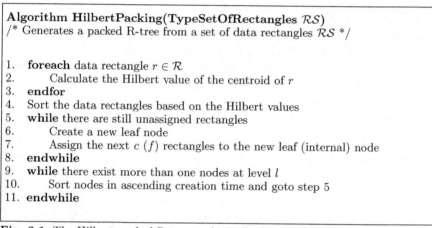

Algorithm HilbertPacking(TypeSetOfRectangles $\mathcal{RS}$)
/* Generates a packed R-tree from a set of data rectangles $\mathcal{RS}$ */

1. **foreach** data rectangle $r \in \mathcal{R}$
2.   Calculate the Hilbert value of the centroid of r
3. **endfor**
4. Sort the data rectangles based on the Hilbert values
5. **while** there are still unassigned rectangles
6.   Create a new leaf node
7.   Assign the next c (f) rectangles to the new leaf (internal) node
8. **endwhile**
9. **while** there exist more than one nodes at level l
10.   Sort nodes in ascending creation time and goto step 5
11. **endwhile**

Fig. 3.1. The Hilbert packed R-tree packing algorithm.

The packing algorithm terminates when it reaches a level that contains a single node. Then this node becomes the root of the Hilbert packed R-tree. The resulting tree has near 100% storage utilization, because the majority of the nodes are full, except from the last node in every level, and perhaps the root that can contain at least two entries. Consequently, less space is required for the index in comparison to the dynamic R-tree, which has nearly 70% storage utilization.

Experiments showed that the latter method achieves significantly better performance than the original R-tree [81], with quadratic split, the R*-tree [19] and the Packed R-tree by Roussopoulos and Leifker [199] in point and window queries. Moreover, Kamel and Faloutsos proposed a formula to estimate the average number of node accesses, which is independent of the details of the R-tree maintenance algorithms and can be applied to any R-tree variant.

3.3 The STR R-tree

STR (Sort-Tile-Recursive) is a bulk-loading algorithm for R-trees proposed by
Leutenegger et al. [134]. Let N be a number of rectangles in two-dimensional
space. The basic idea of the method is to tile the address space by using VS
vertical slices, so that each slice contains enough rectangles to create approximately $\sqrt{N/c}$ nodes, where c is the R-tree node capacity. Initially, the number
of leaf nodes is determined, which is $n_l = \lceil N/c \rceil$. Let $VS = \sqrt{L}$. The rectangles are sorted with respect to the x-coordinate of the centroids, and VS
slices are created. Each slice contains $VS \cdot c$ rectangles, which are consecutive
in the sorted list. In each slice, the objects are sorted by the y-coordinate of
the centroids and are packed into nodes (placing c objects in a node).

The method is applied until all R-tree levels are formulated. The STR
method is easily applicable to high dimensionalities. In particular, for $d > 2$
dimensions, STR first sorts the hyper-rectangles according to the first coordi-
nate of their center [134]. Then it divides the input set into $VS = \lfloor n_l^{\frac{1}{d}} \rfloor$ slabs,
where $n_l = \lfloor N/c \rfloor$ (c is the node capacity). A slab consists of a run of $c \cdot \lfloor n_l^{\frac{d-1}{d}} \rfloor$
consecutive hyper-rectangles from the sorted list. Each slab is next processed
recursively using the remaining $d - 1$ coordinates.

Experimental evaluation performed in [134] has demonstrated that the STR
method is generally better than previously proposed bulk-loading methods.
However, in some cases the Hilbert packing approach performs marginally
better. An intuitive illustration for the comparison between Hilbert Packed
R-tree and STR is depicted in the left and right parts of Figure 3.2, respectively. These figures show the leaf MBRs produced by the three algorithms,
for a spatial dataset. Evidently, STR achieves a much better result, with less
overlapping between the MBRs. A similar behavior is observed in Figure 3.3
for another dataset, comparing the leaf-level MBRs for the R-tree, the R*-tree,
and the STR.

Fig. 3.2. Left: result of Hilbert Packed R-trees; Right: result of STR.

It has to be noticed that Garcia et al. [72] proposed an R-tree node restructuring algorithm for post-optimizing existing R-trees and improving dynamic
insertions, which incurs an optimization cost equal to that of STR. The resulting R-tree outperforms dynamic R-tree versions, like the Hilbert R-tree, with
only a small additional cost during insertions. Moreover, an analytical model

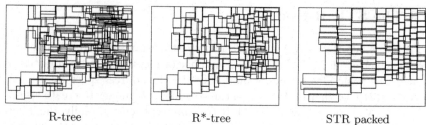

R-tree   R*-tree   STR packed

Fig. 3.3. MBRs of leaf nodes for R-tree, R*-tree and STR Packed R-tree.

to predict the number of disk accesses for buffer management is described by Leutenegger and Lopez [135], which evaluates the quality of packing algorithms measured by query performance of the resulting tree.

3.4 Top-Down Packing Techniques

Unlike the aforementioned packing algorithms that build the tree bottom-up, there are some methods that follow a top-down approach to build the index. We describe two methods in this category, namely the VAMSplit R-tree and the Top-Down Greedy Split.

The VAMSplit R-tree, proposed in [244] to index high-dimensional vectors, performs a recursive decomposition of the data objects based on the *maximum variance criterion*. Basically, this structure is a variation of the VAMSplit k-d-tree, also proposed in [244]. In every step, the construction algorithm determines a *split dimension* and a *split position* in the selected dimension, according to the maximum variance criterion. The authors detected that the maximum variance criterion achieves better search performance than the *maximum spread criterion*. Figure 3.4 illustrates an example for 2D space, where the use of the maximum variance achieves a more promising split than the maximum spread.

The decomposition method is recursively applied until the objects in the resulting buckets can be hosted by a leaf node. The leaf nodes created using the recursive decomposition of the data objects are organized by means of an R-tree-like directory. In [244] a performance evaluation has been reported that compares the VAMSplit R-tree with the VAMSplit k-d-tree, the SS-tree, and the R*-tree with respect to CPU and I/O efficiency for memory-resident and disk-based implementations. It has been shown that the VAMSplit R-tree shows the best performance for the datasets and the parameter values used in the experimental setup.

Another R-tree-like indexing scheme produced using a top-down space decomposition is the Top-Down Greedy Split (TGS) method [70], which has been proposed to handle both points and rectangles. The TGS method recursively applies a splitting process that partitions a set of rectangles into two subsets by

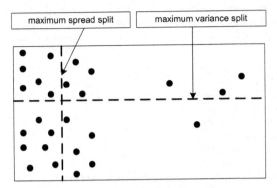

Fig. 3.4. Maximum variance vs. maximum spread.

applying an orthogonal cut to an axis selected by some criteria. This process must satisfy the following properties:

1. the value of an objective function should be minimized, and
2. one subset has a cardinality $i \cdot S$ for some i, so that the resulting subtrees are packed.

The method is recursively applied to both subsets. The objective function has the form $f(r_1, r_2)$, where r_1, r_2 are the MBRs of the two subsets produced. The performance evaluation of the method reported in [70] has demonstrated that the TGS approach is generally better than previously proposed packing algorithms and results in R-trees that have better query processing performance. Figure 3.5 illustrates the basic steps of the TGS packing algorithm.

Recently, a promising new method has been proposed by Lee and Lee [131] for packing an R-tree in a top-down manner. As the number of objects N is known in advance, the method calculates the height of the desired tree as:

$$h = \lceil \log_M N \rceil$$

As the storage utilization will be 100% for most of the nodes, it can be anticipated that the root will be partially filled. The number of data items in one subtree of the root will be:

$$N_{subtree} = M^{h-1}$$

By the next equation we can determine the number of root entries as:

$$S = \lfloor \sqrt{\frac{N}{N_{subtree}}} \rceil$$

Then the problem is to partition the data items in S groups by splitting the space in S vertical slices. Accordingly, each entry of the root has to be partitioned into M subgroups, i.e., the entries of the lower level, and each of the latter set of subgroups recursively until each smaller group contains only M items.

Algorithm TopDownGreedy(TypeSetOfRectangles $\mathcal{R}$)
/* Generates a packed R-tree from a set of data rectangles $\mathcal{R}$ and
a user supplied cost function $f(r_1, r_2)$ */

1. Set $N = |\mathcal{R}|$
2. Set S=maximum number of rectangles per subtree
3. Set $M =$ maximum number of entries per node.
4. **if** $N \leq S$, then terminate
5. **foreach** dimension d
6.   **foreach** ordering ord
7.   **for** i=1 to $\lceil N/M \rceil - 1$
8.   Let r_1 be the MBR of first $i \cdot S$ rectangles
9.   Let r_2 be the MBR of the remaining rectangles
10.   **if** $f(r_1, r_2)$ gives better result
11.   Remember d, ord and i
12.   **endif**
13.   **endfor**
14.   **endfor**
15. **endfor**
16. Split rectangles at the best position determined
17. Call **TopDownGreedy** for the two sets of rectangles

Fig. 3.5. The TGS packing algorithm.

Lee and Lee [131] do not give experimental results, only qualitative conclusions. As MBR overlapping is eliminated, it is anticipated that it will be better than STR from the search performance point of view; that is why the variation is named Overlap Minimizing Top-down (OMT) R-tree.

3.5 Small-Tree-Large-Tree and GBI

The previous packing algorithms build an R-tree access method from scratch. The small-tree-large-tree method (STLT) [42] focuses on the problem of bulk insertions of new data into an already-existing R-tree. The main objective is to minimize the insertion time (i.e., active applications that use the R-tree should not be impacted significantly by the insertion of these new data), while maintaining the good quality of the R-tree (i.e., during query processing) as much as possible.

The STLT algorithm assumes that the new data to be inserted are skewed, i.e., they correspond to a localized portion of the data space instead of being spread all around it. This assumption is crucial for the performance of STLT. Assuming this, the new data can be bulk-loaded into a (small) R-tree. Let the height of this new (small) R-tree be h_r and the height of the original (large) R-tree be h_R. STLT considers the MBR of the root of the small R-tree as an individual entry and applies the R-tree insertion algorithm to locate where to insert this MBR. It has to be noted that the MBR should be tried to be inserted at level $h_R - h_r$, not in a leaf node of the large R-tree. When such a position is found, then the entire subtree is inserted at this point. The procedure is exemplified in Figure 3.6.

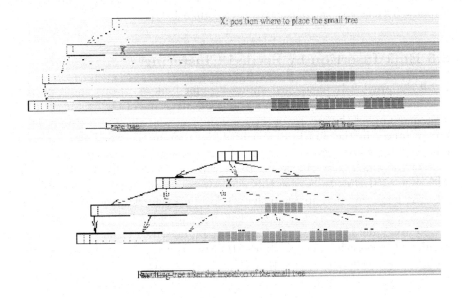

Fig. 3.6. An example of the STLT algorithm.

Evidently, the insertion of the small tree within a node of the large tree may cause the overflow of this node. To handle this case, STLT applies one of the following methods:

– It attempts to merge sibling entries of the overflowed node to create free space. This is carried out by merging the two closed nodes (according to the distance of their centroids), whose combined number of children is less than the fanout of the overflowed node.
– If merging is not possible, then STLT tries to delete one of the sibling nodes and reinsert it, so make room for a new entry (the small R-tree). The sibling to be deleted is selected by finding the distance between each child node from the center of its MBR and by choosing the farthest such distance.
– In case deletion cannot be performed, STLT finally resorts to splitting the overflowed node (splitting may be propagated up to the root node).

Obviously, the efficiency of the resulting index depends on the data distribution of the small R-tree. If the objects in the small tree cover a large part of the data space, then using the STLT approach will result in increasing overlap in the resulting index. Therefore, the method is best suited for skewed data distributions.

STLT is extended in [47], where the Generalized R-tree Bulk-Insertion Strategy (GBI) is proposed. GBI inserts new incoming datasets into active R-trees as follows: it first partitions the datasets into a set of clusters and outliers, then it constructs a small R-tree for each cluster, finding suitable places in the original R-tree to insert the newly created R-trees, and finally it bulk-inserts the new R-trees and the outliers in the original R-tree.

3.6 Bulk Insertion by Seeded Clustering

In all the previously mentioned approaches for bulk-insertions, input objects are clustered without taking into account the structure of the existing R-tree. This may impact the quality of the resulting tree and affect query processing. For instance, in the STLT approach, if the root of the small tree covers a relatively large area, then the corresponding node in the large tree (where the root of the small tree will be inserted) will require significant enlargement. Although GBI tries to resolve this, the several small trees that are inserted into the large one may increase the overlap between the nodes of the latter, because there is no guarantee that their roots are not overlapping.

To overcome the aforementioned shortcomings, Lee et al. [132] proposed a different approach, called bulk-insertion by seeded clustering (SCB). Their bulk-insertion algorithm consists of the following stages:

1. A seeded tree is built, considering only the first few levels of the target R-tree;
2. The seeded tree is used to cluster the objects to be inserted into clusters. This way, the structure of the existing tree is taken into account; and
3. Each cluster forms a separate R-tree and each is placed into a suitable place in the target R-tree.

The intuition behind the consideration of the existing R-tree through the seeded tree is exemplified with the case depicted in Figure 3.7. In this figure, the rectangles drawn with solid lines are the MBRs of two existing nodes, A and B. The points drawn with circles, are the ones that have to be inserted in the tree. By clustering the points without considering the structure of the existing R-tree, the two points in the upper-left corner would be assigned to one cluster and the remaining ones (in the lower-right corner) will be assigned to a second cluster. When trying to insert the two clusters in the R-tree, the second cluster will cause the MBR of node B to expand. The expansion is drawn with dashed lines. In contrast, if the input points are clustered through the seeded tree, then node A will include the three points that are covered by its MBR and node B will include the other two points. In this case, no expansion is required.

More particularly, the first k levels of the existing R-tree are used to shape the seeded tree[1]. For each object that has to be inserted, we find a path from

---

[1] In the experiments performed in [132], the seeded tree is constructed by the first two levels of an R-tree that has height equal to four.

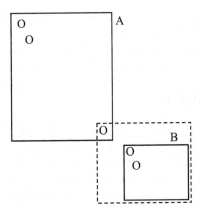

Fig. 3.7. An example of node expansion, when the R-tree structure is not considered.

the root of the seeded tree to a leaf of the seeded tree, which consists of nodes whose MBRs fully cover the object. Then, the object is assigned to the found leaf. If more than one path exists, the first one is selected arbitrarily. If no such path exists, the object is classified as an outlier (experimental results in [132] show that fewer than 0.1% of objects end up as outliers). When the previous procedure is performed for each input object, then the leaves of the seeded tree to which at least one point has been assigned correspond to clusters. The points in each cluster form a small R-tree (using any existing bulk-loading algorithm). The collection of these small R-trees is placed within the existing R-tree. When an R-tree is placed, we have to consider that the existing R-tree has to have all its leaves in the same level. For this reason, the node under which the root of each small R-tree will be inserted, has to be at appropriate level. Moreover, assume that the root S of a small R-tree has less than m entries (m is the minimum allowed number of entries in an internal R-tree node) and that this root will be inserted under node N in the existing tree. To overcome node underflow, SCB distributes the entries of S among its sibling nodes in N (only siblings that overlap with S are considered). In the end, when all small R-trees have been placed, the set of outliers is inserted one by one, following the normal insertion algorithm of the R-tree.

An optimization followed by SCB tries to reduce the node overlapping due to an insertion of the small trees. Reduction of overlapping is achieved in a post-processing step through repacking the node contents. In brief, let N be a node in the existing tree, under which the root S of a small R-tree will be placed. The entries of N are divided into two categories: those that overlap with S and those that do not overlap. The entries of the former category are repacked by creating nodes that enclose the elements in this category using a bulk-loading algorithm.

Experimental results in [132] show that SCB outperforms GBI, in terms of both insertion and query costs. More interestingly, the query performance of SCB is even better than that of the case where the objects are inserted one by one (with the normal insertion algorithm). SCB is the first bulk-insertion algorithm that achieves this, because existing ones (e.g., GBI) do not perform better than the case of one-by-one insertions.

3.7 The Buffer R-tree

Arge et al. [16] proposed the Buffer R-tree (BR-tree) for performing bulk update and queries. BR is based on the buffer tree technique [14] and exploits the available main memory. Let N be the number of data rectangles, M the number of rectangles that fit in main memory, and f the number of rectangles that fit into a disk page (block). On every $\lfloor \log_f(\frac{M}{4 \cdot f}) \rfloor$-th level of the tree, buffers are attached to all nodes of the level. Assuming that leaf nodes reside at level $l = 0$, a buffer of size $\frac{M}{2 \cdot f}$ blocks is assigned to every node residing at level $i \cdot \lfloor \log_f(\frac{M}{4 \cdot f}) \rfloor$, where $i = 1, 2, \ldots$. A node with an attached buffer is called a *buffer node*.

The attached buffer enables the operations to be performed in a "lazy" or deferred manner. For example, assume that a new rectangle r must be inserted. Traditional insertion algorithms initially locate the appropriate leaf and then store the new rectangle. In case of an overflow, special actions are taken. The BR-tree uses a different approach. The insertion is not performed immediately. Instead, we wait until a block of rectangles has been collected, and then this block is stored in the buffer of the root node. If the root buffer contains more than $M/4$ rectangles, a specialized procedure is executed to free some buffer space. Therefore, for each rectangle residing in the full buffer we locate the next appropriate buffer node (respecting the branching heuristics) and store the rectangle. This process is applied until the first $M/4$ rectangles of the buffer have been propagated to other buffer nodes. When we reach a leaf, the rectangle is inserted and appropriate actions are taken if there is a leaf overflow (e.g., a split operation is performed).

Evidently, for some insertions no I/O operation is performed. However, for some insertions the cost may be high because of the potential repetitive application of the buffer-emptying procedure. The total number of I/O operations is reduced significantly because many rectangles are propagated to the next buffer nodes simultaneously. This leads to fewer I/O operations for the Buffer R-tree compared to the traditional individual insertions.

The BR-tree supports bulk insertions, bulk deletions, bulk loading, and batch queries. Analytical results reported in [16] show the efficiency of the BR-tree. Among the theoretical results we highlight the following:

- an R-tree can be bulk-loaded in $O(\frac{N}{f} \cdot \log_{M/f} \frac{N}{f})$ I/O operations;
- a set of n rectangles can be bulk-inserted into a Buffer R-tree containing N data rectangles in $O(\frac{n}{f} \cdot \log_{M/f} \frac{n+N}{f} + \frac{N}{f})$ I/O operations;
- a set of n rectangles can be bulk-deleted from an existing Buffer R-tree containing N rectangles, in $O(\frac{n}{f} \log_{M/f} \frac{N}{f} + \frac{N}{f} + Q(n))$ I/O operations, where

$Q(n)$ is the number of I/O operations required to locate the n rectangles by using batch queries; and

— a set of n queries can be executed on an R-tree containing N rectangles in $O(\frac{Q}{f}\log_{M/f}\frac{N}{f} + \frac{N}{f})$ I/O operations, where $Q\log_f N$ is the number of tree nodes accessed by the normal R-tree query algorithm.

Experimental results illustrate the superiority of the BR-tree over the other methods. The BR-tree requires smaller execution times to perform bulk updates and produces a better-quality index in terms of query processing performance. Moreover, it allows for simultaneous batch updates and queries.

3.8 R-tree with Low Stabbing Number

DeBerg et al. [56] proposed an R-tree construction procedure, which leads to satisfactory worst-case bounds for the case of point queries and window queries with small ranges. The main idea behind their approach is based on the *stabbing number*. For a set of rectangles in the plane, the stabbing number is defined as the maximum of rectangles that contain (i.e., are stabbed by) a query point. Evidently, regarding the number of node reads for a point query, the worst case is equal to the stabbing number of all data rectangles.

The construction is done according to the so-called *striped order* [56]. This order is defined by assuming a set of vertical stripes that intersect the rectangles. Assuming that we start the numbering from the leftmost non-empty rectangle and ending at the rightmost one, the strip order is derived. Given the strip order, an R-tree is constructed similar to the case of existing bulk-loading algorithms, e.g., the Packed R-tree [199].

For a given set of N rectangles, let st be the stabbing number and ρ_x the x-scale factor (i.e., the ratio of the largest x-extent to the smallest x-extent among all rectangles). For a given m, where m is the minimum number of entries that can be accommodated in an R-tree node, deBerg et al. [56] proved that an R-tree can be constructed such that the number of nodes that will be visited for a point query at worst case is $O((st + \log n)\log n/\log m)$. When st and ρ_x are constant, which is the expected case for most practical applications, the aforementioned bound is optimal. Nevertheless, no comparison is performed in [56] against other methods for the average case.

3.9 Merging R-trees

In the previously described approaches, a large amount of new data were either accommodated in an existing index (bulk-insertion) or used to build a new index from scratch (bulk-loading). A third case of dealing with large amounts of data, in which one needs to unify data-sets indexed by separate (auxiliary) data structures into a single indexed data-set, is proposed in [240] and is called *R-tree merging*. Although one can argue that the problem of merging can be treated with either bulk-inserting the data of one tree into the other or just bulk-loading, from scratch, a new tree, both actions ignore the useful information that the existing trees already carry. In contrast, the algorithm in [240] works as follows: given two R-trees, the algorithm constructs a new one by a linear top-down traversal of the smallest one. This does not make any assumptions on data distribution (unlike existing approaches like STR); it just capitalizes on the information that the input R-trees carry: whole subtrees of one of the input trees are accommodated whenever possible, while the entirety of the tree can be inserted as a single entry in the ideal case. This process is driven by applying certain criteria for deciding whether each handled subtree is going to be left intact or decomposed to its individual entries.

During merging there may be a large number of elements inserted in the receiving tree, therefore multiple elements may be inserted into one node at the same time. Therefore, the split of a node needs to be generalized, to be able to handle nodes with an arbitrary number of entries. In [240] such a generalization is performed by redefining the minimum and maximum number of entries that each of the two resulting nodes may receive. Remember that, when dealing with $M + 1$ entries, each of the resulting nodes may receive from m to $M + 1 - m$ of those (recall that M and m are the maximum and minimum, respectively, number of entries that a node can contain). In the generalized case of V entries contained inside the overfull node, [240] finds the minimum v and maximum $V - v$ number of entries that each of the new nodes may contain, by keeping the minimum number of entries in the new nodes and the total number of entries of the overfull node under a constant ratio, and making this ratio the same as in the original, non-generalized case. In particular:

$$v = \left\lfloor \frac{V m}{M + 1} \right\rfloor$$

This way, the original case remains as is, and after that there is a gradual increase of the minimum value.

Since the overflowed node may contain an arbitrary number of entries, the resulting nodes may also contain an arbitrary number of entries. Thus, they can be overflowed themselves. Therefore, the splitting process has to work in such a way, that in the end there are no overflowed nodes. This is achieved by executing recursively the generalized split for the nodes that it produces, until all the nodes that remain contain no more than M entries.

Finally, the algorithm for the insertion of one R-tree into the other works recursively, where each instance always operates on one particular node of the receiving tree. The insertion begins at the root of the tree and recursively descends until it reaches the leaf level. With this algorithm however, multiple paths can be followed inside the tree, because a massive quantity of elements is inserted, organized as an already existing tree. The general idea behind it is the following: the algorithm attempts to insert whole subtrees of the giving tree whenever possible, while the entirety of the giving tree can be inserted as a single entry in the ideal case. Nevertheless, in each node of the receiving tree for which the algorithm is executed, certain criteria are used to decide whether each handled subtree of the giving tree is going to be left intact or decomposed to its individual entries, which can point to smaller subtrees or single elements. The criteria used in [240] are the following:

Area criterion. If the subtree is destined to a lower level of the receiving tree than the current one, the following procedure is followed: the subtree is routed to the child node whose MBR admits the least area enlargement to include it, and that enlargement is recorded. Then, each of the individual entries of the subtree is likewise routed to the child where it causes the least area enlargement, whereas the sum of area enlargements caused to each child (*not* the sum of area enlargements caused by each entry) is recorded as well. If the first recorded value is less than or equal to the second, then the subtree is propagated as a whole to the suitable child; otherwise, it is decomposed to its entries.

Overlap criterion. If, on the other hand, the subtree is destined to the current level, thus to the current node, a different approach is followed: first, the overlap enlargement that would be caused to the current node, if the subtree were inserted into it, is recorded. Then, as in the previous case, the entries of the subtree are distributed to the children where they would cause the least area enlargement, and the overlap enlargement that is caused to *the current node* by such a distribution is recorded. If the first recorded value is less than or equal to the second, and less than or equal to the area of the subtree's MBR, then the subtree is inserted as a whole to the current node; otherwise, it is decomposed to its entries.

The experimental evaluation of [240] indicates that the aforementioned algorithm is efficient with respect to its execution time and that the resulting trees demonstrate very good query performance.

3.10 Summary

The pioneering work of the Packed R-tree defined (one year after the original R-tree was proposed) the area of bulk-loading algorithms for R-tree variants. One must also recognize the intuition behind the use of space-feeling curves (e.g., in the Hilbert packed R-tree), as a simple yet effective approach of clustering spatial objects. However, these approaches may find difficulty when dealing with high-dimensional spaces. The STR R-tree and the Top-Down Greedy Split try to overcome some of the deficiencies of these early works. As in the case of dynamic variants, it is fortunate that approaches have been proposed that offer guaranteed worst-case performance. First, the R-tree with low stabbing number addresses the worst-case bound with respect to point queries. On the other hand, the algorithm for bulk-loading the PR-tree suffices also in the case of static variants and offers the same guarantees for the worst-case.

Moving to bulk updates, STLT defined this problem whereas GBI tried to overcome the dependency of STLT with respect to skewed data. The Buffer

R-tree can be considered as an elegant solution, and in fact it is one of the best approaches for the problem of bulk update. Finally, it is interesting to notice the problem of merging two existing R-trees, which cannot be considered a special case of bulk-update, because both the R-trees are about the same size. In this field, R-tree merging is worth mentioning.

Part II

QUERY PROCESSING ISSUES

4. Fundamental Query Processing Techniques

In this chapter, we present the basic techniques for processing spatial queries with R-trees. This includes methods for range and topological queries (which find data that satisfy a query region, along with their topological relations with respect to this region), nearest-neighbor queries (which find data closest to a query point), and spatial join queries (which find pairs of data that satisfy a condition, e.g., "determine all hotels that are placed near a square"). For each query type we present all the techniques and their variations that have been proposed in related research. Since the usefulness of the aforementioned query types is significant, several more complex extensions have been proposed. However, in this chapter we focus on the fundamental techniques and leave the examination of the more complex extensions for the next chapter.

4.1 Two-step Processing

The processing of spatial queries presents significant requirements, due to the large volumes of spatial data and the complexity of both objects and queries. Efficient processing of spatial queries capitalizes on the proximity of the objects, achieved by the R-tree, to focus the searching on objects that satisfy the queries. Besides efficiency, one of the main reasons for the popularity of R-tree indexes stems from their versatility, because they can efficiently support many types of spatial operators. The most common ones are listed in the following and comprise basic primitives for developing more complex operations in applications based on management of spatial data (like GIS, cartography, etc):

Topological operators: find all objects that, e.g., overlap or cover a given object.

Directional operators: find all objects that, e.g., lie north of a given object.

Distance operators: find all objects that, e.g., lie less than a given distance from a given object (range query), or find the k objects nearest to a given object (k-nearest-neighbor query).

For instance, let a collection of ten 2-dimensional rectangles, denoted as $r_1, \ldots, r_{10}$, which is depicted in the left part of Figure 4.1, be organized with the R-tree that is given in the right part of Figure 4.1 (the MBRs are also depicted). Given a query point a, the answer to the query that finds all objects that cover a (topological operator) is r_{11} and r_{12}. Also, for the query point

b, the answer to a query that finds all objects in the north of b (directional operator) is r_8. Focusing on the nearest-neighbor query (distance operator), given the query point c, r_5 will be found. Finally, considering the range query, let the query point d and a distance that is the radius of the circle depicted with dashed line in Figure 4.1. Apparently, the range query (distance operator) finds r_9 and r_{10}.

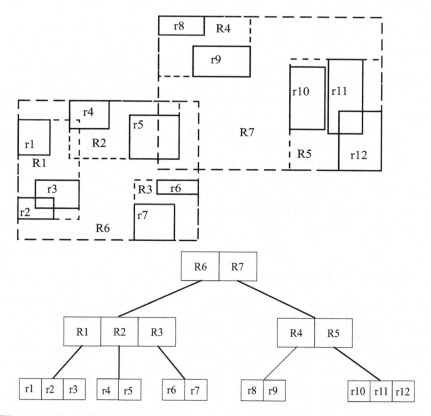

Fig. 4.1. Example of an R-tree.

As described, the R-tree abstracts objects with complex shapes (polygons, polygons with holes, etc.) by using their MBR approximations. To answer queries containing the aforementioned operators, a two-step procedure is followed [33]:

1. **Filter step:** the collection of all objects whose MBRs satisfy the given query is found, which comprises the *candidate set*.
2. **Refinement step:** the actual geometry of each member of the candidate set is examined to eliminate false hits and find the answer to the query.

This procedure is illustrated in Figure 4.2. It has to be noticed that, in general, the filter step cannot determine the inclusion of an object in the query result.

Nevertheless, there are few operators (mostly directional ones) that allow for the finding of query results from the filter step. This is shown in Figure 4.2 by the existence of hits (i.e., answers to the query) in the filter step.

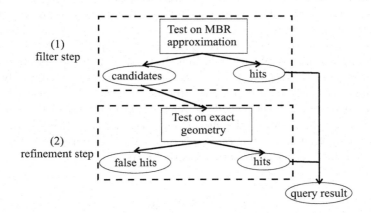

Fig. 4.2. Two-step query processing procedure.

Although examples for the aforementioned operators have been given from the context of queries that are applied on one spatial relation (selection queries), they can be used within spatial join queries as well. A spatial join query finds the set of objects from two (two-way joins) or more (multi-way joins) spatial relations that satisfy a given predicate (e.g., overlap, within-distance, etc.).

In the following, we will describe in more detail the query processing techniques that have been developed for each query type. Since the refinement step is orthogonal to the filtering step, the developed techniques have mainly focused on the latter. For this reason, henceforth we follow this approach by focusing on the filter step of each query type. More details on representations different from the MBR and their impact on the refinement step can be found in [34].

4.2 Range and Topological Queries

The most common operation with an R-tree index is a range query, which finds all objects that a query region intersects. In many cases the query region is a rectangle and the query is called a window query. The processing of a range/window query is defined in [81]. It commences from the root node of the tree. For each entry whose MBR intersects the query region, the process descends to thecorresponding subtree. At the leaf level, for each MBR that intersects the query region, the corresponding object is examined (refinement step). It has to be mentioned that point queries (i.e., find all objects that contain a query point) can also be treated as a range query, because the query point can be considered as a degenerated rectangle.

The intersection operator, which is examined by the range query, can be considered a special case of a more detailed retrieval of topological relations. Papadias et al. [175] developed a systematic description of the topological information that MBRs convey about the corresponding spatial objects and proposed an algorithm to minimize the I/O cost of topological queries, that is, queries that involve topological relations. In particular, the intersection test of the range query corresponds to the *disjoint* or *non-disjoint* condition between the indexed objects (called primary objects, i.e., those contained in the R-tree) and the query object (called the reference object). Although the *disjoint* relation is left unchanged, the *non-disjoint* relation is refined further with the following relations: *meet, equal, overlap, contains*, and *covers*. Figure 4.3 depicts all possible relations between two objects.

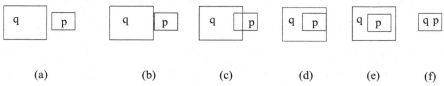

(a)   (b)   (c)   (d)   (e)   (f)

Fig. 4.3. Topological relations: (a) disjoint(q, p); (b) meet(q, p); (c) overlap(q, p); (d) covers(q, p); (e) contains(q, p) or inside(p, q); (f) equal(q, p).

The topological relation between two MBRs does not necessarily coincide with the topological relations between the two corresponding objects, because MBRs are approximate representations. Therefore, given two objects, the corresponding MBRs satisfy, in general, a number of possible relations [175]. For instance, to find all primary objects that *cover* a reference object q, all the reference objects whose MBRs satisfy the relation *covers, contains* or *equal* with respect to the reference object have to be examined. In contrast, for the relation *equal*, only the reference objects whose MBR is *equal* to the reference object's MBR have to be examined. In order to perform a topological query with an R-tree, [175] defines the more general relations that will be used for downward propagation at the intermediate nodes. Let $RN.mbr$ denote the MBR of the entire node (i.e., the father MBR), $e.mbr$ the MBR of a node's entry, q the reference (query) object, and $q.mbr$ its MBR. Table 4.1 illustrates the relationships that have to be tested. By testing the illustrated conditions, the search space can be pruned by discarding nodes that do not satisfy the given conditions. For convenience, we denote this approach as PTSE (from the names of the authors).

Experimental results in [175] indicate that the topological relations can be divided into three categories, with respect to the incurred I/O cost. The first category contains the relation *disjoint*, which requires the larger cost (almost equal to the scanning of the entire R-tree contents); the second contains relations *meet, overlap, inside* and *covered by*, which require medium cost, and

Table 4.1. Relations for the propagation of topological queries.

Possible relation	Relations to be tested
equal($e.mbr,q.mbr$)	equal($RN.mbr,q.mbr$) ∨ covers($RN.mbr,q.mbr$) ∨ contains($RN.mbr,q.mbr$)
contains($e.mbr,q.mbr$)	contains($RN.mbr,q.mbr$)
inside($e.mbr,q.mbr$)	overlap($RN.mbr,q.mbr$) ∨ covers($q.mbr,RN.mbr$) ∨ inside($RN.mbr,q.mbr$) ∨ equal($RN.mbr,q.mbr$) ∨ covers($RN.mbr,q.mbr$) ∨ contains($RN.mbr,q.mbr$)
covers($e.mbr,q.mbr$)	covers($RN.mbr,q.mbr$) ∨ contains($RN.mbr,q.mbr$)
covers($q.mbr,e.mbr$)	overlap($RN.mbr,q.mbr$) ∨ covers($q.mbr,RN.mbr$) ∨ equal($RN.mbr,q.mbr$) ∨ covers($RN.mbr,q.mbr$) ∨ contains($RN.mbr,q.mbr$)
disjoint($e.mbr,q.mbr$)	disjoint($RN.mbr,q.mbr$) ∨ meet($RN.mbr,q.mbr$) ∨ overlap($RN.mbr,q.mbr$) ∨ covers($RN.mbr,q.mbr$) ∨ contains($RN.mbr,q.mbr$)
meet($e.mbr,q.mbr$)	meet($RN.mbr,q.mbr$) ∨ overlap($RN.mbr,q.mbr$) ∨ covers($RN.mbr,q.mbr$) ∨ contains($RN.mbr,q.mbr$)
overlap($e.mbr,q.mbr$)	overlap($RN.mbr,q.mbr$) ∨ covers($RN.mbr,q.mbr$) ∨ contains($RN.mbr,q.mbr$)

the third the relations *equal*, *cover*, and *contains*, which require small cost. The performance of the three R-tree variants, namely original R-tree, R*-tree, R$^+$-tree, is also examined in [175] with respect to topological queries. For small and medium MBRs, R$^+$-tree turned out to perform slightly better than R*-trees, whereas both were found to significantly outperform the original R-tree. For large MBRs, the performance of R$^+$-tree deteriorates and R*-tree requires the smaller I/O cost. Finally, compared to the straightforward case where a range query is first executed and then the topological relations are examined only at the refinement step, the approach of [175] shows an improvement of up to 60%.

4.3 Nearest-Neighbor Queries

The problem of finding k Nearest Neighbors from R-trees has been introduced by Roussopoulos et al. [197]. They describe a branch-and-bound search procedure to avoid the examination of the entire index contents. This approach is based on distance metrics that are developed in [197], which measure the optimistic and pessimistic distances between the R-tree contents and the query point.[1]

Metrics for Nearest-Neighbor Search. Given a query point Q and an object O represented by its MBR $O.mbr$, [197] describes two metrics. The first is called MINDIST and corresponds to the minimum possible distance of Q from O. The second is called MINMAXDIST and corresponds to the minimum

---

[1] The nearest-neighbor query can be also extended to non-point objects, by providing appropriate distance measures. See [88] for more details.

of the maximum possible distances from Q to a vertex of $O.mbr$. These two metrics comprise a lower and an upper bound on the actual distance of O from Q, respectively. Their definition is given in the following. It has to be mentioned that an d-dimensional Euclidean space is assumed, where each rectangle R is represented by the two endpoints $S = [s_1, \ldots, s_d]$ and $T = [t_1, \ldots, t_d]$ of its major diagonal, and it is denoted as $R = (S, T)$. For efficiency and simplicity, the Euclidean distances are squared.

Definition 4.3.1 (MINDIST). *Given a point Q and a rectangle $R = (S, T)$, the minimum distance, denoted as MINDIST(Q, R), is defined as:*

$$\text{MINDIST}(P, R) = \sum_{i=1}^{d} |q_i - r_i|^2$$

where:

$$r_i = \begin{cases} s_i & \text{if } q_i < s_i \\ t_i & \text{if } q_i > t_i \\ q_i & \text{otherwise} \end{cases}$$

Definition 4.3.2 (MINMAXDIST). *Given a point Q and a rectangle $R = (S, T)$, MINMAXDIST(Q, R) is defined as:*

$$\text{MINMAXDIST}(Q, R) = \min_{1 \leq k \leq d} \left(|q_k - rm_k|^2 + \sum_{\substack{i \neq k \\ 1 \leq i \leq d}} |q_i - rM_i|^2 \right)$$

where:

$$rm_k = \begin{cases} s_k & \text{if } q_k \leq \frac{s_k + t_k}{2} \\ t_k & \text{otherwise} \end{cases}$$

and

$$rM_i = \begin{cases} s_i & \text{if } q_i \geq \frac{s_i + t_i}{2} \\ t_i & \text{otherwise} \end{cases}$$

In other words, MINDIST(Q, R) is the distance from Q to the closest point on the boundary of R, which does not necessarily have to be a corner point. MINMAXDIST(Q, R) is the distance from Q to the closest corner of R that is adjacent (i.e., connected with an edge of R) to the corner that is farthest from Q. Figure 4.4 illustrates an example of the MINDIST and MINMAXDIST metrics between a 2-dimensional query point Q and two MBRs. It has to be noticed that for the rectangle that includes Q, according to Definition 4.3.1, MINDIST is equal to 0.

4.3.1 A Branch-and-Bound Algorithm

The branch-and-bound R-tree traversal algorithm presented in [197] uses the aforementioned metrics to order and prune the search tree. The search ordering

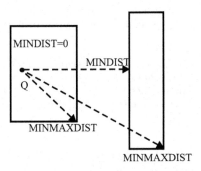

Fig. 4.4. Example of MINDIST and MINMAXDIST.

determines the node visits during the tree traversal. As described in [197], MINDIST produces more optimistic ordering than MINMAXDIST, but there may exist cases of datasets (depending on the sizes and layouts of MBRs) where the latter produces less-costly traversals. For a query point Q, the pruning of node visits during the searching is performed according to the following heuristics:

H1: an MBR M with MINDIST(Q, M) greater than the MINMAXDIST(Q, M') of another MBR M', is discarded because it cannot contain the NN. This is used in *downward pruning*.

H2: an actual distance from Q to a given object O, which is greater than the MINMAXDIST(Q, M) for an MBR M, can be discarded because M contains an object O' that is nearer to Q. This is also used in *downward pruning*.

H3: every MBR M with MINDIST(Q, M) greater than the actual distance from Q to a given object O is discarded because it cannot enclose an object nearer than O. This is used in *upward pruning*.

The algorithm for finding the 1-nearest neighbor is presented in Figure 4.5. It commences from the root node and initializes variable Nearest to infinity (this step is not shown). At a non-leaf node, the procedure finds the MINDIST (according to [197] MINMAXDIST can be used as well) for the node's children MBRs (step 10) and sorts them, along with the corresponding pointers to children nodes, into an active branch list (step 11). Then, pruning of types 1 and 2 is performed (step 12). For each member of the active branch list the procedure is applied recursively (step 15). At the leaf level (steps 1-8) the actual distance function is used (step 3) and the Nearest variable is updated accordingly (steps 4-7). Finally, upward pruning of type 3 is applied (step 16).

For finding the k-nearest neighbors ($k > 1$), the previous procedure can be easily modified to maintain the current k closest objects (along with the corresponding distances) and by pruning with respect to the furthest object each time.

Algorithm NNSearch(TypeNode *Node*, **TypePoint** *Point*, **TypeObj** *Nearest*)
1. **if** *Node* is a leaf
2.   **for** i=1 **to** *Node.count*
3. $dist = \text{objectDIST}(Point, Node.branch[i].rect)$
4.   **if** $dist < Nearest.dist$
5. $Nearest.dist = dist$
6. $Nearest.rect = Node.branch[i].rect$
7.   **endif**
8.   **endfor**
9. **else**
10.   Call **genBranchList**(*branchList*)
11.   Call **sortBranchList**(*branchList*)
12. $last = \textbf{pruneBranchList}(Node, Point, Nearest, branchList)$
13.   **for** $i = 1$ **to** *last*
14. $newNode = Node.branch[branchList[i]]$
15.   Call **NNSearch**(*newNode*, *Point*, *Nearest*)
16. $last = \textbf{pruneBranchList}(Node, Point, Nearest, branchList)$
17.   **endfor**
18. **endif**

Fig. 4.5. Nearest-Neighbor Search Algorithm.

4.3.2 An Improvement to the Original Algorithm

Cheung and Fu [45] have observed that a more efficient version of the branch-and-bound algorithm can be derived when pruning with respect to the number of node accesses is considered. Their approach is based on the observation that only the third pruning heuristic H3 is necessary to maintain the same number of pruned (i.e., not visited) nodes[2]. However, this pruning heuristic has to be applied in a different position, resulting to a modified nearest-neighbor search algorithm. For these reasons, the NNSearch procedure of Figure 4.5 is modified by removing step 12 (which applies pruning heuristics H1 and H2) and repositioning step 3 (pruning heuristic H3) before the recursive application of step 15. Thus, the for-loop of steps 13–17 is given in Figure 4.6.

---

13.   **for** $i = 1$ **to** *last*
14.   Apply Pruning Heuristic 3
15. $newNode = Node.branch[branchList[i]]$
16.   Call **NNSearch**(*newNode*, *Point*, *Nearest*)
17.   **endfor**

Fig. 4.6. Modification in the NNSearch.

The motivation for the modified algorithm is as follows. Heuristic H2 discards an object O if its actual distance from the query point Q is larger than

---

[2] This observation was independently made by [88].

the MINMAXDIST of Q from another MBR. Evidently, the node that contains O cannot be pruned at this point, because it has already been read; thus heuristic H2 does not attain the reduction of node visits. Moreover, Cheung and Fu [45] prove that if a node is pruned by heuristic H1, then it is also pruned by heuristic H3 (when applied at step 14). Thus, the modified algorithm of [45] attains the same number of visited nodes with the original branch-and-bound algorithm. Moreover, based on [88], it can be noticed that the first pruning heuristic is applicable only for finding one nearest neighbor (i.e., $k = 1$), because it bounds the distance at which only the closest object can be found. Conclusively, by avoiding the examination of the first and second heuristic, the modified algorithm of [45] is solely based on MINDIST, and it saves the CPU cost for the computation of the MINMAXDIST. The latter cost may become significant for high dimensional spaces, because its complexity cost belongs in $O(d)$, where d is the number of dimensions.

4.3.3 Incremental Nearest-Neighbor Searching

Hjaltason and Samet [88] presented the problem of incremental nearest-neighbor searching with R-trees. Incremental nearest-neighbor queries find the data objects in their order of distance from the query object (*ranking*). For instance, we have a set of cities C and the query: "find the nearest city to $q \in C$ whose population is larger than 1 million people". By obtaining the neighbors incrementally, they can be examined against the specified criterion. This operation is defined as *distance browsing* [88]. It is different from searching for pre-specified k nearest neighbors, because k cannot be known in advance.

The algorithm for incremental nearest-neighbor searching is based on maintaining the set of nodes to be visited in a priority queue. The entries in the queue are sorted according to the MINDIST metric. It is assumed that the actual objects (e.g., polygons) are stored separately at the data level, as long as each object is completely contained by its corresponding bounding rectangle. Thus, at the leaf-level of the R-tree the object-bounding rectangles (i.e., the MBRs of the data objects) can advocate pruning. The algorithm is depicted in Figure 4.7.

In the IncNNSearch procedure, step 8 reports the next nearest neighbor each time. In step 5 an object O is enqueued only if there are elements in the priority queue with distances less than the distance of O from the query point Q. Otherwise, O is the next nearest neighbor (step 8).

For the analysis of the incremental nearest-neighbor searching algorithm, [88] makes the key observation that any algorithm for the R-tree must visit all the nodes that intersect the search region and notices that the incremental algorithm visits exactly these nodes (this is further described in the following when the previous nearest-neighbor algorithms are also considered). Based on the assumption of low dimensionality and uniform data distribution, it is proven in [88] that the expected number of leaf node accesses to find the k nearest neighbors is $O(k + \sqrt{k})$. It is explained that the $O(\sqrt{k})$ factor is due to leaf nodes that are intersected by the search region but do not contain

---

Algorithm IncNNSearch(TypePoint Q**)**
1.   enqueue($PriorityQueue$, root's children)
2.   **while** $PriorityQueue$ **not** empty
3. $element \leftarrow$ dequeue($PriorityQueue$)
4.   **if** $element$ is an object O or an object bounding rectangle $O.mbr$
5.   **if** $element ==$ $O.mbr$ **and not** $PriorityQueue$ empty
                and objectDist(q, O) $>$ First($PriorityQueue$)$.key$
6.   enqueue($PriorityQueue$, O, objectDist(q, O))
7.   **else**
8.   Output $element$ /*or the associated object*/
9.   **endif**
10.   **else if** $element$ is leaf node
11.   **foreach** object bounding rectangle $O.mbr$ in element
12.   enqueue(PriorityQueue, $O.mbr$, dist($q, O.mbr$))
13.   **endfor**
14.   **else**   /*non-leaf node*/
15.   **foreach** entry e in $element$
16.   enqueue($PriorityQueue$, e, dist(q, e))
17.   **endfor**
18.   **endif**
19. **endwhile**

Fig. 4.7. Optimal Nearest-Neighbor Search Algorithm.

points that satisfy the query. An important factor for the complexity of the algorithm is the cost of the priority queue operations. In case its size gets very large, it may not be possible to be accommodated entirely in main memory. The analysis made this issue illustrates that for 2-dimensional data following uniform distribution, the expected size of the queue is $O(\sqrt{k})$ (at the time point when k points have been reported). For the case of skewed and high-dimensional data, [88] proposes that the queue should be divided in several tiers. One of them remains in main memory while the others lie on secondary storage. When the contents of the main-memory tier are exhausted, they are replaced by the contents of the other tiers.

Evidently, the incremental nearest-neighbor search algorithm can be applied to the problem of finding the k nearest neighbors (for a specified k), because it can terminate after having found the first k neighbors. For this problem, however, the approach of [88] differs from [197]. The branch-and-bound algorithm of Section 4.3.1 traverses the index in a depth-first fashion. Once a node is visited, its processing has to be completed even if other (sibling) nodes are more likely to contain the nearest-neighbor object; thus at each step only local decisions can be made.

In contrast, the described algorithm in [88] makes global decisions by using the priority queue to maintain the nodes that are going to be visited, and chooses among the child nodes of all nodes that have been visited, instead of the current one (as in the case of [197]). Thus, it uses a best-first traversal of the tree and prunes the visits to nodes according to pruning heuristic H3.

Interestingly enough, Berchtold et al. [22] have proposed an analogous k nearest-neighbor searching algorithm that is based on the approach of [86] (apparently, the incremental algorithm of [88] for the case of the R-tree is the extension of [86]). They called the described algorithm Optimal Nearest-Neighbor Search. The "optimality" of the incremental algorithm is with respect to the number of R-tree node visits, and not to the nearest-neighbor problem itself [22, 88]. In particular, let Q be the query point and O_N the nearest neighbor; then the NN-sphere of Q is defined as a sphere with center Q and radius equal to the distance of Q from O_N. Therefore, in [22] it is proven that the "optimal" algorithm (i.e., incremental nearest-neighbor algorithm) visits exactly those nodes whose MBR intersects the NN-sphere. Thus, the incremental algorithm visits the minimum number of nodes necessary for finding the nearest neighbor.

4.3.4 Comparison of Nearest Neighbor Algorithms

From the description of the aforementioned k-nearest-neighbor algorithms (original branch-and-bound KNN [197], the modified MNN [45], and the incremental INN [88]) it follows that there are three design issues that affect the performance of the nearest-neighbor searching:

1. the criterion of ordering node visits,
2. the manner of ordering node visits (i.e., traversal type), and
3. the pruning heuristics.

Experimental results in [197] (also verified by [88]) indicate that, with respect to the first issue, ordering by MINDIST results in more than a 20% improvement (especially when searching in dense areas of the space) compared to MINMAXDIST. This result has been verified only with 2-dimensional bulk-loaded datasets [197]. In these cases, MINDIST is expected to attain a good prediction, because the dead space within MBRs is reduced. In dynamic and high-dimensional data, where deletions can affect the dead space of MBRs, MINMAXDIST (or a combination of the two metrics [197]) can perform better.

For the second issue, the ordering of node visits is done in a depth-first manner in [45, 197], whereas a best-first approach is adopted in [88]. With respect to the third issue, MNN [45] uses only the MINDIST for pruning (heuristic H3). Similarly, INN performs pruning according to MINDIST (heuristic H3), whereas the original KNN algorithm [197] uses all three heuristics. Table 4.2 summarizes the selection made by each algorithm for these issues.

Experimental results in [88] illustrate the superiority of INN over KNN. Considering the distance browsing operation, KNN has to be repeatedly applied, because k is not known beforehand, whereas INN after a point, reaches a stage where it accesses only about one object per reported neighbor; thus it significantly outperforms KNN in this case.[3] For the problem of the k nearest-

---

[3] It has to be noticed that in [88] an optimization was considered for KNN, using previous search results for pruning during the repeated invocation of the algorithm.

Table 4.2. Characterization of nearest-neighbor search algorithms.

	KNN	MNN	INN
Ordering	MINDIST or MINMAXDIST	MINDIST	MINDIST
Traversal type	Depth-first	Depth-first	Best-first
Pruning heuristics	H1,H2,H3	H3	H3

neighbor search (when k is specified), experimental results in [88] indicate an improvement of 20%-30% with respect to execution time, compared to KNN (differently from [197], and [88] KNN is tested for dynamic and not bulk-loaded data). INN also shows good scalability to very large datasets, achieving a speedup from 1.8 to 5.8 over KNN. Nevertheless, the comparison for high-dimensional data is left as an open issue (where it has to be considered that the size of the priority queue may increase significantly and stored on disk). The sensitivity of the nearest-neighbor search procedure against other factors is given by some other experimental results that are presented in [197]. They show that the number k of nearest neighbors searched for, is the dominant term in the components of the constant of proportionality, and the resulted number of node accesses scales linearly to this factor. Also, the aforementioned cost increases linearly with the height of the tree.

4.4 Spatial Join Queries

Given two spatial datasets $A = \{a_1, \ldots, a_n\}$ and $B = \{b_1, \ldots, b_m\}$ (a_i, b_i are spatial objects), the spatial join computes all pairs (a_i, b_j), where $a_i \in A$ and $b_j \in B$ that satisfy a spatial predicate, like the topological operators *overlap* and *covers* (see Section 4.2 for a discussion on topological operators). For instance, such queries can find all rivers that cross cities. Based on the two-step processing scheme (presented at the beginning of Section 4), the R-tree facilitates the filter step, that is, the determination of all pairs (MBR(a_i), MBR(b_j)) that satisfy the required operator. Spatial join queries, different from selection queries (range and nearest neighbor) that are single-scan, are characterized as multiple-scan queries, because objects may have to be accessed more than once. Therefore, this type of query poses increased requirements for efficient query processing. In the sequel of this section, we examine the case of two-way join, whereas multi-way join is examined in the next chapter.

4.4.1 Algorithm Based on Depth-First Traversal

Brinkhoff et al. [35] presented the first algorithm for processing spatial joins using R-trees. Let T_1 and T_2 be the joined R-trees. The basic form of the algorithm traverses the two R-trees in a depth-first manner, each time testing the entries of two nodes RN_1 and RN_2, one from each tree. Let $e_1 \in RN_1$ and $e_2 \in RN_2$. If their MBRs do not intersect, then further examination of the corresponding subtrees can be avoided. Otherwise, the algorithm proceeds

recursively to the entries of the subtrees. This presents a *search pruning* criterion that capitalizes on the clustering properties of the R-tree. The description
of the basic form of the algorithm is given in Figure 4.8.

Algorithm RJ(TypeNode RN_1, TypeNode RN_2)
1.   **foreach** $e_2 \in RN_2$
2.   **foreach** $e_1 \in RN_1$ with $e_1.mbr \cap e_2.mbr \neq \emptyset$
3.   **if** RN_1 is leaf node   /* RN_2 is also a leaf */
4.   **output**(e_1, e_2)
5.   **else**
6.   Call **RJ**$(e_1.ptr, e_2.ptr)$
7.   **endif**
8.   **endfor**
9.   **endfor**

Fig. 4.8. Basic Depth-First Spatial Join Algorithm.

In procedure RJ it is assumed that both trees are of equal height (step 3).
Reference [35] describes that when the trees have different heights and the
algorithm reaches a leaf node (whereas the other node is not a leaf), then
window queries on the subtrees rooted at the non-leaf node are performed
with the MBRs of the entries belonging to the leaf node. Nevertheless, the
experimental results in [35] indicate that window queries do not profit very
much from the proposed optimizations, which will be described in the sequel;
thus the performance of the join query may be impacted in this case. Also, to
avoid multiple rereading of nodes as much as possible, an LRU buffer is used.
With this setting, the basic form of the R-tree join algorithm is I/O-bounded
for small page sizes and CPU-bounded for large ones. Thus, [35] presents two
methods for tuning CPU and I/O time.

CPU-time Tuning. In the basic form of the algorithm, each node entry is examined against all entries of the other node. For this reason, two optimizations
are proposed in [35].

1. **Restricting the search space.** Let two nodes, RN_1 and RN_2, and $I =
   RN_1.mbr \cap RN_2.mbr$ the intersection rectangle. This optimization is based
   on the observation that only the entries $e_1 \in RN_1$ and $e_2 \in RN_2$ for which
   $e_1 \cap I \neq \emptyset$ and $e_2 \cap I \neq \emptyset$ have to be examined, because they are the only
   ones that can have a common intersection. Therefore, the basic form of
   the algorithm, given in Figure 4.8 has to be modified. Before step 1, the
   intersection rectangle I is found and a linear scan of all node entries is
   performed to find those that intersect I. Then, the algorithm is applied
   only to this subset of entries. Experimental results in [35] show that the
   factor of improvement due to this optimization is significant (between 4.6
   and 8.9).
2. **Spatial sorting and plane sweep.** Given two nodes RN_1 and RN_2, let
   $\mathcal{RS}_1$ and $\mathcal{RS}_2$ represent the collection of the MBRs of the node entries,

where $\mathcal{RS}_1 = \langle e_1^1, \ldots, e_1^n \rangle$ and $\mathcal{RS}_2 = \langle e_2^1, \ldots, e_2^m \rangle$. Also, let $\pi_x(t)$ denote the projection of a rectangle t on the x axis. $\mathcal{RS}_1$ and $\mathcal{RS}_2$ are sorted with respect to the lower x-coordinate values of e_1^i and e_2^i, respectively. The sequences are processed using a plane-sweep algorithm. Without harming the generality, let the sweep-line be initially moved to the first rectangle $e_1^1 \in \mathcal{RS}_1$. Then $\mathcal{RS}_2$ is sequentially scanned until a rectangle $e_2^h \in RS_2$ is found that has lower x-coordinate larger than the upper x-coordinate of e_1^1. In this case, the interval $\pi_x(e_1^1)$ intersects $\pi_x(e_2^j)$ for $1 \leq j \leq h$. If $\pi_y(e_1^1)$ also intersects $\pi_y(e_2^j)$, then e_1^1 intersects e_2^j (for high-dimensional spaces, all the remaining dimensions have to be examined). Then, e_1^1 is marked as processed, the sweep-line is moved to the next unmarked rectangle among $\mathcal{RS}_1$ and $\mathcal{RS}_2$ with the smaller lower x-value, and the procedure is repeated until one of the two sequences has been exhausted. The sorted node of entries is not maintained in the nodes during insertions or deletions.

I/O-time Tuning. The reduction of I/O cost, compared to the basic form of the algorithm, is achieved in [35] with the computation of a read schedule, which controls the way nodes are fetched from the disk into the buffer. The following local optimization policies are proposed, which are based on spatial locality; they try to maintain the buffer nodes whose MBRs are close in space.

1. **Local plane-sweep order with pinning.** It is based on the plane-sweep sequence, that was described for the tuning of CPU time, to derive the read-schedule (thus, no additional cost is required). For a pair of entries (e_1, e_2) obtained by the schedule and after the processing of the corresponding subtrees, the degree of the MBRs of both entries is computed. The degree of an MBR is the number of intersections between it and the MBRs of entries belonging to the other tree that have not been processed until this time point. The MBR with the maximum degree is found and the corresponding node is pinned in the buffer. Then the spatial join between the pinned node and all other nodes is computed. The next pair of entries is obtained from the read-schedule, and the procedure is repeated. Due to pinning, pages whose MBR frequently intersects other MBRs are completely processed to avoid their rereading.

2. **Local z-order.** With this optimization, the intersections between the MBRs of the two nodes are first computed. Then the MBRs are sorted with respect to a space-filling curve, like the Peano curve, opting to bring together MBRs that are closer in space (note that this is preserved by the space-filling curve for low-dimensional space only). As in the previous case, the pinning of nodes is applied. With respect to I/O cost, local z-order performs slightly better for small buffer sizes compared to the local plane-sweep order. For larger buffer sizes, the latter performs better. However, the local plane-sweep order does not require additional cost, whereas the local z-order requires computation of the values for the space-filling curve. The experimental results in [35] illustrate that both the aforementioned

optimizations (plane-sweep and z-ordering) achieve up to 45% fewer disk accesses, compared to the basic form of the algorithm.

The overall experimental results (those that evaluate all the described optimizations) indicate that the optimized form of the spatial join performs about 5 times faster than the basic one (notice that the basic form is CPU-bounded, whereas the optimized one is I/O-bounded)[4].

4.4.2 Algorithm Based on Breadth-First Traversal

Unlike the depth-first traversal of [35], Huang et al. [92] propose the synchronous traversal of both R-trees in a breadth-first manner, for the processing of spatial joins. This approach is based on the observation that the method of [35] does not have the ability to achieve a global optimization for the ordering of node visits, because the local optimizations (read-scheduling) performed in [35] do notcapture the access pattern of nodes beyond the currently examined nodes. The BFRJ (Breadth-First R-tree Join) algorithm of [92] opts for such global optimizations.

The basic form of the BFRJ algorithm commences from the two root nodes of the R-trees. It performs a synchronized traversal in terms of the examined levels. BFRJ uses the same search pruning criterion as in [35], i.e., the examination of the subtrees of two nodes can be avoided if the MBRs of the nodes do not intersect. The results, i.e., pairs of intersected entries, at each level l are maintained in the *intermediate join index* (IJI_l). When it completes the join for all tuples at IJI_l, it proceeds to the next level, until the leaf level is reached. If the two R-trees do not have the same height, then when reaching the leaf level of one tree, BFRJ proceeds by descending the levels of the other tree, until the leaf level is reached for this tree. At this point, the resultant IJI (at the leaf level) comprises the output of the algorithm.[5] The basic form of BFRJ is depicted in Figure 4.9.

At steps 2 and 6, BFRJ uses the same optimizations as [35] does for the tuning of CPU time (i.e., restriction of search space and plane sweep). Nevertheless, [92] proposes three new global optimizations for the tuning of I/O time. Due to these optimizations, experimental results in [92] indicate an improvement in terms of disk accesses, compared to the approach of [35]. This improvement is mainly at intermediate buffer sizes (because for small buffer sizes the performance of both methods deteriorates, whereas for large buffer sizes both algorithms perform similarly). At level l, the global optimizations of BFRJ are based on IJI_{l-1} to schedule the reading of nodes, and they are described as follows:

---

[4] It has to be noticed that in [149] an improvement of the join execution time has been reported, which applies a grid-based heuristic instead of plane-sweeping. However, no consideration was paid for the case of a buffer overflow.

[5] Based on [92], the examination of this case is omitted in the following, because it can be addressed easily; thus, R-trees of the same height are assumed.

Algorithm BFRJ(Tree T_1, Tree T_2)
1. $RN_1 = \text{root}(T_1)$, $RN_2 = \text{root}(T_2)$
2. $\text{IJI}_0 = \{(e_1, e_2) \mid e_1 \in RN_1, e_2 \in RN_2, e_1.mbr \cap e_2.mbr \neq \emptyset\}$
3.   **for** $i = 1$ **to** $h - 1$ //same height assumed
4.   **foreach** $(e_1, e_2) \in \text{IJI}_i$
5. $RN_1 = e_1.ptr$, $RN_2 = e_2.ptr$
6. $\text{IJI}_{i+1} = \text{IJI}_{i+1} \cup \{(e_1', e_2') \mid e_1' \in RN_1, e_2' \in RN_2, e_1.mbr \cap e_2.mbr \neq \emptyset\}$
7.   **endfor**
8.   **endfor**
9.   **output** IJI_i /* the IJI of leaf-level */

Fig. 4.9. Breadth-First R-tree Join Algorithm.

1. **IJI Ordering.** If an MBR appears $k > 1$ times in IJI_{l-1}, then it will be referenced k times at level l. Given a fixed size LRU buffer, the appearances of this MBR may be widely scattered within IJI. In this case, it will probably be paged out during its subsequent processing, thus it will have to be fetched from disk multiple times. BFRJ orders the contents of IJI by trying not to spread their multiple appearances too widely. Since each member of IJI corresponds to two MBRs, this form of clustering may have to be performed concurrently for both of them. In [92] several options are considered for the processing with respect to: (a) the lower x-coordinate of the first R-tree, (b) the sum of the centers (for each member of IJI, the x-coordinates of the centers of the two MBRs are calculated, and their sum is taken), (c) the center point (the x-coordinate of the bounding rectangle that includes both MBRs of each IJI member), and (d) the Hilbert value of the center (similar to theprevious case, but the Hilbert value instead of the x value is considered). Experimental results in [92] show that option (a) is better for small buffer sizes, whereas (b) outperforms all others for medium and large buffer sizes (because its storage locality spreads wider to cover both MBRs).

2. **Memory Management for IJIs.** If enough main memory is available, then the contents of IJI can be entirely stored in it. However, in this case the available buffer size for the join computation shrinks. For this reason, [92] examines the storage of IJI contents on disk as well. In this case, the contents are stored only after the corresponding level has been completely written. However, with this option the shuffling of the IJI contents between disk and main memory cannot be avoided. Experimental results indicate that, as expected, the storage in main memory performs better for larger buffer sizes (when there is still enough memory for the join process), whereas for small buffer sizes it is outperformed by the storage on disk.

3. **Buffer management of IJI.** The first global optimization (IJI ordering) cannot eliminate the probability of multiple node references. The multiple readings of a node can be further minimized, if the buffer can predict

which node will be fetched again in the sequel. Therefore, the buffer can purge nodes that have completed their processing. This is achieved by maintaining for each node a counter, which corresponds to the number of the node's appearances in IJI. Each time a node is processed, its counter is reduced by one. Thus, the nodes whose counter is equal to 0 can be purged.

For a comparison between the two described spatial join algorithms, Table 4.3 summarizes the options followed by each one.

Table 4.3. Characterization of spatial join algorithms.

	Brinkhoff et al. [35]	Huang et al. [92]
Traversal type	Depth-first	Breadth-first
CPU time	Restrict search space, plane-sweep	Restrict search space, plane-sweep
I/O time	Plane-sweep/pinning, z-ordering	IJI ordering, memory and buffer management for IJI

4.4.3 Join Between an R-tree-Indexed and a Non-Indexed Dataset

In case that an intermediate query result (e.g., of a range query) participates in the join, an R-tree will not be available for it. A straightforward approach to perform the join in this case is to apply multiple range queries, one for each object in the non-indexed dataset, over the R-tree of the other dataset. Evidently, this approach is efficient only when the size of the intermediate dataset is very small.

An R-tree can be created (e.g., with bulk-loading) for the non-indexed dataset to apply the already described algorithms for joining two R-trees [186]. This approach, however, may introduce a non-negligible cost, required for the R-tree creation. In order to improve the latter approach, Lo and Ravishankhar [139] propose the use of the existing R-tree as a skeleton to build the *seeded tree* for the non-indexed dataset. Also, the *sort-and-match* algorithm [181] sorts the objects of the non-indexed dataset (using spatial ordering), creates leaf nodes that can be accommodated in main memory, and examines each of them with leaves of the existing R-tree of the other dataset with respect to the join condition. Arge et al. [17] propose the *Priority Queue-Driven Traversal* (PQ) algorithm, which combines the index-based and non-indexed-based approaches. Mamoulis and Papadias [145] propose the *slot index spatial join* (SISJ), which applies a hash-join using the structure of the existing R-tree to determine the extents of the spatial partitions.

By additionally considering data that are indexed with Quadtrees, [54] proposes an algorithm that joins a Quadtree with an R-tree data structure. Moreover, Hoel and Samet [86] present a performance comparison of PMR Quadtree join against join for several R-tree-like structures. All the aforementioned methods employ specialized techniques to handle the non-index dataset, which do not directly relate to query processing for existing R-trees. For this reason, further details on them are omitted; the interested reader is referred to the given references.

4.5 Summary

Range and nearest-neighbor searching are fundamental in all data structures. For this reason they attracted a lot of interest in R-trees. The range-searching algorithm of the original R-tree is used in most of the variants. Only by significantly changing the original structure can one develop more efficient range searching. Regarding the nearest-neighbor algorithms, as described, several approaches have been proposed. The algorithm proposed by Hjaltason and Samet [88] is optimal in the number of accessed nodes. Its "browsing" ability is also very appealing, because this paradigm of query is suitable for many applications. However, it is still an open problem to define an optimal algorithm with respect to the overall cost, considering also the cost to manipulate the auxiliary data structures (such as the priority queue). The importance of the spatial join operation resulted in the existence of many join algorithms, which consider several factors (e.g., the type of traversal, the number of joined trees, the number of datasets for which an R-tree is already built, etc.). The research on nearest-neighbor and join algorithms influenced other types of more complex queries, because NN queries and spatial join queries can be considered as primitives for more complex operations (e.g., data mining queries).

5. Processing More Complex Queries

The query processing techniques studied in the previous chapter can be considered fundamental. In recent research, however, several more complex extensions have been proposed, which consider additional aspects. In this chapter, we consider such extensions and present them in the same order as in the previous chapter. Therefore, we first describe extensions to range queries, next we consider extensions to nearest-neighbor queries, and finally we present extensions to spatial join queries. These queries require significant I/O and CPU cost, and therefore sophisticated methods have be applied to reduce processing cost. Finally, approximate query processing techniques are presented that sacrifice accuracy for better performance.

5.1 Categorical Range Queries

As already described, traditional range queries find all objects intersected (covered, etc.) by a query region. In a large number of applications, objects may come aggregated in (disjoint) groups. In this case, an interesting variation of the basic range queries is to search for groups (instead of individual objects themselves) that are intersected by the query region. For instance, consider a set of locations, where each one is associated with its spatial coordinates and its soil type (a common case of thematic layers in GIS). A possible query is to find all soil types of locations that are within a query window. This type of query is denoted Categorical Range Query (CRQ). Another common name is Chromatic Range Query. CRQs have been comprehensively studied in the research fields of computational geometry and main-memory data structures. A first approach to handle CRQs in large spatial databases has been proposed in [153].

A CRQ can be considered as a special range query. As such, it can be processed by first executing the regular range query, i.e., finding individual objects (not categories) within the query region, followed by filtering its output set to select the distinct categories. However, this approach does not take into account the difference between the selectivity (i.e., size of output set) of the CRQ and of the regular range query. In spatial databases, objects that are close in space may share the same value for a categorical attribute (e.g., forest-cover type); thus the selectivity of the CRQ can be much larger (i.e., smaller output size) than with a the regular range query. In such a case, by first processing the plain range query and then filtering with respect to the categorical attribute, the cost is high.

Based on R-trees, [153] develops a multi-tree index that integrates in an efficient way the spatial dimensions and the categorical attribute. This approach is based on the broad concept of the augmentation of nodes with additional information to accelerate queries. The augmentation scheme is based on the notion of maximal/minimal points. Figure 5.1 illustrates an example of a set of two-dimensional points and the corresponding maximal/minimal points.

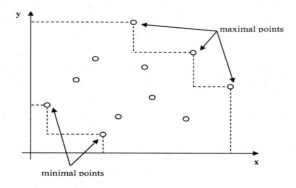

Fig. 5.1. Example of maximal/minimal points.

Each category in a subtree of the R-tree is separately represented through its maximal/minimal points, and the collection of such points for all categories in a subtree comprises the information, which augmentation is based. In particular, the R-tree is augmented with auxiliary data structures that are maintained at each internal (i.e., not leaf) node entry. Each entry e in an internal R-tree node is of the form: $\langle e.\text{mbr}, e.\text{ptr}, e.\text{max\_btree}, e.\text{min\_btree} \rangle$, where $e.\text{max\_btree}$ and $e.\text{min\_btree}$ are pointers to the roots of B$^+$-trees that store the maximal and minimal, respectively, points in the subtree of e (the other two elements, $e.\text{mbr}$ and $e.\text{ptr}$, have their regular meaning). Within the B$^+$-trees, the maximal and minimal points are ordered according to their category values, which comprise the search keys in each B$^+$-tree. Therefore, the two B$^+$-trees of a node entry e are probed with respect to category values, and the maximal and minimal points can be retrieved.

The top part of Figure 5.2 illustrates a sample dataset (the description of categories is also depicted) and the bottom part shows the corresponding multi-tree index. Note that the R-tree nodes are depicted with solid lines whereas the B$^+$-tree ones are drawn with dashed lines. The points in the leaves of the R-tree are stored along with their category, but there is no ordering with respect to the category values. In contrast, in the B$^+$-tree nodes the entries are the maximal/minimal points and they are ordered with respect to their category value. For instance, in node P, the maximal points for category 1 are points p_3 and p_4, and for category 2 it is point p_5. For the same node, the minimal points are: p_1 for category 1 and p_6 for category 2.

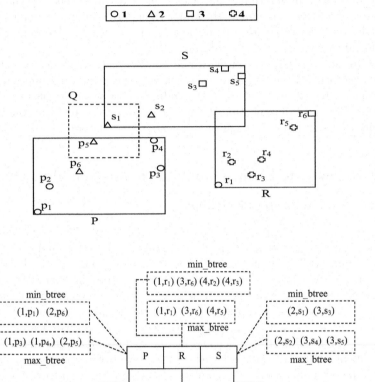

Fig. 5.2. Top: example of a dataset. Bottom: the corresponding augmented R-tree.

Due to the properties of maximal and minimal points, branches of the R-tree can be pruned during the examination of a CRQ. For example, consider the query rectangle Q depicted in the top part of Figure 5.2 and the R-tree in the bottom part of Figure 5.2. Starting from the node whose MBR is rectangle P, the contents of its max_btree (the B-tree with the maximal points) and min_btree (the B-tree with the minimal points) are examined. Point p_5 is contained in Q, thus category 2 is included in the output set. No point is found for categories 3 and 4, whereas we cannot determine from points p_1, p_3, and p_4 whether category 1 exists in Q. Therefore, we proceed to the leaf child of P, where no point from category 1 is found to be contained in Q. The searching continues at the internal nodes, testing the entry whose MBR is rectangle S;

the entry with MBR R is skipped because R is not intersected by Q. In this node, we are searching for categories 1, 3, and 4 because 2 has been output. There are no maximal or minimal points for categories 1 and 4, whereas for category 3 we can determine that it does not exist in Q (because the minimal point s_3 dominates maximally the upper-right corner of Q). Therefore, we need not descend to the subtree of this node, and the searching terminates having included category 2 in the output set.

Experimental comparison with real and synthetic data in [153] illustrates the superiority of the proposed approach over the plain range query and naive scheme for R-tree augmentation. Depending on the value of relative selectivity of the CRQ, the aforementioned approach can achieve performance improvements up to an order of magnitude, for large real datasets.

5.2 Reverse and Constrained Nearest-Neighbor Queries

5.2.1 Reverse Nearest Neighbors

Reverse nearest-neighbor (RNN) queries find the set of database points that have the query point as the nearest neighbor. The RNN and NN problems are asymmetric. If the nearest neighbor of a query point q is a data point p, then it does not hold in general that q is the nearest neighbor of p (i.e., q is not necessarily the reverse nearest neighbor). The aforementioned problem has been introduced in [115], but it was restricted to static data and specialized data structures. Stanoi et al. [219] have developed a reverse nearest-neighbor algorithm for the R-tree, which can handle dynamic data efficiently.

The algorithm of [219] is based on the notion of *space dividing lines*. For the 2-dimensional space, each point can be associated with three lines around it. They are denoted l_1, l_2 and l_3, where l_1 is parallel to the x-axis, and the angles between l_1 and l_2, l_2 and l_3, and l_3 and l_1 are $2\pi/3$. The top part of Figure 5.3 illustrates the arrangement of the three space dividing lines, which determine six regions (denoted as $S_1, \ldots, S_6$).

According to [219], for a query point q and the corresponding region S_i, either the nearest neighbor of q in S_i is also the reverse nearest neighbor, or there does not exist a reverse nearest neighbor in S_i. Therefore, for each of the S_i regions, the nearest neighbor of the query point has to be found. This set of points for all regions determines a candidate set that has to be examined so as to identify the reverse nearest neighbor. Hence, for the 2-dimensional space, this limits the choice of RNN(q) to one or two points in each of the six regions [219]. The corresponding algorithm is depicted in Figure 5.4. Note that the computations corresponding to all six regions are performed in a single traversal and not separately for each region.

Conditions Determined by Space Dividing Lines. Given one of the six regions S_i, the conditional nearest neighbor finds the nearest neighbor of the query point in S_i. This procedure is based on the observation that the examination of points that belong in MBRs that are out of S_i, can be pruned.

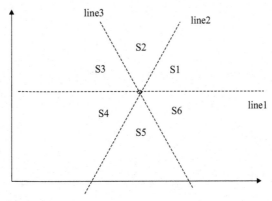

Fig. 5.3. Space dividing lines.

Algorithm RNNSearch(TypePoint q**)**
1. $RNNResult = \emptyset$
2. $CandidateList =$ **CondNNSearch**(q)
3.   Call **EliminateDuplicates**$(CandidateList)$
4.   **foreach** $p \in CandidateList$
5.   Call **NNSearch**(p, r) /*$r = NN(p)$*/
6.   **if** objectDist$(p, q) \leq$ objectDist(p, r)
7. $RNNResult = RNNResult \cup p$
8.   **endif**
9.   **endfor**
10. **return** $RRNResult$

Fig. 5.4. Reverse Nearest-Neighbor Search Algorithm.

However, for an MBR that belongs to S_i, their overlapping is done either fully or partially. This leads to five possible cases, which are illustrated in the top part of Figure 5.5 for, e.g., the S_2 region:

1. MBR A: fully contained (all four vertices within S_2).
2. MBR B: three vertices are in S_2. Thus, there exist some data points in B that are also contained in S_2.
3. MBR C: two vertices are in S_2. Thus, at least one data point of C is also in S_2 (because an entire edge of C is in S_2 and there exist at least one point on that edge).
4. MBR D: only one vertex is in S_2. No implication can be done on the existence of points in D that also belong in S_2.
5. MBR E: no vertices in S_2, but part of E overlaps S_2. No implication can be done on the existence of points in D that also belong in S_2, *nor* on the not existence.

With the consideration of these cases, the conditional nearest-neighbor searching traverses the tree and prunes out the sections that cannot lead to an answer either because: (a) their MBRs do not belong in the examined region, or (b)

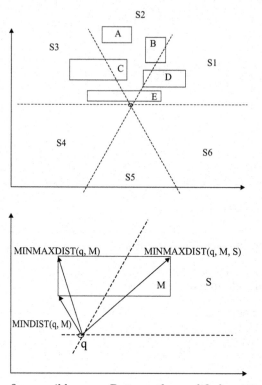

Fig. 5.5. Top: the five possible cases. Bottom: the modified metrics.

it can be determined that other points in the region are closer to the query point.

The approach of [219] for conditional searching is based on the algorithm of [197]. The latter pruning condition is achieved with a modification of the pruning heuristics of [197] (given in Section 4.3.1). Let q be the query point and M the examined MBR. The difference is due to the fact that MINMAXDIST(q, M) may be irrelevant if M is only partially contained by the region S. Hence, [219] proposes a new metric, denoted as MINMAXDIST(q, M, S), which is the distance from the query point to the furthest vertex of M on its closest face included in S. This is illustrated in the bottom part of Figure 5.5, where it is shown that MINMAXDIST(q, M) is with respect to the upper-left vertex of M (not belonging in S), whereas MINMAXDIST(q, M, S) is with respect to the upper-right vertex, which belongs in S. On the other hand, MINDIST(q, M, S) is maintained equal to MINDIST(q, M), regardless of whether the corresponding vertex is in or out S, as long as M overlaps with S. Summing up, Table 5.1 [219] illustrates all these cases.

Table 5.1. Definition of MINMAXDIST(q, M, S) and MINDIST(q, M, S).

# vertices in S	MINDIST(q, M, S)	MINMAXDIST(q, M, S)
0 $(M \cap S = \emptyset)$	∞	∞
0 $(M \cap S \neq \emptyset)$	MINDIST(q, M)	∞
1		
2	MINDIST(q, M)	distance to furthest
3		vertex on closest face in S
4		

5.2.2 Generalized Constrained Nearest Neighbor Searching

The conditional nearest-neighbor searching that is determined by constraints due to space dividing lines is extended by Ferhatosmanoglou et al. [66] to consider more general constraints. They define the constrained nearest-neighbor (CNN) queries as nearest-neighbor queries that are constrained to a specified region (determined by a convex polygon [66]). For instance, let a 2-dimensional map, depicted in the top part of Figure 5.6, contain several cities that are represented by points. Given the query point q, a CNN query finds the nearest city south of q.[1] Evidently, in unconditional nearest-neighbor search, the result would be city a. In contrast, the result of the CNN query is city b. Therefore, CNN queries can combine directional and distance operators. Moreover, CNN queries can involve multiple constraint regions [66].

A straightforward approach for the CNN problem may comprise a 2-phase algorithm. For instance, incremental nearest-neighbor searching [88] can output nearest points in the order of their distance, testing at the same time if they satisfy the given constraint. The searching is terminated when the nearest point that fulfills the constraint (for the k-CNN this is extended until the k-th such point is found). However, this approach may unnecessarily retrieve a large number of points that do not belong in the query region before finding the desired one. Another 2-phase approach can first apply a range query with the specified constrained region and then search for the nearest neighbors in the results of the range query. Depending on the selectivity of the range query, this approach may also unnecessarily retrieve a large number of points that will be discarded during searching for the nearest neighbors.

For these reasons, [66] proposes a new approach that merges the conditions of nearest neighbor and regional constraints in one phase. It is based on an extension of the work described for the reverse nearest neighbor, which considers general areas defined by polygons instead of the regions determined by space dividing lines. CNN again considers the five possible cases for the overlap between the query region and an MBR, which were described in Section 5.2.1. The MINDIST and MINMAXDIST metrics, however, are modified in a different way.

---

[1] Although this constraint does not explicitly determine a convex polygon, as described in [66] the combination of the directional line with the space boundary gives the desired polygon.

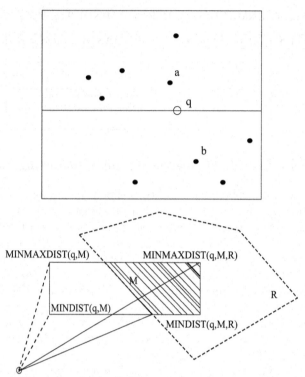

Fig. 5.6. Top: an example of CNN query; Bottom: the modified metrics for CNN.

We have a query (i.e., constraint) region *Reg*, a query point *q*, and an MBR *M*. Also, let the I_R polygon be the intersection between *Reg* and *M*, i.e., $I_R = Reg \cap M$ (several well-known techniques exist to identify the intersection polygon). Having calculated the edges of the I_R polygon, [66] defines MINDIST(*q, M, Reg*) to be the minimum of all distances from *q* to these edges. This case is illustrated in the bottom part of Figure 5.6, where MINDIST(*q, M, Reg*) offers a tighter bound than MINDIST(*q, M*). Similarly, MINMAXDIST as defined by [197] does not hold when *M* is only partially contained in *Reg*. Therefore, [66] defines MINMAXDIST(*q, M, Reg*), which is computed only over the edges of *M* that are completely contained in *Reg* (to identify the distance that guarantees the inclusion of a point from *M* in *Reg*). This case is illustrated in the right part of Figure 5.6, where the shaded area represents I_R, the original metrics are depicted with dashed lines and the modified ones with solid lines.

The CNN algorithm is developed in [66] on the basis of the IncNNSearch algorithm, described in Section 4.3.3, and the proof of its "optimality" is based on the approach followed in [22]. The experimental results in [66] compare the performance of CNN with the 2-phase approach that considers the incremental nearest-neighbor searching (the other 2-phase approach, which is the combination of range and nearest-neighbor query, is not examined). The general conclusion from these results is that, as expected, CNN outperforms the 2-phase approach when smaller constraint regions are used, whereas both methods perform similarly for large regions (that cover a large percentage of the data space).

5.3 Multi-way Spatial Join Queries

The spatial join algorithms that were examined in Section 4.4 focus on the case of two datasets. In GIS applications, large collections of spatial data may have several thematic contents, thus they may involve the join between multiple inputs. multi-way spatial join queries, proposed by Mamoulis and Papadias [144] (an earlier version was presented in [171]), involve an arbitrary number of R-trees. Given n datasets $\mathcal{RS}_1, \ldots, \mathcal{RS}_n$ (each indexed with an R-tree) and a query Q, where Q_{ij} represents the spatial predicate that should hold between $\mathcal{RS}_i$ and $\mathcal{RS}_j$, the multi-way join query finds all tuples $\{(r_{1,w}, \ldots, r_{i,x}, \ldots, r_{j,y}, \ldots r_{n,z}) \mid \forall i, j : r_{i,x} \in RS_i, r_{j,y} \in RS_j, r_{i,x} \ Q_{ij} \ r_{j,y}\}$. Therefore, multi-way spatial join queries can be considered as a generalization of pairwise spatial join queries that were presented in Section 4.4. Query Q can be represented by a graph G_Q whose nodes correspond to the data sets $\mathcal{RS}_i$ and edges to join predicates Q_{ij}. In general, the query graph can be a tree (graph without cycles), a graph with cycles or a complete graph – also called *clique* (every node connected to each other). For instance, Figure 5.7 depicts these three different cases of a query graph along with a tuple that satisfies the corresponding predicates (henceforth, based on [144], it is assumed for simplicity that each predicate Q_{ij} corresponds to the spatial operator *overlap*).

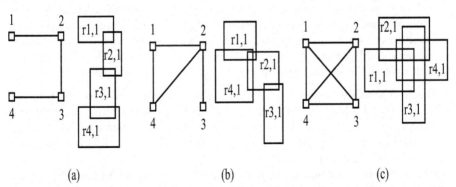

Fig. 5.7. Examples of multi-way queries: (a) Acyclic (chain) query; (b) Query with cycle; (c) Complete graph (clique) query.

One method to perform multi-way spatial joins is the combination of a sequence of pairwise joins (PJM). The order of pairwise joins is determined by the minimization of expected I/O cost (in terms of page accesses). In this sequence, a pair does not necessarily correspond to a join between two R-trees (i.e., indexed datasets). Therefore, (i) RJ or BFRJ (see Section 4.4) is applied when both inputs are indexed, (ii) Slot Index Spatial Join (SISJ) [145] is applied when only one dataset is indexed, and (iii) Hash spatial Join (HJ) [140] when none of the datasets is indexed (i.e., they are intermediate results). The optimal execution plan is selected from the estimation of output size and I/O cost of the algorithms. Queries with cycles are addressed by being transformed to tree expressions using the most selective edges of the graph and filtering the results with respect to the other relations in memory [144].

A different approach from PMJ is also described in [144, 171], called Synchronous Traversal (ST). ST starts from the root nodes and synchronously traverses the R-trees. It proceeds only with the combination of nodes that satisfy the query predicates Q_{ij} until reaching leaf nodes. ST is facilitated by the R-tree structure to decompose the problem into smaller *local* ones at each level. If $f_{\max}$ is the maximum node fanout, then in the worst case each local problem examines $(f_{\max})^n$ combinations. The local problem is defined by:

- A set of n variables, $v_1, \ldots, v_n$, each corresponding to an R-tree.
- A domain RS_i, for each variable v_i that consists of the entries $\{e_{i,1}, \ldots e_{i,f_i}\}$ of node RN_i in the T_i tree (f_i is the fanout of RN_i).
- Each pair of variables (v_i, v_j) is constrained by predicate *overlap*, if Q_{ij} is true.

Based on [144], a binary assignment $\{v_i \leftarrow e_{i,x}, v_j \leftarrow e_{j,y}\}$ is consistent iff (Q_{ij} is true) $\Rightarrow$ ($e_{i,x}$ overlaps $e_{j,y}$). A solution of a local problem is an n-tuple $\tau = (e_{1,w}, \ldots, e_{i,x}, \ldots, e_{j,y}, \ldots, e_{n,z})$ such that $\forall\, i,j\{v_i \leftarrow e_{i,x}, v_j \leftarrow e_{j,y}\}$ is consistent. The objective of ST is finding all assignments of entries to variables so that all predicates are satisfied. The complete algorithmic description of ST is given in Figure 5.8 (it is assumed that all trees have the same height).

Park et al. [182] made the observation that the optimization techniques of the original two-way R-tree join algorithm are still required in the case of multi-way join, and they proposed the M-way join algorithm. Furthermore, Mamoulis and Papadias [144] proposed two optimizations for the ST algorithm, which exploit the spatial structure of the multi-way join problem:

Static Variable Ordering (SVO). This heuristic preorders the problem variables by placing the most constrained one first. Thus, variables are sorted in decreasing order of their degree. SVO is applied once (before performing ST) and produces a static order that is used in find-combinations and space-restriction procedures.

Plane-Sweep combined with Forward Checking (PSFC). PSFC is an improved implementation of procedure find-combinations, which decomposes a local problem into a series of smaller problems, one for each event of the sweep line. With this heuristic, the overhead of searching and backtracking in large domains is avoided.

Experimental results in [144] show that the improvement due to SVO is significant when the first few variables are more constrained, whereas this does not apply for complete query graphs. The combination of SVO-PSFC presents

---

Algorithm ST(TypeGraph G_Q, Array of TypeNode A)
1.   **for** $i=1$ **to** n
2. D_i = space-restriction(G_Q, A, i)
3.   **if** $D_i = \emptyset$
4.   **return** /* no qualifying */
5.   **endif**
6.   **endfor**
7.   **foreach** $\tau \in$ **find-combinations**(G_Q, D)
8.   **if** N are leaves
9.   **output** τ
10.   **else**
11.   Call ST$(G_Q, \tau.\text{ref}[\,])$
12.   **endif**
13.   **endfor**

Procedure space-restriction(TypeGraph G_Q, Array of TypeNode A, i)
1. $RN_i = A[i]$
2. $D_i = \emptyset$
3.   **foreach** $e_{i,x} \in RN_i$
4.   valid = true
5.   **foreach** node RN_j with a link between i and j in G_Q /*Q_{ij} = true*/
6.   **if** $e_{i,x} \cap RN_j.\text{mbr} == \emptyset$
7.   valid = false /* pruned */
8.   **break**
9.   **endif**
10.   **endfor**
11.   **if** valid == true
12. $D_i = D_i \cup e_{i,x}$
13.   **endif**
14.   **endfor**

Fig. 5.8. Synchronous R-tree traversal multi-way join algorithm.

significant reduction in both I/O and CPU cost, compared to the version of ST that does not use these optimizations (PSFC performs better with increasing page size). In general, the savings in CPU cost are considered more significant in [144], because ST is CPU bounded.

The experimental comparison between ST and PJM illustrates that data density does not affect the CPU time of ST; in contrast, PJM is greatly impacted. Therefore, dense data are best processed by ST, whereas sparse data and queries (i.e., not complete graph queries) favor PJM. In the latter case ST still achieves lower I/O cost, but its CPU cost increases significantly due to the large number of examined variables. For these reasons, [144] concludes that ST and PJM are complementary, because each outperforms the other under different conditions. Thus, depending on the data and query density, a combination should be used.

Based on the cost estimation of PJM and ST, [144] uses optimization with dynamic programming to derive the query execution plan. Each time, either ST or PJM is selected for the intermediate executions. As indicated by experimental results in [144], with this approach, execution plans, which are slightly more expensive (12% in the worst case) than the optimal one, are selected. Nevertheless, if n (the number of input R-trees) is larger than 10, the cost of the dynamic programming is prohibitive. For this reason, [144] also describes a randomized search algorithm for finding the execution plan of large queries, i.e., for large n.

5.4 Incremental Distance-Join and Closest-Pair Queries

5.4.1 Incremental Distance Join

Given two spatial datasets $\mathcal{RS}_1$ and $\mathcal{RS}_2$, distance join queries find the subset of the Cartesian product $\mathcal{RS}_1 \times \mathcal{RS}_2$, which satisfies an order that is based on distance. Hjaltason and Samet [87] present an incremental approach for processing distance join and distance semi-join queries (the latter is a variant of the former and finds for each object in $\mathcal{RS}_1$ the nearest object in $\mathcal{RS}_2$). The incremental algorithms for these queries described in [87] report the results one by one, with respect to the distance ordering. The spatial join algorithms that have been described in Section 4.4, focused on the overlap operator. However, they can be easily extended to handle the distance (i.e., within) operator for the distance-join query. Nevertheless, in contrast to the incremental algorithm, they will first have to compute the entire result and then to sort it before starting the output. Evidently, the focus of the incremental algorithm is on starting the output of results as early as possible.

Basic Form of Incremental Algorithm. For two R-trees T_1 and T_2, the Incremental Distance-Join Algorithm (IDJ) maintains a set $\mathcal{P}$ of pairs (each pair has one item from T_1 and one item from T_2). Initially, $\mathcal{P}$ contains the root nodes of the two trees. During the processing of $\mathcal{P}$'s entries, each time a pair $p \in P$ is encountered that contains a node entry e (i.e., not a data object), it is replaced by all pairs resulting by substituting e with all its children nodes. The elements of $\mathcal{P}$ have to be kept sorted according to the distance between the two corresponding items of the element, so that pairs are processed in order of their distance and the results are reported in the required order. To achieve this, $\mathcal{P}$ is implemented as a priority queue, where the key that orders the elements is the distance between the two pairs. Consequently, the element at the head of $\mathcal{P}$ is retrieved each time. When $\mathcal{P}$'s items are both data objects, then the pair is output as the next result, because no subsequent pair will have a smaller distance. Otherwise, as described, if one item of the pair in the head is a node, then all resulting pairs are inserted in queue, by replacing the item with all the children nodes of the corresponding node. This procedure is depicted in Figure 5.9. Notice that the ProcessNode procedure (also depicted) uses the same basic loop as the incremental nearest-neighbor algorithm of Section 4.3.3, where Item$_2$ corresponds to the query object.

Algorithm IDJ(Tree T_1**, Tree** T_2**)**
1. $Queue \leftarrow (0, (R_1.root, R_2.root))$
2.   **while** $Queue$ **not** empty
3. $elem \leftarrow Queue$
4.   **if** both items of $elem$ are data objects
5.   **Output**$elem$ /*elem $= (O_1, O_2)$*/
6.   **else if** both items OBRs
7. $dist = \text{objectDist}(O_1, O_2)$
8.   **if** $Queue$ empty **or** $dist \leq \text{Front}(Queue).dist$
9.   **Output** (O_1, O_2)
10.   **else**
11. $Queue \leftarrow (D, (O_1, O_2))$
12.   **endif**
13. **else if** first item of elem is node
14.   Call **ProcessNode**($Queue, elem, 1$)
15. **else**
16.   Call **ProcessNode**($Queue, elem, 2$)
17. **endif**

Procedure ProcessNode(TypeQueue, $Queue$**, TypeElem** $elem$**, int** $order$**)**
     /* $elem = (i_1, i_2)$ */
1.   **if** $order == 1$
2. $Node = i_1$, $\text{Item}_2 = i_1$
3.   **else**
4. $Node = i_2$, $\text{Item}_2 = i_1$
5.   **endif**
6.   **if** $Node$ is leaf
7.   **foreach** entry $O.mbr$ of $Node$
8. $Queue \leftarrow (\text{dist}(O.mbr, \text{Item}_2), (O.mbr, \text{Item}_2))$
9.   **endfor**
10. **else**
11. **foreach** child pointer ptr of Node
12. $Queue \leftarrow (\text{dist}(ptr, \text{Item}_2), (ptr, \text{Item}_2))$
13. **endfor**
14. **endif**

Fig. 5.9. Basic form of Incremental Distance-Join Algorithm.

Optimizations to the Basic Form. In [87] two types of optimizations are described over the basic form of the algorithm, with respect to the tie-breaking criteria and the order of node processing.

For elements with the same distance (i.e., the value of the key of the element in the priority queue) two choices can be made, which affect the traversal pattern:

Depth-first-like traversal: when it is required to produce results as soon as possible, elements containing data objects or MBRs can be given priority over other elements with the same distance. Also, for elements containing non-leaf items, priority can be given to nodes at smaller levels (i.e., deeper in the tree).

Breadth-first-like traversal: when a large number of results is required, elements that contain nodes at higher levels can be given priority among the elements with the same distance.

Besides tie-breaking, another factor that affects the incremental distance-join algorithm is with respect to the order of processing the node items, when a pair (RN_1, RN_2) with non-leaf nodes is retrieved from the head of the priority queue. In [87] three options are presented:

Basic: the one used by the basic form of the algorithm, given in Figure 5.9, where RN_1 is arbitrarily chosen to be processed. However, with this option, T_1 (the first R-tree) will be traversed down to the leaf level before the nodes of T_2 will be started to being processed.

Even: in order to achieve a more even traversal of the two trees, the node at a higher level (i.e., at shallower depth) is chosen to be processed.

Simultaneous: differently from the previous two options, this one processes both RN_1 and RN_2 simultaneously. Evidently, further optimizations, like the plane-sweep algorithm, can be used in this case. A similar approach has been followed in [216].

The evaluation of all the described options is given in [87] through experimental results. The performance in all cases is dominated by the number of distance calculations and the priority queue size. These results indicate that the best performance is achieved by the combination of Even and Depth-First-like traversal.

Specifying a Distance Range. During the processing of the distance join, the priority queue may become very large. For the implementation of the priority queue, [87] describes an approach that is analogous to the one presented in Section 4.3.3, which divides the queue in a number of partitions. One partition is kept in main memory, and its contents are replaced by the other partitions, which are maintained on disk. Nevertheless, most of the pairs will have a large distance and will probably never be retrieved by the queue, depending on the number of requested results. In order to limit the number of entries in the priority queue, [87] proposes the use of restrictions based on a minimum and a maximum specified distance that the query results have to satisfy. The examination of a pair against the specified minimum and maximum distance is done with the use of the MINDIST and MINMAXDIST metrics (see Section 4.3). These modifications are incorporated in the algorithm as follows. Before enqueuing a pair $(O.mbr, Item_2)$ at step 8, the MINDIST$(O.mbr, Item_2)$ and MINMAXDIST$(O.mbr, Item_2)$ are examined against the user-specified constraints. The same is applied at step 12, before the insertion of a pair $(c, Item_2)$.

If no such constraints on the distance can be posed by the user, [87] sets an upper bound on the number of examined pairs (in the same way that the "STOP AFTER" clause of SQL reports only a specified number k of results). This is done by estimating a lower bound for the distance $Dist_{max}$, which can be used to impose the required constraint.

Experimental results in [87] show that by setting a limit to the distance, the performance is improved considerably. On the other hand, an upper bound on the required number of pair results pays off only if it is not very large. However, this is a sensible assumption in many real world applications.

5.4.2 Distance Semi-Join Query

As mentioned, the distance semi-join query is a special case of the distance-join query, because for each pair (O_1, O_2) in the result, the object O_1 appears only once (i.e., it does not appear in any other pair). In order to achieve this, [87] uses a set S_I to keep track of all first objects in each pair that is output. The following options are being described for this purpose:

Outside: computes the distance join and eliminates duplicates in a post-processing phase.

Inside: in the incremental distance-join algorithm, if for a dequeued element (O_1, O_2) O_1 is an object that has been examined already (i.e., it belongs in S_I), then this pair is discarded. Furthermore, the ProcessNode procedure can ignore entries that correspond to objects that are members of S_I.

Local: inside the ProcessNode procedure, for a pair of the form (O_1, RN_2) where O_1 is a data object and RN_2 is a non-leaf node entry, finding the closest object to O_1 that exists in the subtree of RN_2 downward pruning can be performed according to the MINMAXDIST.

GlobalAll: for each node and data object in the first R-tree, the smallest $Dist_{max}$ distance that has been encountered so far, is maintained. A new pair (O_1, O_2) is enqueued only in the case that its distance is smaller than $Dist_{max}$ for O_1. Since the GlobalAll option may require significant memory space, $Dist_{max}$ can be maintained for nodes only. This variation is called GlobalNode.

The previous options are examined experimentally in [87]. These results indicate that the Outside option is outperformed by the Inside option, when a large number of pair results are required. Regarding the other three options, GlobalAll presents the best performance. It is interesting to notice that the distance semi-join is also compared with the straightforward approach of applying multiple nearest-neighbor queries, one for each object of the first R-tree. The results of [87] show that the incremental algorithm outperforms the straightforward one (up to 40% improvement).

5.4.3 Finding Closest Pairs

As already described, the incremental distance-join algorithm can be easily modified to produce up to k pairs [87]. In this case, the algorithm finds the k closest pairs between the two datasets, that is, the pairs of objects from the two datasets that have the k smallest distances between them ($k = 1$ yields to the classic closest-pair problem of computational geometry). For instance, given a collection of archeological sites and holiday resorts, the k closest-pair query finds sites that have the k smallest distances to a resort, so tourists are easily accommodated.

Corral et al. [50] propose an approach, called CP, for closest-pair queries that is different from the one in [87]. Two types of algorithms are being described as follows. (We present the case for $k = 1$, because the extension to $k > 1$ is easy, according to [50]. Also, we assume that the trees have the same height.):

Recursive algorithm based on sorting distances. This algorithm, call STD, descends the two R-trees, starting from the root nodes, and keeps track of the closest distance $Dist_c$ found so far. When two internal nodes are accessed, the MINMAXDIST is calculated for all pairs formed by their contents. Thus, $Dist_c$ can be updated (a kind of downward pruning) if it is larger than one such distance. Also, the MINDIST is calculated for each pair, and the pairs are sorted with respect to it. The descending to subtrees proceeds with this order, but only for those pairs whose MINDIST is smaller than $Dist_c$. When reaching the two leaves, the actual object distances are calculated, and $Dist_c$ can be updated[2].

Non-recursive algorithm based on heap. Similar to [87], this algorithm, called HEAP, maintains the pairs to be examined within a heap structure, sorted with respect to MINDIST metric. However, differently from [87], HEAP considers only pairs that have MINDIST smaller than $Dist_c$. Moreover, similar to STD, HEAP updates $Dist_c$ with respect to the MINMAXDIST metric.

Therefore, it can be concluded that STD is a type of depth-first closest-pair algorithm, which considers local optimizations. In contrast, HEAP and the incremental distance-join algorithm belong to the type of best-first algorithms, which consider global optimizations. Recall that these two different algorithmic types have also been described for nearest neighbor and join queries. Evidently, closest-pair queries combine the characteristics of both these types of queries.

Regarding the tie-breaking criteria, [50] describes several, however the best performance is achieved by resolving ties by giving priority to the pair whose elements have the largest MBR. Also, different tree heights are addressed with two methods: (a) Fix-at-root stops the downward propagation in the tree with the lower level and continues the propagation in the other tree, until a pair of nodes at the same level is found. (b) Fix-at-leaves works in the opposite way from the former. Experimental results in [50] show that the fix-at-root method presents better performance.

The comparison between STD and HEAP, which is experimentally performed in [50], indicates that HEAP outperforms STD for very small buffer sizes and for datasets with large overlapping. However, for medium and large

---

[2] Note that STD is formed by a number of optimizations, which are presented separately in [50], namely Naive, Exhaustive and Simple Recursive. Herein we only present STD because it is the final form of these intermediate versions, and because it outperforms them significantly [50].

buffer sizes, STD clearly compares favorably to HEAP, because it can take better advantage of the available buffer space. This conclusion holds for both small and large values of k. STD and HEAP are also compared with the incremental distance join algorithm of [87]. Two options are considered for the latter according to the order of processing, Even and Simultaneous (see Section 5.4.1). Differently from the results in [87], those in [50] show that the Simultaneous option leads to better results, especially for very large k (because Even focuses on the as-quick-as-possible production of results, which is achieved better for small k, as explained in [87]). Nevertheless, STD outperforms both Simultaneous and Even, by a factor of 20% to 50%. Heap also outperforms the incremental algorithm, but compared to Simultaneous, it performs better only for small buffer sizes. These results are explained in [50], based on the observation that the incremental algorithm is likely to insert a large number of pairs in the corresponding priority queue, especially for large values of k. In contrast, HEAP maintains a smaller number of pairs,[3] and STD does not use such an additional structure (it is recursive). Thus, the large size of the priority queue results in an increased I/O overhead for the incremental algorithm, due to the partitions of the queue that are stored on disk (see Section 5.4.1). A detailed performance evaluation considering the impact of buffering in the performance of closest-pair queries has been reported in [55].

5.5 All Nearest-Neighbor Queries

For two datasets A and B that contain points, which are indexed by two R-trees T_A and T_B, the all nearest-neighbor query (ANN) finds for each $a \in A$ its nearest neighbor $NN(a) \in B$. This query finds several applications in geographical information systems or urban planning and resource-allocation applications, e.g., find all the nearest warehouses for each supermarket. ANN queries have also been used in [154], to speed-up clustering.

A simplistic approach to process ANN queries is to perform a single NN query on T_B for each point of A. Evidently, this approach will lead to prohibitive cost. Although approaches to optimize multiple similarity queries have been proposed, they assume that the number of queries is small enough to fit in main memory. However, in case of ANN queries, the number of queries is equal to the number of points in A, thus this assumption may not hold. Another approach to process ANN queries may be based on finding all closest pairs (see Section 5.4.3). However, it turns out that this approach, for ANN queries, is much worse than the aforementioned simplistic method. For these reasons, Zhang et al. [250] proposed new techniques to process ANN queries when A and B datasets are indexed with R-trees.[4]

---

[3] The comparison between the size of the priority queue (incremental algorithm) and the heap structure (HEAP algorithm) is not given explicitly in [50].

[4] They also addressed the case when one or both datasets are not indexed. Nevertheless, herein we focus on the case of indexed datasets.

The first technique is based on the *multiple nearest-neighbor* (MNN) algorithm. MNN applies a NN query on T_B for each point in A. In order to avoid the drawbacks of the simplistic approach, MNN takes into account the ordering of points in A. Points of A that are close to each other comprise consecutive NN queries, so that an LRU buffer can be used effectively, because such points are expected to fetch about the same nodes from T_B. To achieve this, MNN capitalizes on the clustering that is already performed in T_A, thus points in the same leaf in T_A form consecutive NN queries. Moreover, to further improve spatial locality, the leaf nodes of T_A are examined according to the Hilbert value of their MBR's center. MNN is expected to be efficient in terms of I/O time. However, in terms of CPU time, it requires a very large number of distance calculations.

To resolve the problem of MNN, *batched NN* (BNN) is proposed, which retrieves the nearest neighbors of multiple points at a time. In particular, BNN divides the points of A into n disjoint partitions $G_{A_1}, G_{A_2}, \ldots, G_{A_n}$. For each G_{A_i}, T_B is traversed only once, leading to drastic reductions in the number of distance calculations.

Let the currently examined group be G_A. Distance $globaldist(G_A, B)$ stores the maximum $NNDist(a_i, B)$ for all points $a_i \in G_A$, i.e., it is the largest radius (with respect to the corresponding nearest-neighbor spheres) of the points in G_A. T_B is traversed by visiting nodes according to increasing MINDIST from G_A. This allows the pruning of all subtrees rooted to an entry e_B, for which $mindist(G_A, e_B) > globaldist(G_A, B)$. In a leaf RN_B, a simplistic approach would compute the distance of all points in G_A to all points in RN_B. However, Zheng et al. [250] exploit the following pruning criteria:

– Do not consider all $a_i \in G_A$, for which $NNdist(a_i, B) < mindist(a_i, RN_B)$.
– Do not consider all $b_j \in RN_B$, for which $mindist(G_A, b_j) > globaldist(G_A, B)$.

Furthermore, the remaining points to be considered in RN_B are sorted according to their coordinate, for the axis with the largest RN_B's MBR projection. If a point $a_i \in G$ (from those remaining from consideration) is on the left of some b_j and $NNdist(a_i, B) < dist(a_i.x, b_j.x)$, then no point $b_m \in RN_B, m > j$ can be the nearest neighbor of a_i. The same holds for the symmetric case, i.e., when a_i is on the right of b_j, all $b_m, m < j$ can be pruned. By exploiting this observation, further pruning can be done, as described in [250].

Evidently, the way the points of A are grouped is crucial for the performance of ANN queries. The following criteria have to be considered while performing such a grouping [250]:

1. The number of points in each group should be maximized to decrease the resulting number of NN queries that have to be performed (i.e., fewer groups lead to fewer queries).
2. The MBR of each group should be minimized, because a smaller MBR can be more effective for pruning (with respect to the previously described pruning criteria).

3. The number of points in each group should be such that they can be stored entirely in main memory.

Clearly, the first criterion can be in conflict with the other two. To consider these criteria as much as possible, the clustering of points into nodes in the R-tree T_A is exploited. In particular, BNN starts from the root of T_A and visits its nodes according to the Hilbert value of their MBR's center. When a leaf is reached, its points are inserted into the current group. The inclusion of points into the current group stops when a criterion is violated. As a consequence, the points of a leaf may belong to different groups.

Experimental results in [250] indicate that BNN queries are up to an order of magnitude faster than ANN queries when using the all-closest-pair algorithm. Moreover, BNN queries are more efficient than MNN queries, because they retain the low I/O cost of batching, and they attain significant savings in terms of CPU time.

5.6 Approximate Query Processing on R-trees

Depending on the query nature and data properties, exhaustive processing of some spatial queries (e.g., multi-way spatial joins) can be prohibitively expensive due to the exponential nature of the problem. Therefore, approximate solutions are important in the spatial query processing context, because such solutions can provide good bounds of the optimum result (sacrificing accuracy) and, in practice, they can be obtained by users much faster than the precise ones. Most of the known approximate algorithms on R-trees can be classified into one of the two following approximate techniques: *search space reduction* and *heuristic search*.

For the search space reduction techniques, when it is not computationally feasible to enumerate all the possible cases, we may systematically enumerate only a partial fraction using different methods. The computational cost required by an algorithm can be reduced if the search space is restricted by some means, at the possible expense of exact optimality.

The most representative search space reduction techniques, which guarantee that the quality result is bounded by some constant in terms of distance error are the ε-approximate and the α-allowance technique. Their main characteristics are described here:

ε-**approximate technique.** Given any positive real ε ($\varepsilon \geq 0$) as maximum distance relative error to be tolerated, the result of a query is $(1 + \varepsilon)$-approximate if the distance of its i-th item is within relative error ε (or a factor $(1 + \varepsilon)$) of the distance of the i-th item of the exact result of the same query. Note that for $\varepsilon = 0$, the approximate algorithm behaves as the exact version and outputs the precise solution.

α-**allowance technique.** When the pruning mechanism is applied, an item X is discarded if $MINDIST(X) + \alpha(z) > z$, where z ($z \geq 0$) is the current pruning distance value and $\alpha(z)$ is an allowance function. In order to apply this approximate method, $\alpha(z)$ is assumed to satisfy that $\alpha(z) \geq 0$ for all z and $z_1 \leq z_2$ implies that $z_1\alpha(z_1) \leq z_2a(z_2)$. Typical forms of $\alpha(z)$ are: $\alpha(z) = b$ (b is a non-negative constant), and $\alpha(z) = z \cdot \gamma$ (g is a constant with $0 \leq \gamma \leq 1$, i.e., a positive real in the interval $[0,1]$). If $\alpha(z) = b$, the absolute distance error of the approximate result is bounded by b. On the other hand, if $\alpha(z) = z \cdot \gamma$, the relative distance error of the approximate result is bounded by γ [53]. The exact algorithm is obtained when $\gamma = 0$. The usage of this approximate technique is more appropriate than ε-approximate for easy adjustment of the quality of the result by users, because α-allowance uses a bounded parameter ($0 \leq \gamma \leq 1$), whereas ε-approximate uses an unlimited upper bound ($\varepsilon \geq 0$).

These techniques can be utilized by algorithms for distance-based queries using R-trees, such as: distance-range queries, k-NNQ [197], KCPQ [50], buffer queries [40], k-way distance-join queries [51]. For example, if we consider the α-allowance technique ($\alpha(z) = z \cdot \gamma$, for $0 \leq \gamma \leq 1$), the iterative and non-incremental approximate branch-and-bound algorithm for processing k closest pairs for two datasets indexed by R-trees is illustrated in Figure 5.10, where it is assumed that both R-trees are of the same height. Moreover, z is the distance value of the k-th closest pair found so far, which is set to infinity in the beginning.

The α-allowance technique and N-consider (it considers only a specific percentage $0 < N_I \leq 1$ of the total number of entries from the internal R-tree node, following the normal processing order) has been applied under limited time in k-CPQ algorithms using R-trees for high-dimensional data [53] and spatial data in k-way distance-join query algorithms [51]. For high-dimensional data, this hybrid technique reported excellent results (reduced response time, preserving a high degree of accuracy in the approximate result) for KCPQ using $\gamma = 1.0, N_I = 0.5$ with unlimited time. In the case of a k-way distance-join query (it is a very expensive query, when the number of input spatial datasets is increased, in terms of response time), the same values for approximate parameters (γ and N_I) reported excellent results as well, i.e. a good balance between cost and quality of the approximate result is obtained. Obviously, in both cases, the quality of the best approximate result found so far using the approximate algorithm is successively improved as long as more computation time is given.

In order to measure the quality/accuracy of the approximate result, two metrics were taken into account in [53] and [51]: *Average Relative Distance Error (ARDE)* and *Quality of the Approximate Result (QAR)*. In order to obtain ARDE, the exact result for the query is obtained off-line, then the approximate algorithm is applied, and the average relative distance error of all elements of the results is calculated. QAR obtains the percentage of elements in the approximate solution that also appear in the exact result (i.e., values of QAR close to 1.0 indicate a good quality of the approximate solution, because QAR=1.0 corresponds to the value for the exact result).

Algorithm AHEAP

/* Determines the k closest pairs between two datasets
indexed by R-trees, based on the α-allowance approximate technique */
1.   Start from the roots of the two Rtrees; initialize H
/* H is a minimum binary heap with references to pairs of R-tree nodes
accessed so far from the two different R-trees and their MINMINDIST value
$(< MINMINDIST(M_i, M_j), Addr\,RP(M_i), Addr\,RQ(M_j) >)) $ */
2.   if two internal nodes are accessed
3.   apply the distance-based plane-sweep technique [50] to obtain ENTRIES
         /* ENTRIES is the reduced set of pairs of candidate entries */
4.   Insert into the minimum binary heap H, the item
         $< MINMINDIST(M_i, M_j), Addr\,RP(M_i), Addr\,RQ(M_j) >$ from
         ENTRIES having $MINMINDIST(M_i, M_j) \le z * (1\gamma)$
5.   endif
6.   if two leaf nodes are accessed
7.   apply the distance-based plane-sweep technique to obtain ENTRIES
8.   foreach (p_i, q_j) having $MINMINDIST(p_i, q_j) < z$
9.   remove the root of the $Kheap$
             /* heap holds pairs of points ordered by min distance */
10.   insert the new pair of points (p_i, q_j)
11.   update this data structure and z
12.   endfor
13. endif
14. if the minimum binary heap H is empty
15.   return
16. else
17.   get the item $<$MINMINDIST, $Addr\,RP, Addr\,RQ >$
         on top of the minimum binary heap H
18.   if this item has the MINMINDIST values larger than $z \cdot (1\gamma)$
19.   return
20.   else
21.   goto step 2 and repeat for this item
22.   endif
23. endif

Fig. 5.10. The AHEAP algorithm for α-allowance approximate computation of k closest pairs.

The most representative heuristic search techniques that can be used in algorithms on R-trees to reach good enough results (but not necessary optimal) for spatial queries, are: local search, simulated annealing, and genetic algorithms. They can be applied on algorithms for multi-way spatial joins [145] and k-way distance-join queries [51] using R-trees, due to the exponential nature of the problems. In particular, local search and genetic algorithms have been successfully used on multi-way spatial joins to report fast inexact results, using R-trees as the underlying spatial access method [169]. For example, in the approximation context, local search is applied to improve the quality of initial approximate solutions obtained by some means. In [169] an Indexed Local Search (ILS) for approximate processing of multi-way spatial joins that uses indexes (R-trees) to improve solutions was proposed. The outline of the ILS algorithm under limited time is illustrated in Figure 5.11.

Algorithm ILS

1. $bestSolution = S_\infty$
2.   **while not** (Time threshold)
3. S = random seed
4.   **while not** (LocalMinimum(S))
5.   determine an R-tree T_i
6. S = **findBestSolution**(Root of T_i, S)
7.   **if** cost(S) < cost(S)
8. $S = S$
9.   **endif**
10.   **endwhile**
11.   **if** cost(S) < cost($bestSolution$)
12.   bestSolution $= S$
13.   **endif**
14.   **endwhile**

Fig. 5.11. The ILS algorithm.

There have been many attempts to include some deterministic features in local search and to achieve a more systematic exploration of the problem space. In graph terminology, memory mechanisms guarantee that the algorithm will not find the same nodes repeatedly by keeping a list of visited nodes. These nodes become forbidden (*tabu*) in the graph, forcing the algorithms to move to new neighborhoods. *Guided Indexed Local Search (GILS)* [169] combines these ideas by keeping a memory, not of all the solutions visited, but of the assignments at local minima. In particular, the pseudo-code of GILS is similar to ILS. Their difference is that GILS generates one random seed only during its execution and has some additional code for penalty assignment.

Simulated annealing, in the approximation context, follows a similar procedure to local search, but it also accepts uphill moves with a certain probability. This probability is gradually decreased with the time and the algorithm finally accepts only downhill moves leading to a good local minimum. By using these ideas and the scheme suggested in [95], the ILS algorithm can be easily adapted to obtain the Indexed Simulated Annealing Search (ISAS), which can be applied to report approximate results for multi-way spatial joins using R-trees [145].

Genetic algorithms (evolutionary algorithms) can be viewed as a specific type of heuristic, so they may work well on some problems and less well on others. It is not always clear that it provides better performance on specific problems than a simpler method such as local search with random restarts. A practical drawback of this approach is the fact that there are usually many algorithmic parameters (such as the number of chromosomes, specification of how chromosomes are combined, etc.) that must be specified, and it may not be clear what the ideal settings are for these parameters for a given problem. In [169], the *Spatial Evolutionary Algorithm (SEA)* for approximate processing of multi-way spatial joins that takes advantage of spatial indexes and the problem structure to improve solutions was proposed. In this algorithm, three genetic operations (selection, crossover, and mutation) are used. These operations are repeatedly applied to obtain a population (i.e., a new set of solutions) with better characteristics and they are presented in [169]. In general, the SEA algorithm first computes the similarity of the solutions (evolution) and then performs offspring allocation (using, for example, the tournament approach), crossover, and mutation. During the initial generations, crossover plays an important role in the formation of new solutions. As time passes its role gradually diminishes and the algorithm behaves increasingly like ILS, because mutation becomes the main operation that alters solutions. The outline of SEA under limited time is given in Figure 5.12.

From the experimental results in [169], SEA outperformed ILS and GILS, although it requires more time to reach high-quality solutions due to the application of the genetic operations on a large population of solutions. Nevertheless, ILS and GILS can be usefully applied in cases where there is very limited time for processing. Moreover, ILS performs better than GILS, except for queries involving many variables.

Another randomized search alternative is *random sampling*. In general, a random search method selects solutions from underlying space randomly and outputs the best feasible solution obtained in such trials. If feasible solutions are easily constructed, it is usually advantageous to restrict the search space to a feasible region. Therefore, a random search method generates permutations randomly and outputs the best one as an approximate solution. However, a plain random strategy may be rather inefficient, and to improve its efficiency the probability distribution function used for random generation is sometimes biased in a direction that tends to give good solutions.

One of the most representative contributions on random sampling using R-trees for spatial databases is [163], where two fundamental approaches to spatial sampling with spatial predicates were discussed, depending on whether they *sample first* (first generate a sample point uniformly from the bounding

---

Algorithm SEA

1. $\mathcal{P}$ = generate initial set of solutions $\{S_1, S_2, , S_P\}$
2.   **while not** (Time threshold)
3.   compute crossover point cp
4.   **foreach** $S_i \in \mathcal{P}$
5.   evaluate S_i
6.   **if** S_i is the best solution found so far
7.   keep S_i
8.   **endif**
9.   **endfor**
10.   **foreach** $S_i \in \mathcal{P}$
11.   compare S_i with W other random solutions in $\mathcal{P}$
12.   replace S_i with the best among the $W+1$ solutions
13.   **endfor**
14.   **foreach** $S_i \in P$
15.   with probability μc change S_i as follows:
16.   determine set of variables to keep their current values
17.   re-instantiate the remaining variables using their values
                  in another solution S_j ($S_j \in \mathcal{P}$)
18.   **endfor**
19.   **foreach** $S_i \in P$
20.   with probability μm change S_i as follows:
21.   determine an T_j
22. $S_i = $ **findBestSolution**(Root of T_j, S_i)
23.   **endfor**
24. **endwhile**

Fig. 5.12. The SEA algorithm.

box, then check the spatial predicate) or evaluate the *predicate first* (choose a polygon at random with probability proportional to area, then choose a point within the polygon, calculate its stabbing number (number of polygons that cover a point), and accept the point with probability proportional to its stabbing number). The Sample First algorithm consists of a loop in which a random point is generated and then performs a point location query on the tree; if the point is reached, it is accepted into the sample; otherwise it loops until a point is accepted (and this procedure is repeated until the desired sample size is obtained). The general scheme of the Predicate First is as follows: the algorithm searches the tree beginning at the root, at each node a branch is randomly chosen; if the branch is a leaf node; then a point at random from the region is chosen and return; otherwise if the branch points to another internal node, this procedure is recursively applied. We must highlight that for R-trees, in order to uniformly sample a point we cannot simply choose a random path through the R-tree; we must compensate for the fact that some points are contained in more than one leaf, and therefore would be included in the sample with a higher probability. These approaches were described in the context of R-trees, detailing the sample first, acceptance/rejection tree, partial area tree, and spatial reservoir tree (adapting the classic reservoir sampling algorithm to support spatial sampling) algorithms.

The work on [163] is focused on uniform random sampling, in which every point has the same probability of being included in the sample. It does not consider the density-biased sampling, in which the probability that a point will be included in the sample depends on the density of its location. Spatial indexes (like the R-tree and its variants) achieve a clustering of objects within their nodes, which preserves the local density information and can provide improved density approximations. Moreover, the index can comprise means for efficiently accessing the examined points. In [155] the problem of Density Biased Sampling (DBS) from spatial indexes was considered, exploiting its clustering properties to provide density-biased samples of improved quality and with low execution time for the sampling procedure. The latter paper proposed an algorithm based on the local density information that the nodes of spatial indexes preserve, and techniques for producing the sample according to the requirements of DBS. With this algorithm, the sampling quality is preserved with respect to a variety of factors (skew, noise, and dimensionality) and the exploitation of spatial indexes helps in avoiding the overhead of existing methods in terms of sampling time. The algorithm is called *Selective Pass* and it is a method for DBS from an R-tree the main characteristics being the avoidance of reading nodes that will not contribute to the final sample. In the experimental results of [155], the authors show that the SP algorithm significantly outperformed the extended acceptance/rejection algorithms in terms of efficiency.

5.7 Classification of R-tree-Based Query Processing Algorithms

In this section, we give a summary and classification of all R-tree-based query processing methods described in Chapters 4 and 5. The classification is given in Figure 5.13 and uses the same notation for the names of the algorithms as the one used throughout the previous sections. The links between the contents of Figure 5.13 represent the relationships among them.

Four general types of spatial queries were presented, namely range, topological, nearest neighbor, and join queries. The algorithm for the range query (denoted Gutt from the author of [81]) is the first searching algorithm that was developed for the R-tree. Topological queries (the corresponding algorithm is denoted as PTSE by the authors of [175]) form a generalization of the range query. Nearest-neighbor (NN) queries include KNN [197] and its improved version MNN [45], which find the k-nearest neighbors. Moreover, based on KNN, RNN [115, 219] finds the reverse nearest neighbors. A different approach is followed by INN [88], which incrementally finds the nearest neighbors in the order of their distance from the query object. By generalizing the constraints of RNN, and based on INN (to achieve its "optimality"), CNN [66] finds the near-

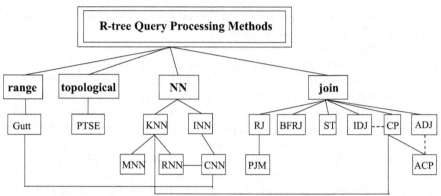

Fig. 5.13. Classification of the described R-tree-based query processing methods.

est neighbors according to a query constraint. Therefore, constrained nearest-neighbor queries is a combination of range and nearest-neighbor queries. The spatial join query between two R-trees is addressed by RJ (depth-first) [35] and BFRJ (breadth-first) [92]. For the multi-way join, PJM [144] is based on RJ to perform multiple pairwise joins, whereas ST traverses all trees at the same time. IDJ [87] (analogously to INN) focuses on the distance join (i.e., operator *within*) and finds the results incrementally, in the order of the distance between them. Closest-pair queries (CP) [50] find the k closest pairs between two indexed datasets, and can be considered as a combination of both nearest neighbor and join queries. IDJ can also lead to closest-pair searching; for this reason there is a connection between CP and IDJ. Finally, approximate techniques for distance-join computation (denoted as ADJ) [51] and closest-pair queries (denoted as ACP) [53] can be classified under the corresponding non-approximate techniques. Since ADJ and ACP are based on similar approaches for approximation, we illustrate their relationship with a dashed line between them.

5.8 Summary

Regarding extensions to range queries, we should mention the impact of computational geometry in spatial databases, which in this case is reflected by the approach for categorical range queries. This work can be extended to other query types as well, e.g., categorical nearest-neighbor and categorical spatial join queries. Reverse nearest-neighbor queries are another example where interesting geometrical properties are taken into account to develop pruning criteria. The spatial join query is more complex, and for this reason, it has attracted a lot of interest and, thus, many extensions have been proposed. The algorithms for processing and optimizing multi-way spatial join queries present an accomplished approach, which fulfil the requirements posed by existing DBMS for dealing with spatial data. Incremental distance join, closest-pair queries, and all-nearest-neighbor queries combine concepts from both spatial join and nearest-neighbor searching. All the aforementioned complex queries pose new challenges compared to the fundamental ones and are considered very important in modern applications.

Part III

R-TREES IN MODERN APPLICATIONS

6. R-trees in Spatiotemporal Databases

Spatiotemporal database systems aim at combining the spatial and temporal characteristics of data. There are many applications that benefit from efficient processing of spatiotemporal queries such as: mobile communication systems, traffic control systems (e.g., air-traffic monitoring), geographical information systems (GIS), multimedia, and location-based services (LBS). The common basis of these applications is the requirement to handle both the space and time characteristics of the underlying data [217, 232, 246]. These applications pose high requirements concerning the data and the operations that need to be supported, and therefore new techniques and tools are needed for increased processing efficiency.

6.1 Preliminaries

Spatiotemporal access methods (STAMs) provide the necessary tools to query spatiotemporal data. Spatiotemporal data are characterized by changes in location or shape with respect to time. A large number of the proposed methods are based on the well-known R-tree structure.

The research conducted in access methods and query processing techniques for spatiotemporal databases is generally categorized in the following areas:

- query processing techniques for past positions of objects, where past positions of moving objects are archived and queried, using multi-version access methods or specialized access methods for object *trajectories*, and
- query processing techniques for present and future positions of objects, where each moving object is represented as a function of time, giving the ability to determine its future positions according to the current characteristics of the object movement (reference position, velocity vector).

The incorporation of time increases the number of query types that can be posed by users. A user may focus on a specific time instance or may be interested in a time interval. Spatiotemporal queries that focus on a single time instance are termed *time-slice queries*, whereas if they focus on a time interval, they are termed *time interval queries*. If we combine these choices with spatial predicates and the ability to query the past, the present, or the future, spatiotemporal queries can be very complex, and significant effort is required to process them. Assume that we maintain a database of aircrafts, and we record the position of each aircraft and the corresponding time instance. We present a list of example queries that could be posed to such a database:

- Which aircrafts crossed the 3D region R at time instance t_x?
- Which aircrafts crossed the 3D region R between the time interval $[t_{start}, t_{end}]$?
- Which were the k nearest neighbors of aircraft a at time instance t_x?
- Given the current motion characteristics of the aircrafts, predict the nearest neighbor of aircraft a at some time instance t_x in the near future.
- Which aircrafts will cross the 3D region R between $[t_{start}, t_{end}]$?
- Determine the pairs of aircrafts (a_i, a_j) such that their distance at time instance t_x was less than 5 Km.

By considering the aforementioned query examples, it is evident that the fundamental query types discussed in Chapters 4 and 5 (range, nearest neighbors, join, closest pairs) can be combined with either time-slice or time interval queries, for past, present, or future, in order to form more complex queries.

Spatiotemporal topology queries involve complete or parts of object trajectories and include semantics, such as entrance, crossing, etc. [189]. Undoubtedly, these queries cannot be decomposed in combinations of coordinate-based queries because their processing requires knowledge of the trajectory evolution in time. More precisely, whether an object enters (leaves, bypasses etc.) an area is detected only if one or more trajectory segments are examined. Topology queries are important in several applications of spatiotemporal databases (e.g., fleet management systems) but costly in processing. Index support for this query type is not straightforward because the trajectory concept should be preserved in the index. Figure 6.1 illustrates examples of spatiotemporal topology queries.

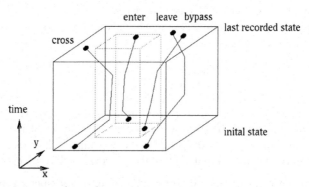

Fig. 6.1. Spatiotemporal topology queries.

In the sequel, we introduce a number of STAMs and query processing techniques related to spatiotemporal applications, such as bitemporal spatial applications, trajectory monitoring, and moving objects. All methods are based on the concept of the R-tree access method.

6.2 The RT-tree

The RT-tree [249] is the earliest effort to incorporate time information into the R-tree access method. Basically, the RT-tree is a regular R-tree augmented by temporal information in each node entry. However, the tree construction process is governed by the spatial information, and therefore the processing of temporal queries requires considerable computation effort.

Each object in the RT-tree has a spatial and a temporal extent. For an object that is inserted at time t_x its temporal extent is initialized to $[t_x, t_x)$. As long as the spatial information of the object remains unchanged, this temporal extent is increased in every time instance. If the spatial information of an object changes at time instance t_y $(y > x)$, then a new entry is created and its temporal extent is initialized to $[t_y, t_y)$. Evidently, if the objects change their spatial extents frequently, a large number of entries will be created for a single spatial object, resulting in huge consumption storage.

Figure 6.2 illustrates an example, showing the set of entries handled by an RT-tree for three time instances t_1, t_2, and t_3. In the first two time instances, both spatial objects maintain their original spatial information. In the third time instance, however, both objects change their spatial extents, resulting in two additional entries, which are inserted into the RT-tree.

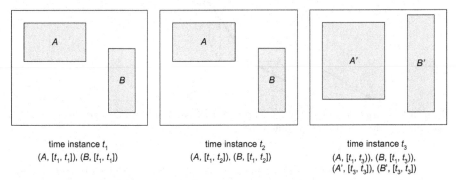

time instance t_1
$(A, [t_1, t_1]), (B, [t_1, t_1])$

time instance t_2
$(A, [t_1, t_2]), (B, [t_1, t_2])$

time instance t_3
$(A, [t_1, t_3]), (B, [t_1, t_3]),$
$(A', [t_3, t_3]), (B', [t_3, t_3])$

Fig. 6.2. Entries handled by an RT-tree for three time instances.

The inefficiency during temporal queries and the large amount of storage required by the RT-tree motivated a significant number of researchers to invest in the development of more efficient spatiotemporal access methods.

6.3 The 3D R-tree

The 3D R-tree, proposed in [238], considers time as an additional dimension and represents two-dimensional rectangles with time intervals as three-dimensional boxes. This tree can be the original R-tree [81] or any of its variants discussed in Chapters 2 and 3.

The 3D R-tree approach assumes that both ends of the interval $[t_{start}, t_{end})$ of each rectangle are known and fixed. If the end time t_{end} is not known, this approach does not work well. For instance, assume that an object extends from some fixed time until the current time, *now* (refer to [48] for a thorough discussion on the notion of *now*). One approach is to represent *now* by a time instance sufficiently far in the future. This leads to excessive boxes and consequent poor performance. Standard spatial access methods (SAMs), such as the R-tree and its variants, are not well suited to handle such "open" and expanding objects. One special case where this problem can be overcome is when all movements are known a priori. This would cause only "closed" objects to be entries of the R-tree.

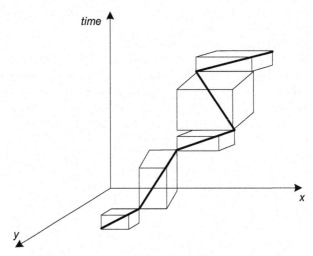

Fig. 6.3. Trajectory of a moving point and three-dimensional boxes generated by considering time as an extra dimension.

The 3D R-tree was implemented and evaluated analytically and experimentally [238, 241], and it was compared with the alternative solution of maintaining a spatial index (e.g., a 2D R-tree) and a temporal index (e.g., a 1D R-tree or a segment tree). Synthetic (uniform-like) datasets were used, and the retrieval costs for pure temporal (during, before), pure spatial (overlap, above), and spatiotemporal operators (the four combinations) were measured. The results suggest that the unified scheme of a single 3D R-tree is obviously superior when spatiotemporal queries are posed, whereas for mixed workloads, the decision depends on the selectivity of the operators.

6.4 The 2+3 R-tree

One possible solution to the problem of "open" geometries is to maintain a pair of two R-trees [159]:

- a 2D R-tree that stores two-dimensional entries that represent current (spatial) information about data, and
- a 3D R-tree that stores three-dimensional entries that represent past (spatiotemporal) information; hence the name 2+3 R-tree.

The 2+3 R-tree approach is a variation of an original idea proposed in [125] in the context of bitemporal databases, and which was later generalized to accommodate more general bitemporal data [27, 28].

As long as the end time t_{end} of an object interval is unknown, it is indexed by the (2D) *front* R-tree, keeping the start time t_{start} of its position along with its ID. When t_{end} becomes known, then:

- the associated entry is migrated from the front R-tree to the (3D) *back* R-tree, and
- a new entry storing the updated current location is inserted into the front R-tree.

Should one know all object movements a priori, the front R-tree would not be used at all, and the 2+3 R-tree reduces to the 3D R-tree presented earlier. It is also important to note that both trees may need to be searched, depending on the time instance related to the posed queries.

6.5 The Historical R-tree

Historical R-trees (HR-trees, for short) have been proposed in [158], implemented and evaluated in [159], and improved in [222] (Efficient HR-tree). This spatiotemporal access method is based on the overlapping technique. In the HR-tree, conceptually a new R-tree is created each time an update occurs. Obviously, it is not practical to physically keep an entire R-tree for each update. Because an update is localized, most of the indexed data and thus the index remain unchanged across an update. Consequently, an R-tree and its successor are likely to have many identical nodes. The HR-tree exploits exactly this phenomenon and represents all R-trees only logically. As such, the HR-tree can be viewed as an acyclic graph, rather than as a collection of independent tree structures.

With the aid of an array pointing to the root of the underlying R-trees, one can easily access the desired R-tree when performing a time query. In fact, once the root node of the desired R-tree for the time instance specified in the query is obtained, the query processing cost is the same as if all R-trees were kept physically. Figure 6.4 illustrates an HR-tree example.

The concept of overlapping trees is simple to understand and implement. Moreover, when the number of objects that change location in space is relatively small, this approach is space efficient. However, if the number of moving objects from one time instance to another is large, this approach degenerates to independent tree structures, because no common paths are likely to be found.

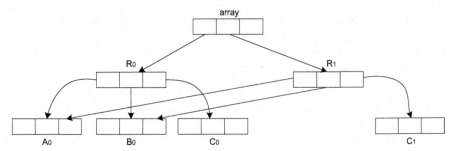

Fig. 6.4. An example of an HR-tree.

In [159] a performance comparison has been reported among the HR-tree, the 2+3 R-tree, and the 3D R-tree approach, using synthetic datasets generated by the GSTD data generator [235]. They assumed spatiotemporal data specified as follows:

- the dataset consisted of two-dimensional points, which were moving in a discrete manner within the unit square,
- updates were allowed only in the current state of the (hence, chronological) database,
- the timestamp of each point version grew monotonically following a transaction time pattern, and
- the cardinality of the dataset remained fixed as time evolved.

The HR-tree was found to be more efficient than the other two methods for time-slice queries, whereas the reverse was true for time interval queries. Also, the HR-tree usually led to a rather large structure because of node replication, even for small changes in data.

6.6 The R^{ST}-tree

The R^{ST}-tree [201] is capable of indexing spatio-bitemporal data with discretely changing spatial extents. In contrast to the indexing structures described previously, the R^{ST}-tree supports data that has two temporal dimensions and two spatial dimensions. The *valid time* of data is the time(s)—past, present, or future—when the data are true in the modeled reality, while the *transaction time* of data is the time(s) when the data were or are current in the database [98, 218]. Data for which both valid and transaction time are captured are termed *bitemporal*.

A characteristic of temporal data is that time intervals associated with objects may be *now-relative*, meaning that their end-points are strongly related to the current time. For example, assume a personnel database. When a new employee is hired, we do not know the exact time that this person will leave the company. Therefore, the personal data remain valid from a specific start time until the current time. The right end-point, t_{end}, of the valid interval is not known. The same holds for transaction time, because we do not know in advance when the corresponding data of the new employee will be deleted from the company database. As pointed out in [201], this characteristic of the time attribute has no counterpart in space.

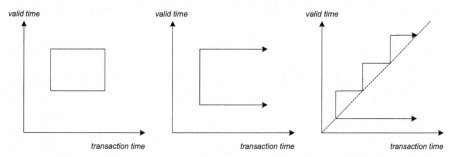

Fig. 6.5. Example regions formulated by valid time and transaction time attributes.

The valid time and transaction time attribute combination may produce different regions, as illustrated in Figure 6.5. The R^{ST}-tree manages to handle such regions more efficiently than the 3D R-tree, which is proven by the tentative performance comparison reported in [201].

6.7 The Partially Persistent R-tree

In [113] an R-tree variation is proposed, called Partially Persistent R-tree (PPR-tree), which is based on the concept of *partial persistency* [125]. It is assumed that in spatiotemporal applications, updates arrive in time order. Moreover, updates can be performed only on the last recorded instance of the database, in contrast to general bitemporal data.

The PPR-tree is a directed acyclic graph of nodes with a number of root nodes, where each root is responsible for recording a subsequent part of the ephemeral R-tree evolution. Object records are stored in the leaf nodes of the PPR-tree and maintain the evolution of the ephemeral R-tree data objects. Each data record is augmented to include the two *lifetime* fields *insertion time* and *deletion time*. The same applies to internal tree nodes, which maintain the evolution of the corresponding directory entries.

A leaf (data) entry or an internal node entry is called *alive* for all time instances included in the corresponding lifetime interval. A leaf node or an internal node is called alive if no split has been performed on that node. In order to guarantee the efficiency of the structure, there is a restriction on the minimum number of alive entries that must be contained in a node. This enables the concentration of alive entries in a bounded number of nodes, improving the I/O efficiency of the method.

The PPR-tree is formulated by applying a sequence of update operations in specified time instances. Assume that an update operation must be performed at time instance t_x. As a first step, the leaf where the update must be performed is searched, by considering the lifetime intervals of internal and leaf entries. Therefore, only entries that are alive at time t_x are examined. When the appropriate leaf node has been located, the following actions are performed:

– in case of an insertion, a new entry is added to the leaf with lifetime interval $[t_x, now)$,
– in case of a deletion, the lifetime interval of the corresponding entry is updated by substituted *now* with t_x.

Insertions and deletions may lead to structural changes of the PPR-tree. More specifically, during an insertion the located leaf node may be full, and therefore it cannot accommodate the new entry. This effect is called *node overflow*. After a deletion, the number of alive entries in a node may become less than the specified threshold. This situation is characterized as *weak version underflow*. Both cases require structural modifications to the PPR-tree, which are initiated by performing a split on the corresponding leaf node.

In [113] algorithms for range and NN processing are given. Moreover, experimental results are offered indicating the efficiency of the proposed approach in comparison to other techniques.

6.8 The MV3R-tree

To overcome the shortcomings of the 3D R-tree and the HR-tree, Tao and Papadias [223] proposed the MV3R-tree (multi-version 3-dimensional R-tree), consisting of a multi-version R-tree and a small auxiliary 3D R-tree built on the leaves of the former. The multi-version R-tree is an extension of the multi-verion B-tree proposed by Becker et al. [18]. The intuition behind the proposed access method is that timestamp queries can be directed to the multi-version R-tree, whereas interval queries can be handled by the 3D R-tree.

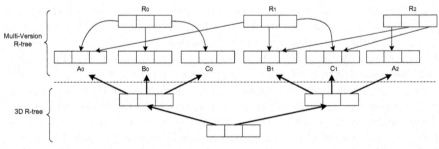

Fig. 6.6. An example of an MV3R-tree.

An MV3R-tree example is illustrated in Figure 6.6. The multi-version R-tree is composed of nine nodes (three internal nodes and six leaf nodes). The 3D R-tree is built on the leaf nodes of the multi-version R-tree, and it is composed of three nodes. Since the number of leaf nodes in the multi-version R-tree is small in comparison to the number of entries, the size of the 3D R-tree is relatively small. This favors interval queries. On the other hand, the space requirements of the multi-version R-tree are higher, but the time domain discrimination achieved favors timestamp queries.

Each node contains entries of the form $< mbr, p, t_{start}, t_{end} >$, where mbr is the MBR enclosing all entries of the corresponding subtree, and p is the pointer to the next level node. The time instances t_{start} and t_{end} denote the time that the entry was inserted and deleted, respectively, from the database. If the entry lies in a leaf node, then p points to the detail description of the corresponding object.

The construction process of the MV3R-tree uses different heuristics to handle insertions in internal and leaf nodes. Insertions are performed by the multi-version R-tree. The insertion heuristics try to avoid redundancy at the leaf level as much as possible, because the number of leaf nodes is considerably larger than the number of internal nodes. Moreover, by increasing the number of leaf nodes, there is an increase in the number of nodes of the 3D R-tree. The insertion heuristics deal with two types of split policies: (a) version split, and (b) key split. A *version split* causes redundancy, and therefore it should be avoided, specifically for leaf nodes. A *key split* works in a way similar to the split operation in the R-tree access method. After inserting a new entry, the structure of the 3D R-tree is adjusted accordingly in a bottom-up manner, in order to satisfy the MBR constraints of the structure.

Deletions are handled carefully to avoid performance deterioration. If a deletion does not cause any structural changes, then simply the attribute t_{end} is set to the current time and no other modifications are performed. An entry is physically deleted only if the attribute t_{start} is equal to the current time. Node underflows are handled differently for internal and leaf nodes. If an internal node underflows, its entries are reinserted into the structure. If a leaf node underflows, there is an attempt to borrow live entries from sibling nodes to avoid cascading version splits due to reinsertion. If such entries cannot be found, then reinsertion is applied as a last resort.

Through an extensive experimentation for up to 20% dataset *agility*,[1] the MV3R-tree turned out to be efficient in both timestamp and interval queries with relatively small space requirements, in comparison to the HR-tree and 3D R-tree.

---

[1] The agility of a dataset is the percentage of the objects that change their position in the next timestamp.

6.9 The TB-tree

Access methods like the 3D R-tree and the MV3R-tree try to preserve spatial proximity of objects, which is a fundamental property to guarantee I/O efficiency during query processing. However, these structures cannot guarantee efficiency when we require the history of a set of objects. This is because line segments belonging to the same trajectory may not be close in the dataspace, and therefore they will not be placed in the same leaf page during index construction.

The TB-tree (Trajectory Bundle) [189] has been designed for efficient access to objects' history. The basic characteristic of the TB-tree is that it relaxes the fundamental property of spatial access methods, which states that neighboring objects must be stored in the same leaf node. The TB-tree strictly preserves trajectories by forcing line segments belonging to the same trajectory, to be stored in the same leaf node, ignoring spatial proximity. Therefore, the structure is essentially a set of leaf nodes, each one storing parts trajectories. In order to achieve access to the whole trajectory of an object, leaf nodes belonging to the same trajectory are linked by means of a doubly linked list.

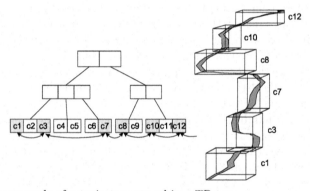

Fig. 6.7. An example of a trajectory stored in a TB-tree.

Evidently, a trajectory is split to more than one leaf node, and a leaf node may contain parts of several trajectories. Figure 6.7 illustrates a trajectory and the part of the TB-tree that stores the trajectory. As long as a trajectory part becomes available, the complete trajectory can be recovered by following the pointers of the doubly linked list.

The performance of the TB-tree access method has been studied in [189]. The results have shown that for queries involving the history of objects, the TB-tree performs very well in comparison to other access methods (such as the 3D R-tree). However, as expected, the performance of the TB-tree for queries involving the spatial and temporal coordinates of objects is worse than that of the 3D R-tree, but still competitive.

6.10 Scalable and Efficient Trajectory Index (SETI)

SETI (Scalable and Efficient Trajectory Index) was proposed in [38] for trajectory indexing and decomposes spatial from temporal dimensions. SETI slices spatial dimension in fixed, non-overlapping partitions and, for each partition, a sparse index is built on temporal dimension. Any SAM can be used for the latter, including R-trees and variations.

The structure of a SETI index is illustrated in Figure 6.8. As already discussed, spatial discrimination is achieved by logically separating space in a number of disjoint spatial cells. Each cell contains only those trajectory segments that fall into its area. If a trajectory segment interests the border of two cells, then it is split into two disjoint sub-segments, which are inserted in the corresponding cells.

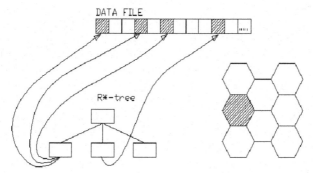

Fig. 6.8. SETI structure.

Trajectory segments are inserted in tuples in a data file, taking into consideration that every data page contains segments covered by the same cell. The *lifetime* of a data page is defined to be the minimum time interval that completely covers the time intervals of all trajectory segments stored in the page. All pages lifetimes corresponding to a spatial cell are indexed by an R*-tree. These *temporal indices* are sparse, because an entry per page (instead of an entry per segment) is stored in the index. Obviously, using sparse indices improves the performance during insertions.

Due to this mechanism (indexed objects are actually 1-dimensional temporal intervals) SETI does not suffer from the dimensionality curse. Another advantage of the structure is that it is an index that can be easily built on top of an existing indexing technique, such as R-trees, and hence implemented easier than the case of implementing a physical indexing scheme.

6.11 The Q+R-tree

The Q+R-tree [248] is an indexing scheme for moving objects, which reduces significantly the update costs. The proposed approach is based on the following observations:

1. Most moving objects do not move at high speeds most of the time. In fact, most of them are in a *quasi-static* state, meaning that they are not absolutely static, but they move in a relatively small region.
2. The movement of objects is guided by several topography constraints. For example, a large building may host many people, who are in a quasi-static state. On the other hand, objects moving at high speeds are usually on roads and highways.

The development of the Q+R-tree index is based on the two aforementioned observations. The update frequency for quasi-static objects is expected to be small, because their velocities are also small. Based on this, the authors propose to handle quasi-static objects by means of an R*-tree, enhanced by the *lazy update* mechanism proposed in [127]. According to the lazy update mechanism, an update occurrs only if an object moves out of the region MBR associated to it. This technique reduces the number of updates considerably. The R-tree enhanced with the lazy update policy is called the Lazy Update R-tree (LUR-tree). On the other hand, the use of an R*-tree to index fast moving objects is not a proper solution because of the high update frequency that these objects pose. To attack this problem the authors propose the use of a Quadtree [203] to index fast-moving objects. The construction of the Q+R-tree index is composed of three phases, which are briefly described here:

1. An R*-tree is constructed to handle all quasi-static moving objects. However, this tree is not built based on the positions of the quasi-static objects as in the usual case. Instead, the tree is formulated according to the topographical characteristics of the dataspace. Thus, the tree is called a *topography-based* R*-tree. For example, if the data space contains buildings, then the upper levels of the R*-tree contain MBRs to organize the MBRs of the buildings. The quasi-static objects are stored in the level.
2. All objects not in the quasi-static state are organized by means of a Quadtree. Therefore, the data space is decomposed hierarchically in quadrants.
3. The topography-based R*-tree and the Quadtree are combined to produce a single access method, the Q+R-tree. Note that both trees correspond to the same area. Therefore, MBRs of the R*-tree may overlap with quadrants in the Quadtree. In such a case, a pointer exists between the quadrant and the MBR to reflect that they overlap. Essentially, a linked list can be used in every quadrant containing the pointers to the overlapping MBRs of the R*-tree. An example is illustrated in Figure 6.9.

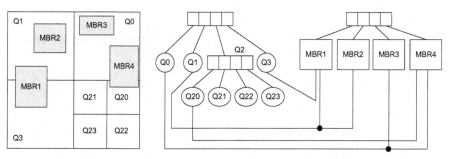

Fig. 6.9. Q+R-tree example.

6.12 The FNR-tree and the MON-tree

The common characteristic of the previously described spatiotemporal access methods is that it is assumed that objects can move freely in any direction without restrictions. However, there are several application domains where the motion of each object must satisfy several spatial constraints. For example, objects moving in a road network must obey specific rules, which are enforced by the underlying *spatial network*. Although access methods for free motion objects can be applied in this case, several optimizations are possible aiming at more efficient query processing.

An R-tree variation, the Fixed Network R-tree (FNR-tree), which takes into account the underlying spatial network, was proposed in [67]. Instead of using a single R-tree to index object trajectories, the FNR-tree utilizes a forest of R-trees. More specifically, the FNR-tree is a two-stage access method, consisting of a 2D R-tree, which organizes a set of 1D R-trees. The 2D R-tree is used to index the spatial data of the network, whereas each of the 1D R-trees corresponds to each leaf of the 2D R-tree and indexes time intervals. As long as there are no structural changes in the spatial network, the 2D R-tree remains fixed, whereas each 1D R-tree changes as objects move.

Each 2D R-tree leaf node contains entries of the form (*lineID*, *mbr*, *orientation*), where *lineID* is the ID of the spatial network segment, *mbr* is the MBR of the line segment, and *orientation* is a flag that describes the exact geometry of the line segment inside the MBR. Each internal node contains entries of the form (*p*, *mbr*), where *p* is the pointer to a child node, and *mbr* is the MBR of the subtree. Each leaf node of the 1D R-tree stores entries of the form (*oID*, *lineID*, t_{start}, t_{end}, *direction*), where *oID* is the ID of the moving object, *lineID* the ID of the line segment, t_{start} is the time instance denoting the time that the moving object has entered the corresponding line segment, t_{end} the time instance that the moving object has exited the line segment, and *direction* is a flag denoting the motion direction. A bird's eye view of the FNR-tree is illustrated in Figure 6.10.

An insertion in the FNR-tree is performed every time a moving object exits from a line segment. The insertion algorithm is executed in two steps: (a) during the first step, the 2D R-tree is searched to locate the leaf node

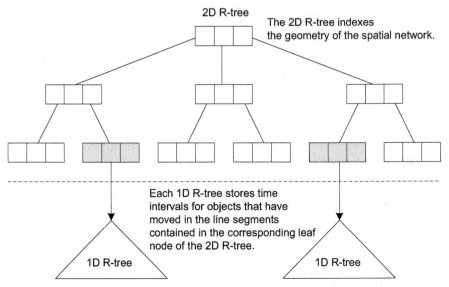

Fig. 6.10. FNR-tree example.

which contains the corresponding line segment (e.g., by using well-known R-tree search techniques), (b) in the second step, an insertion is performed in the 1D R-tree by providing the line segment ID, the moving object ID, the motion direction and the time interval that the object resided in the line segment. Spatiotemporal range search operations are performed by first searching the 2D R-tree and then searching each 1D R-tree determined and applying traditional pruning techniques.

The performance of the FNR-tree has been studied in [67] and compared with that of the 3D R-tree. It has been shown that in most cases the FNR-tree significantly outperforms the 3D R-tree for spatiotemporal range queries and time-slice queries. In some test cases and for a small number of moving objects the 3D R-tree has proven marginally better.

A variation of the FNR-tree, called MON-tree, has been proposed in [7]. Instead of using a 1D R-tree for every leaf node of the 2D R-tree, the MON-tree utilizes a 2D R-tree for every polyline of the spatial network. The authors do not give any performance evaluation results regarding the efficiency of the proposed approach in comparison to the FNR-tree.

6.13 The Time-Parameterized R-tree

The aforementioned access methods focus on providing access paths to present or past values of objects. An access method based on the R-tree structure and that provides access to present and future values is the Time-Parameterized R-tree (TPR-tree) [202]. This method is based on the concept of non-static

MBRs of leaf and internal nodes. In other words, the MBR of an object or a tree node is a function of time. It is assumed that the velocity vector of each object is known. Based on the last location of the object and its velocity vector, one can determine the current object location in space and predict its location in the future.

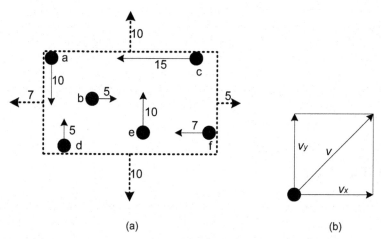

Fig. 6.11. (a) An example of a moving bounding rectangle; (b) mapping the velocity vector to the x- and y-axes.

One basic characteristic of the TPR-tree structure is that the covering MBRs of the internal nodes are rarely minimum (although they are conservative). This means that the empty space is larger than in an R-tree storing stationary objects. Figure 6.11 illustrates an example of a moving MBR. Note that the velocity vector of a moving object plays a very important role in determining the MBR of a node.

The algorithms for insertion, deletion, and node splitting are not very different from those applied to R-tree variations. The most significant difference is the use of integrals, calculated over a time perid, in order to determine area and overlap enlargement of node MBRs. The use of integrals is natural, considering that a choice for node splitting must be performed, taking into consideration the movement of the objects, rather than considering only one time instance. Therefore, all the heuristics that have been successfully applied to R-tree variations are adapted, taking into account the mobility of node MBRs. In order to facilitate this, the TPR-tree is based on the concept of the *time horizon*, which denotes the time interval that the structure remains in good shape, without the need for reorganization. Note that, due to the objects' movement, an MBR can never reduce its area. In the best case an MBR will retain its original area. However, in the general case, the area of a moving MBR increases continuously, resulting in excessive MBR overlap after a long period of time, depending on the mobility of the dataset.

Based on the TPR-tree, [194, 195, 224] propose methods for time-parameterized query processing in databases of moving objects.

In a recent work [192], an efficient variation of the TPR-tree has been proposed, called STAR-tree, that eliminates some basic disadvantages of the structure and shows better performance in query processing. Moreover, in [227] an improved variation of the TPR-tree has been proposed, the TPR*-tree, which outperforms the TPR-tree during predictive query processing.

Recently, in [188] the authors have proposed an indexing scheme to index the past, present and future locations of moving objects using time-parameterized bounding rectangles and the concept of partial persistency. The proposed approach seems promising, because all time instances can be queried using a single access method, instead of using separate index structures for past and future positions. The combined scheme is called the Past Present and Future R-tree (R^{PPF}-tree).

6.14 The VCI R-tree

In [191] the authors propose a novel technique to index moving objects. The resulting indexing scheme, called Velocity Constrained Indexing R-tree (VCI R-tree) is tuned to efficient manipulation of moving objects' velocities. This scheme manages to avoid the update costs of moving objects by using the notion of the maximum speed of each moving object.

The VCI R-tree is a regular R-tree-based index, augmented by an additional field, V_{max}, in each node, to store the maximum allowed speed over all objects covered by this node. In an internal node, the V_{max} field is the maximum of the corresponding fields of its children. In a leaf node, the V_{max} fields are the maximum speed among all objects hosted in the leaf. The V_{max} field is updated accordingly when a split or insertion occurs, by propagating changes upward (this operation resembles the MBR adjustments performed in the regular R-tree structure).

Assume that a VCI index has been built for the current time instance t_0. Evidently, the MBRs in the VCI reflect perfectly the positions of the moving objects at instance t_0. Assume that a range query is issued for a future time instance $t_x > t_0$. By using the V_{max} value in each node we can expand each MBR in every direction by the value $dist_{max} = V_{max} \cdot (t_x - t_0)$. The expanded MBR guarantees the enclosure of the objects covered by the node, because no object can travel faster than V_{max}. Instead of expanding each node MBR, we can expand only the MBR of the query region and obtain the same result.

It is not difficult to prove that this approach avoids false dismissals. However, the MBR expansion may return a significant number of false alarms. In order to eliminate them and return the answer, a post-processing phase is required. During this phase the exact position of each candidate is retrieved to determine if indeed satisfies the query constraints. Evidently, as time progresses the number of false alarms is expected to increase, because the MBR expansion becomes more and more significant. The authors in [191] propose to rebuild the index periodically to reflect more accurately the positions of the moving objects, and reduce the number of false alarms. An alternative procedure that could be followed is to just refresh the index without rebuild. During refreshing, the current positions of the moving objects are determined and then an MBR adjustment is performed in a bottom-up manner.

6.15 Summary

The main goal of a spatiotemporal database system is to manage the spatial and temporal characteristics of the underlying dataset, toward efficient management and query processing of spatiotemporal queries. The utilization of time information poses several challenges, because the assumption that time is an additional dimension does not always lead to elegant and efficient solutions.

The first spatiotemporal access methods that appeared in the literature focused on indexing past and present positions of objects. Recently, some proposals deal with indexing future positions of moving objects, paving the way for predictive query processing. We believe that in the near future more efficient techniques will be proposed, because there is a lot of interest in this direction due to their importance in location-based services and monitoring systems.

7. R-trees for Multimedia, Warehousing and Mining

Modern applications like multimedia, data warehouses, and data mining require the organization and manipulation of complex objects, and pose diverse requirements with respect to the efficient processing of queries. Based on the fact that indexing schemes are ubiquitous to improving the response time of a user query, researchers studied the application of indexing techniques to the aforementioned advanced applications as well. In this chapter, we focus on the application of the R-tree access method to the efficient handling end processing of multimedia queries, data warehousing operations, and data mining tasks.

7.1 R-trees in Multimedia Databases

Multimedia database management systems aim at the effective representation and the efficient retrieval of multimedia objects, such as text, images, audio, and video [141]. The basic characteristics of multimedia objects that makes multimedia query processing challenging are the following:

- Multimedia objects are characterized by significant complexity due to their rich content. This complexity is translated to significant storage requirements and non-trivial algorithms for their management.
- The notion of similarity between two multimedia objects is often difficult to express. Therefore, new algorithms are required to to search multimedia databases based on content.

In the sequel, we present some important techniques that have been proposed to handle and manipulate multimedia objects efficiently. More particularly, we focus on access methods toward efficient similarity query processing. The fundamental idea is to transform multimedia objects to multidimensional vectors, enabling the utilization of multidimensional access methods for efficient retrieval.

7.1.1 Generic Multimedia Indexing (GEMINI)

GEMINI [60] is a generic approach to indexing multimedia objects, for searching multimedia types by content. The problem of searching can be described as follows: given a collection of N objects $O_1, O_2, \ldots, O_N$ and a distance function

$D(O_i, O_j)$ (for $1 \leq i, j \leq N$), the goal is to find all objects that are within ε distance from a query object Q.

The straightforward application of a sequential scan algorithm incurs prohibitive cost in the case where N is large and/or the calculation of the distance function between the objects is costly. For this reason, GEMINI follows an alternative method, which is characterized by two components:

1. An initial "quick-and-dirty" test, which discards most of the objects that do not satisfy the query, and
2. The searching through a spatial access method (SAM), which avoids the shortcomings of the sequential search.

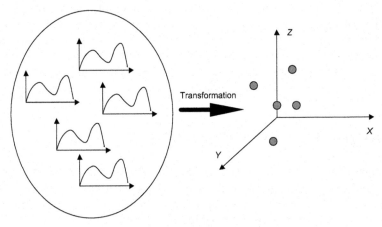

Fig. 7.1. Mapping time series to multidimensional vectors.

Processing Range Queries. Let us now focus on the application of GEMINI in indexing 1-dimensional signal data [6], e.g., stock-rates, music, etc. Assume a sequence S of real values (S_i denotes the i-th item of S). Also, let that the distance between S and a query sequence Q be the Euclidean distance $D(S, Q) = \sqrt{\sum_{i=1}^{len}(S_i - Q_i)^2}$ (*len* is the length of the sequences). The quick-and-dirty test of GEMINI can be applied if from each sequence we can extract a set of features and map them to a feature space, as illustrated in Figure 7.1. The selection of good features will attain two fundamental objectives:

– it causes the occurrence no false dismissals, and
– it incurs as few false alarms as possible.

The first component of GEMINI (quick-and-dirty test) is supported by using as features some of the first coefficients of the discrete Fourier transform (DFT). That is, for each sequence we compute its DFT, keep a number d of the first coefficients, and map them into a 2d-dimensional point (recall that each coefficient is a complex number). The DFT coefficients are good features with respect to the aforementioned objectives. Regarding the first objective, let $F(S_i))$ be the mapped point in the feature space of a sequence S. Also, $D_f(F(S_i), F(S_j))$ denotes the distance between the mapped points in the feature space. Due to Parseval's theorem, it holds that $D_f(F(S_i), F(S_j)) \leq D(S_i, S_j)$. Therefore, no false dismissals occur. Regarding the second objective, DFT has been reported to have the desirable property of energy concentration in the first few coefficients (i.e., the first coefficients carry most of the signal's energy), especially in application domains like stock-markets or music sequences. Therefore, the expected number of false alarms is limited.

The guarantee that no object will be missed from the final answer is given by the lower bounding property between the distance of two objects in the original and the transformed spaces. As long as the distance in the transformed space is less than or equal to the distance in the original space, then no answer will be missed. Figure 7.2 illustrates an example. It is evident that the answer to the range query is composed of objects O_1 and O_3. By inspecting the transformed space we see that object O_2 is also reported as an answer. However, O_3 will be discarded in a subsequent refinement step.

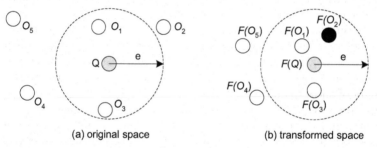

(a) original space   (b) transformed space

Fig. 7.2. Illustration of the lower bounding property.

The second component of GEMINI (use of a SAM to accelerate searching) is advocated by the use of an R-tree structure, which stores the points mapped in the feature space (in this case, the corresponding index has been given the name F-index). The range searching algorithm is outlined as follows:

1. Map the query sequence Q to a point $F(Q)$ in the feature space.
2. Use the R-tree to retrieve all candidate points in the transformed (feature) space that are within distance ε from $F(Q)$.
3. Retrieve the corresponding sequences, compute their actual distance from Q and discard any false alarms.

The work described in [6] has been extended in [63] for the problem of subsequence matching. Also, the work has been extended in [106, 107] to consider the peculiarities of indexing music sequences. Finally, GEMINI has been examined in the context of retrieving similar images by content. This work is described in [61].

Processing Nearest-Neighbor Queries. In addition to the processing of simple range queries, GEMINI can be used to answer nearest-neighbor queries as well. However, the NN problem is more difficult to solve, taking into consideration that in the transformed space the distances among the objects are reduced, due to the lower bounding property. Therefore, we cannot judge on the k nearest neighbors of a query object by only investigating the transformed space.

By a careful look at Figure 7.2(a) it is evident that the two nearest neighbors of the query object Q are the objects O_1 and O_3. However, if we rely only on the transformed space (Figure 7.2(b)), the nearest neighbors of $F(Q)$ are the objects $F(O_1)$ and $F(O_2)$. This means that the determination of the nearest neighbors will be wrong if we investigate only the transformed space. This is natural, taking into account that the lower bounding property of the distance does not imply monotonicity. In order to provide correct results, a more elaborate algorithm is required. Such an algorithm has been proposed in [117], where the authors study the problem of image indexing. The algorithm operates in four phases, which are described here:

Execution of a k-NN query in the transformed space. In this step a k-NN query is executed in the transformed space and the set of k objects closer to the query object is determined.

Determination of the safe distance. Let $dist_1, \ldots, dist_k$ be the distance between the query object and its k nearest neighbors in the transformed space. The algorithm determines the original distance between the query object and each of the k returned objects. Let $dist_{max}$ denote the maximum of these distances.

Range query on the transformed space. Using the query object as the center and the distance $dist_{max}$ as the radius, a circular range query is executed in the transformed space, and all objects that are enclosed are returned as candidates.

False alarm elimination. The final step involves the elimination of false alarms and the determination of the k nearest neighbors in the original space.

The main drawback of the aforementioned method is that it may require significant cost to eliminate false alarms. The number of candidates generated in the third step may be large, leading to increased CPU and I/O cost. Based on this observation the authors in [210] proposed an optimal algorithm with respect to the number of candidates generated. The algorithm is based on an incremental processing of the k nearest neighbors and utilizes a termination criterion to avoid the retrieval of non-promising candidates. Although the performance evaluation of [210] is based on the X-tree access method, any R-tree variation can be used equally well.

7.1.2 High-Dimensional Access Methods

By using suitable transformations, the technique has been successfully applied for other data types as well (e.g., audio, color images, video). In order to organize these multidimensional vectors a spatial access method can be used. Therefore, we see that even if the original data are not spatial in nature, spatial access methods can still be effectively utilized to organize and efficiently query these datasets.

In several cases, many features are selected to represent the multimedia objects. Therefore, each multimedia object is represented by a high-dimensional vector (hundreds of dimensions). It has been observed that for very high dimensionalities, the performance of most hierarchical spatial access methods degenerate into that (or even worse than that) of a sequential scan [24, 138, 157]. The reason for this degeneration is twofold:

1. By increasing the space dimensionality, more space is required to store a single vector, and therefore the index fanout (number of children per node) is reduced considerably resulting in disk accesses increase, and
2. The nice properties of the index structures do not hold, because dimensionality increase results in excessive overlap of intermediate nodes, and therefore the discrimination power of the structure decreases considerably.

Due to this inefficiency, a number of access methods have been proposed in the literature that try to reduce the negative effects of the so-called *dimensionality curse*. In the sequel we examine some of these proposals, which originated from the R-tree access method, but are tuned toward better handling of high-dimensional vectors.

The TV-tree. Lin, Jagadish, and Faloutsos proposed the Telescopic Vector Tree (TV-tree) in [138]. The main characteristic of the method is that it does not utilize all dimensions to construct the tree, but only those that are promising for pruning and discrimination. Each node in a TV-tree represents the MBR (an Lp-sphere) of all of its descendents. Each region is represented by:

− a center, which is a vector determined by the telescoping vectors representing the objects, and
− a radius, which determines the extent of the region.

The center of a region is also a telescopic vector, and the term Telescopic Minimum Bounding Region (TMBR) is used to determine a region with a telescopic vector as its center.

The bounding property of the TV-tree resembles that of the R-tree. The main difference is that it is not necessary to utilize all dimensions. Therefore, a telescopic L_p sphere with center $\vec{c}$ and radius r with dimensionality n, and $\alpha \leq n$ *active dimensions* contains all points $\vec{x}$ such that:

$$c_i = x_i, i = 1, ..., n - \alpha$$

and

$$r^p \geq \sum_{i=n-a+1}^{n} (c_i - x_i)^p$$

Actually, the set of active dimensions contains the dimensions that can discriminate between the objects, in contrast to the inactive dimensions, which cannot distinguish between the node's descendants. The number of active dimensions α of a TV-tree is the (common) number of active dimensions of all its TMBRs.

The search algorithm of the TV-tree is very similar to that of the R-tree access method. Searching starts from the TV-tree root and proceeds by recursively visiting tree branches if the query region intersects the TMBR of a node entry. Since TMBRs are allowed to overlap, multiple tree branches may need to be followed for exact match queries (similarly to R-trees). Spatial joins and nearest-neighbor queries are also supported, and the corresponding algorithms are modified versions of the fundamental R-tree algorithms. The insertion algorithms tries to determine a suitable leaf node to host the new entry. Evidently, a node overflow may take place, which leads to either a number of reinsertions or a node split. We note that a node overflow may occur not only due to the insertion of a new entry, but also due to the potential increase of the number of active dimensions in a telescopic vector. In [138] insertion, deletion, and overflow handling are studied in detail. Moreover, performance results have been reported comparing the TV-tree with the R*-tree access method.

The SS-tree. The Similarity Search Tree (SS-tree) has been proposed by White and Jain [245] as a variation of the R-tree access method to better handle high-dimensional data, aiming at more efficient similarity query processing. The SS-tree supports the use of the weighted Euclidean distance as a similarity measure and therefore considers the Euclidean distance as a special case. This way, correlations among the dimensions can be captured and expressed, avoiding the optimistic assumption that dimensions are independent. Moreover, by using the weighted Euclidean distance, the similarity between two feature vectors can be calculated even if a linear transformation has been applied to the feature vectors.

The SS-tree organizes feature vectors hierarchically, by constructing bounding regions. Each bounding region in an internal node encloses all its descendants. Figure 7.3 illustrates an example of a hierarchical organization of the feature vectors in 2D space. Note the ellipsoidal form of the bounding regions, which is due to the weighted Euclidean distance similarity measure used.

Indexing with SS-trees can be effectively performed if the following issues are handled appropriately:

- The form of the feature vectors must guarantee that the weighted Euclidean distance can be used as a similarity measure, and
- Domain knowledge is available to constrain the types of similarity measures between feature vectors, that likely will be used in user queries. This knowledge can then be used to tune the performance of the SS-tree.

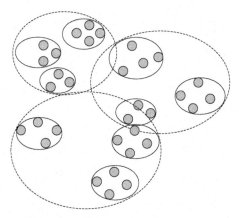

Fig. 7.3. Bounding regions in an SS-tree.

In [245] a performance comparison between the SS-tree and the R*-tree has been reported. The two access methods have been compared using uniformly and normally distributed datasets. Moreover, experiments for real-life data are provided. The SS-tree has been proven a very promising access method with respect to several performance measures, such as the number of leaf accesses and the number of internal node accesses. Moreover, the average storage utilization of the SS-tree is about 85%, whereas that of the R*-tree is around 70%-75%.

In [126] an improved variation of the SS-tree has been proposed, which is called the SS$^+$-tree. The main difference between the two structures is that the SS$^+$-tree utilizes a tighter bounding sphere for each node. This sphere is an approximation at the smallest enclosing sphere. Moreover, a different split algorithm is used.

The SR-tree. The SR-tree has been proposed by Katayama and Satoh in [108]. The structure of the SR-tree is based on those of the R*-tree and the SS-tree. Basically, it is a combination of these two structures, because it utilizes both bounding spheres and bounding rectangles to formulate bounding regions. These bounding regions are organized hierarchically by means of a tree-like directory.

Each bounding region of the SR-tree is the intersection of a bounding sphere and a bounding rectangle. The motivation behind the proposed scheme is summarized as follows:

1. Bounding rectangles have much longer diameters than bounding spheres, especially in high-dimensional spaces. On the other hand, their volume is smaller in comparison to bounding spheres.
2. Bounding spheres, although they have larger volumes, form regions with smaller diameter than bounding rectangles.

By considering both bounding spheres and bounding rectangles, the SR-tree tries to compromise the size of the diameters and the size of the volumes, to a more effective discrimination. Figure 7.4 illustrates the way bounding regions are formed in the SR-tree.

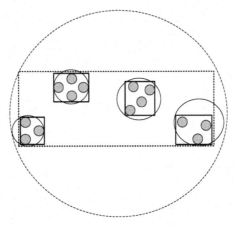

Fig. 7.4. Bounding regions in an SR-tree.

In [108] a performance evaluation among the R*-tree, the SS-tree, and the SR-tree has been reported. The SR-tree performs very well, especially for high-dimensional real-life datasets. One of the potential problems of the SR-tree scheme is that it is more sensitive to node size than the other methods. The fanout of the SR-tree is significantly less than that of the other methods. Therefore, more internal nodes are required to index a set of objects. This is due to the fact that both bounding rectangles and bounding spheres are stored in internal nodes. Moreover, the construction time of the SR-tree is higher than those of the SS-tree and the R*-tree, because more complex operations are required during insertions of new entries and node splits.

The X-tree. Although the aforementioned access methods perform considerably better than the R*-tree scheme, their performance degenerates if the number of dimensions is increased significantly. In very high-dimensional spaces, the discrimination power of the methods degenerates, and in the extreme case their performance is similar to that of sequential scanning of the dataset. The X-tree, proposed by Berchtold, Keim and Kriegel in [24], is tuned to better handle objects in high-dimensional spaces.

Figure 7.5 illustrates an X-tree example. The X-tree is composed of three node types, namely data nodes, normal directory nodes and supernodes. The data (leaf) nodes contain MBRs of the corresponding data objects, in addition to the pointers to the objects' detailed descriptions. Among the internal tree nodes some of them may become supernodes. A *supernode* is a directory node with variable capacity, which can be used to avoid node splitting. However, a supernode is not just a tree node with larger capacity, because it can shrink and grow dynamically as needed. Therefore, the X-tree can be considered as

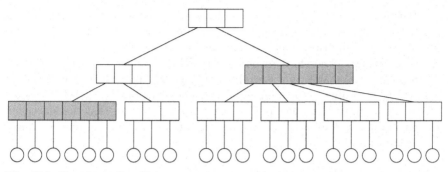

Fig. 7.5. Structure of an X-tree.

a heterogeneous access method, because it is composed of nodes of different types. Supernodes are shown shaded in Figure 7.5.

Supernodes are generated during insertion of new entries, only if there is no way to avoid overlapping. Using supernodes leads to the following advantages of the X-tree over other access methods:

– the average storage utilization is increased, because fewer splits take place,
– the average tree fanout is increased and therefore the tree height is reduced, resulting in fewer disk accesses for point location queries, and
– sequential scanning of the dataset is facilitated for very high-dimensional spaces, when it is not possible to construct a hierarchical access method with minimized overlap between node bounding regions.

Performance evaluation results reported in [24] have shown that the X-tree consistently outperforms the R*-tree and the TV-tree for high-dimensional datasets. For implementation details and the description of the insertion algorithm, the interested reader should consult the corresponding reference.

7.1.3 R-trees and Hidden Markov Models in Music Retrieval

In [100] an application of R*-trees is presented for indexing hidden Markov models (HMMs). An HMM describes a doubly stochastic process in which only the current state affects the choice of the next state (Markov property). A HMM consists of states and edges. For musical pieces, states correspond to note transitions and are represented with an interval and a number, called IOIratio, that is the ratio between two consecutive intervals corresponding to the difference between the onset of two notes [100]. In order to perform effective music information retrieval and to allow for mistakes, a collection of music pieces is represented by their corresponding HMMs, where each information in each state is mapped to an interval between a minimum and a maximum allowed value. Therefore, each state can be represented as a 4-dimensional rectangle. Given a query musical piece, its HMM is extracted and it has to be examined against all stored HMMs. During each test, the states of the query HMM are examined against the states of the stored HMMs, where in the bottom line, the 4-dimensional point corresponding to each state of the query HMM is tested for inclusion by the 4-dimensional rectangle of the stored HMM. To speed-up the aforementioned process, [100] uses an R*-tree to index all stored HMMs. Therefore, given a query HMM, we get a set of points that correspond to its states, and test them against the index. The stored HMMs are ranked according to the number of their matched states (i.e., 4-dimensional rectangles) against the query points. Results in [100] show that the aforementioned approach does not lead to false negatives, whereas it reduces query execution times by a factor of 7.

7.1.4 R-trees and Self-Organizing Maps

An interesting variation of R*-trees, called SOM-Based R*-trees, is proposed by Oh et al. [162]. The SOM-based R*-tree combines Self-Organizing Maps (SOMs) and R*-trees and achieve good query performance in applications like the retrieval of similar images (images are indexed by features). A SOM is a kind of neural network that maps data from a high-dimensional space to a two-dimensional space, by preserving the topology of the feature vector. The mapping is called a *topological feature map*. The topological feature map is generated by performing SOM training. As a result, the vector generated on each node of SOM is produced, which is called a *codebook vector*. Using the topological feature map, similar images are classified to the nearest node, depending on the distance between its feature vector and the collection of codebook vectors. For each node, the classified similar images are organized in a *best-matching image list* (BMIL). Evidently, there exist nodes in SOM to which no image is classified, thus they are empty. Regarding the construction of an R*-tree, a d-dimensional point corresponds to a codebook vector of the topological feature map. We check all codebook vectors. Those corresponding to empty nodes are ignored. For the others, the points that correspond to the codebooks are inserted into the tree. Each point is inserted into the leaf whose centroid is closest to the point to be inserted. Since empty nodes are avoided, the R*-tree index helps locate those nodes that are not empty into the SOM. Therefore, searching this way for similar images is faster than having to examine the entire SOM.

7.2 R-trees in Data Warehousing and Data Mining

Data warehouses are specialized databases that serve as repositories for multiple heterogeneous data sources, organized under a unified schema to facilitate decision making. On-Line Analytical Processing (OLAP) is an analysis technique performed in data warehouses, which is exploratory-driven. Although OLAP is very useful, it mainly works for hypothesis verification. In contrast, data mining works in a (semi-)automatic manner. Data mining (or knowledge discovery in databases) is the process of extracting interesting information or patterns from data in large databases. Both data warehousing and data mining need to access large amounts of data. For this reason, the acceleration of data access is facilitated by indexes. Although specialized indexes have been developed for these new environments (e.g., bitmap indexes), R-tree-like indexes have also been successfully used.

R-tree variations for OLAP and Data Warehouses store summary information in internal nodes and therefore in many cases it is not necessary to search lower tree levels. Examples of such queries are window aggregate queries, where parts of the data space are requested that satisfy certain aggregate constraints. Thus, a window-aggregate (WA) query returns summarized information (e.g., count, max, avg) about objects included within the query window.

An observation that is used for WA queries is that R-tree nodes can be augmented with summarized information. Nodes totally contained by the query window do not have to be accessed, and only those nodes that intersect (not covered by) the query window have to visited. One of the first efforts in this context was the R_a^*-tree variant of which has been proposed for efficient processing of window aggregate queries, where summarized data are stored in internal nodes in addition to the MBR [102].

More particular, the data points have coordinates corresponding to the value of dimensions (assuming, for instance, a star schema). Additionally, they contain a value corresponding to the measure value. An R*-tree is used to index the data points, but the internal node also stores the summarized information, which may help to speed-up searching. Regarding the type of summary information, it can correspond to any distributed or algebraic function (holistic measures are not considered in [102]). The resulting structure is called R_a^*-tree. Figure 7.6 illustrates an example of an R_a^*-tree, where the internal nodes contain summarized information for the *count* and *sum* aggregation functions, which are distributive.

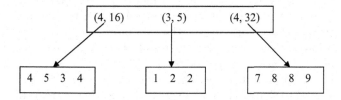

Fig. 7.6. An example of an R_a^*-tree.

The range searching algorithm tries to exploit the summarized information. When the MBR of an internal node is entirely contained within the region of the range query, then the searching to the corresponding subtree is pruned, and the result is updated through the summarized information stored in the covered node. The searching algorithm for the R_a^*-tree is depicted in Figure 7.7 (the *sum* aggregate function is assumed).

Algorithm RangeSearch(TypeNode RN, **TypeRect** Q)

1. sum $\leftarrow 0$
2. **if** RN is leaf
3.   **foreach** entry $e \in RN$
4.   **if** $e.mbr \cap Q \neq \emptyset$
5.   sum $\leftarrow$ sum $+$ e.summary_info
6. **else**
6.   **foreach** entry $e \in RN$
8.   **if** $e.mbr \subseteq Q$ //contained entirely
9.   sum $\leftarrow$ sum $+$ e.summary_info
10.   **else if** $e.mbr \cap Q \neq \emptyset$
11.   sum $\leftarrow$ sum $+$ **RangeSearch**($e.ptr$, Q)
12. **return** sum

Fig. 7.7. The range search algorithm for the R_a^*-tree.

The savings due to R_a^*-tree increase with increasing query size, because larger queries tend to entirely cover more MBRs. This is important for OLAP, because analysts often pose OLAP queries with large ranges. However, the performance of R_a^*-tree still depends on the query size [228], i.e., for large window sizes, more nodes are accessed. To overcome this deficiency, Tao et al. [228] proposed the aP-tree, to process aggregate queries on planar point data. An aP-tree maps points from 2D space to 1D intervals. Given a set of points in the space $[0, M_x] : [0, M_y]$, the y-coordinate of a point is considered the key value, whereas the x-coordinate represents the starting time of the interval. The ending time of all intervals is the current time, i.e., intervals are left open from the right. An example is depicted in Figure 7.8. The query is also mapped, thus instead of a query window q, two vertical line segments q_0 and q_1 are illustrated in the figure, corresponding to two queries for the intervals. If S_1 is the set of intervals that are intersected by q_1 and S_0 the set of intervals intersected by q_0, then the result of the WA query is given by the set difference $S_1 - S_0$.

To efficiently process intersection queries for intervals, the aP-tree uses a structure similar to that of the multi-version B-tree (MVB-tree) [18]. However, it uses an additional field, which stores the aggregate number over the entries in the child node. Insertions are performed as in MVB-trees except that some intermediate entries may be duplicated on the path. The advantage of the aP-tree, compared to R_a^*-tree, is that the query cost is independent of the window size. Although this is attained with an increase in the space cost, the savings in query execution times are much more important.

Analogous techniques have been used in [170] in the case of spatial data warehouses, where the structure of the aggregate R-tree (aR-tree) has been

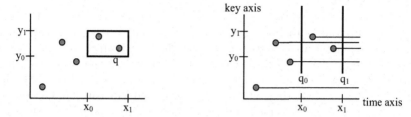

Fig. 7.8. An example mapping points to intervals in the aP-tree.

proposed. In [173] a combination of aggregate R-trees and B-trees has been proposed for spatiotemporal data warehouse indexing. Continuing these efforts, Gowarski and Malczok have proposed the Virtual Memory Aggregate R-tree (VMAT) to overcome the problems of availability of RAM memory limitations when indexing large amounts of data [73, 74].

Roussopoulos et al. [198] proposed the indexing of data cubes with a set of packed R-trees. The data cube [76] is an operator used in OLAP applications and, informally, it is defined as the set of all possible multidimensional projections of a relation, which are stored redundantly to improve query processing. The set of dimensions for a data cube form a multidimensional space and the data values (non-aggregates) correspond to points in this space. The aggregate values are also points, which result from projection of all points from dimensions that do not correspond to the aggregation. The collection of all (data and aggregate) points can be indexed with an R-tree. In this case, the R-tree is called a cubtree [198]. For efficiency, the packing of cubtrees has been examined. Interestingly enough, the algorithm of the Packed R-tree [199] was selected, because for range queries in the cubtree, space-filling curves scatter the projection points, and this result in a bad clustering of points. In order to decide the dimension on which sorting and packing will be based, an algorithm called SelectSortOrder is described in [198], which uses the (expected) cardinalities of the aggregates. Also, for cubes with d dimensions, a significant optimization proposed in [198] is the decomposition of the original cubtree into a forest of d reduced cubtrees that are $(d$-1)-dimensional. This is done by first removing all data points (resulting to a dataless cubtree), and then by organizing the rest points into d groups. The grouping is done with a greedy algorithm, called AllocateLattice [198]. The objective of this algorithm is to combine the groupby members that correspond to each group in a way such that at least one common dimension exists among them. By having at least one common dimension, the undesirable existence of dispersed groupby members is avoided, because it leads to bad clustering of points. Experimental results in [198] show that the reduced cubtrees perform well and have good scalability to large data-cube sizes. Their performance for high dimension, however, is an interesting topic for future examination. Finally, the extension of cubtrees for indexing materialized views in relational OLAP (ROLAP) environments is proposed in [122].

Recently, R-trees have been also used in the context of Data Mining. In particular, Spatial Data Mining systems [83] include methods that gradually refine spatial predicates, based on indexes like the R-tree, to derive spatial patterns, e.g., spatial association rules [114]. Based on the R-tree structure and the closest-pairs query, Nanopoulos et al. [154], developed the C^2P algorithm for efficient clustering, whereas [155] proposed a density-biased sampling algorithm from R-trees, which performs effective preprocessing to clustering algorithms.

7.3 Summary

Due to their nature, multimedia objects are complex, therefore their management is a difficult task. Moreover, the notion of similarity between two multimedia objects in many cases can be considered subjective. The aforementioned reasons pose requirements for new searching techniques for this kind of data. In this chapter, we presented some of the most important similarity searching techniques and specialized accesses methods that have been proposed for multimedia objects. Since objects in multimedia applications tend to have very high dimensionality, we presented several high-dimensional access methods that have been proposed for this purpose.

The need to access large volumes of data is present in both data warehousing and data mining applications. The acceleration of data access in these environments is facilitated by specialized indexes that have been proposed (e.g., bitmap indexes). Nevertheless, R-tree-like indexes still find important applications. We considered variations of the R-tree for the problem of answering aggregate queries and for the efficient storage of data cubes. Finally, we outlined the uses of R-tree-like indexes in data mining applications.

Part IV

ADVANCED ISSUES

8. Query Optimization Issues

Determining the best execution plan for a spatial query requires tools for measuring (more precisely, estimating) the number of (spatial) data items that are retrieved by a query as well as its cost, in terms of I/O and CPU effort. As in traditional databases, spatial *query optimization* tools include cost-based models, exploiting analytical formulae for selectivity and cost of a query, and histogram-based techniques.

In particular for spatial databases supported by R-tree indices, cost-based optimization exploits analytical models and formulae that predict the number of hits among the entries of the R-tree (called *selectivity*) and the cost of a query retrieval, measured in R-tree node accesses (or actual disk accesses, assuming existence of a buffering scheme).

Traditionally, R-tree performance has been evaluated by the ability to answer range queries by accessing the smallest possible number of disk pages (i.e., nodes). Other queries, such as nearest neighbor [197] and join queries [35] are also of great interest for a spatial query optimizer. Recently, a new push in related work has been due to the emerging spatiotemporal applications, where novel variants of R-trees have been proposed.

8.1 Selectivity and Cost Models for Selection Queries

Considering that each R-tree node corresponds to a physical disk page, the cost estimation of a query (i.e., the number of pages accessed to retrieve the query result) turns into the problem of estimating the number of nodes visited during R-tree traversal. Evidently, the actual time required (i.e., the number of disk pages times the time required to read a page resident on disk) could be less than the estimated due to the effect of buffering. Therefore, several models have included buffer parameters in their formulae.

8.1.1 Formulae for Range Queries

The first attempt to estimate the performance of R-trees for range queries was made by Faloutsos et al. [65]. In this paper, the authors make two fundamental assumptions:

1. uniform distribution of data (uniformity assumption), and

2. all R-tree nodes are supposed to be full of data (packed trees).

For point queries, the derived cost formula expresses the fact that the number of nodes to be visited equals the overlap of parent nodes per level or, in other words, the *density* of nodes per level summed up for all but the leaf level (actually, the term density was not used by the authors of [65]; it was used quite later, in [234], as will be discussed). Although the analysis in [65] was restricted by the assumptions on uniformity and packed trees, it served as a framework for almost all related work that followed it. Among the proposed formulae, it was also one about the expected height h of an R-tree:

$$h = \log_f \frac{N}{c} \qquad (8.1)$$

where f is the node capacity (fanout) for parent nodes, c is the capacity of leaf nodes, and N is the number of data entries.

Extending this work, Kamel and Faloutsos [104] and Pagel et al. [167] independently presented the following formula that gives the average cost C_W of a range query with respect to a query window $q = (q_1, \ldots, q_d)$, assuming the dataset is indexed by a d-dimensional R-tree index T and provided that the sides $(s_j, 1, \ldots, s_j, d)$ of each R-tree node s_j are known (the summation extends over all the nodes of the tree):

$$C_W(T, q) = \sum_j \left\{ \prod_{i=1}^{d} (s_{j,i} + q_i) \right\} \qquad (8.2)$$

Equation 8.2 allows the query optimizer to estimate the cost of a query window (measured in number of node accesses) assuming that the corresponding R-tree has been already built, hence, the MBR of each node s_j of the R-tree can be measured. Looking into this formula, it intuitively presents the relation between the sizes of the R-tree nodes and of the query window, on the one hand, and the cost of a range query, on the other. Moreover, the influence of the node perimeters is revealed, which helps us understand the R*-tree efficiency as, it was the first method among the R-tree variants to take into account the node perimeter parameter during its construction phase (see Section 2.2 for relevant discussion and [233] for a performance-wise comparison of the most popular members of the R-tree family until that time).

Extending the work reported in [167], Pagel et al. [168] proposed an optimal algorithm that establishes a lower bound result for the performance of packed R-trees. Through experimental results, it has also been shown that the best known static and dynamic R-tree variants, the packed R-tree by Kamel and Faloutsos [104], and the R*-tree [19], respectively, performed about 10% to 20% worse than the lower bound. Reference [168] defined the problem of measuring the performance of SAMs like R-trees, as follows: for a bucket set B and a query model QM, let $Prob(q \ meets \ B_i)$ be the probability that performing query q forces an access of bucket B_i. Then the expected number of bucket accesses needed to perform query q is called the performance measure PM for QM and is given by:

$$PM(QM, \mathcal{B}) = \sum_{i=1}^{m} \text{Prob}(q \text{ meets } B_i) \qquad (8.3)$$

Reference [168] also formalized the so-called Bucket Set Problem (BSP): given a set of geometric objects, a bucket capacity $b \geq 2$, and a query model QM, determine the bucket set $\mathcal{B}_{opt}$ for which the performance measure PM is minimal. They also distinguished two cases, the simple case (called SBSP), where $b = 2$, and the universal case (called UBSP), where $b \geq 3$, and prove that SBSP can be solved in polynomial time while UBSP is NP-hard. Practically, this means that in R-trees etc. (where $b = M >> 2$), it is not possible to find and integrate an optimal construction algorithm.

The impact of the three parameters that are involved in Equation 8.2, namely the sum of rectangle areas, the sum of rectangle perimeters, and the number of rectangles, is further studied in [166], where formulae for various kinds of range queries, such as intersection, containment and enclosure queries of various shapes (points, lines, circles, windows, etc.) are derived. One of the main conclusions of this paper is that window queries can be considered representative for range queries in general.

However, Equation 8.2 cannot predict the cost of a range query just by taking into consideration the dataset properties, because R-tree properties were involved (namely, the R-tree node extents s_j). Faloutsos and Kamel [62] and Theodoridis and Sellis [234] extend this formula toward this goal. The authors of [62] use a property of the dataset called *fractal dimension*. The fractal dimension of a dataset (consisting of points) can be mathematically computed and constitutes a simple way to describe non-uniform datasets, using just a single number. According to the model proposed in [62], the estimation of the number of disk accesses at level 1 (i.e., leaf level), denoted by $C_W(T^1, q)$, is given by:

$$C_W(T^1, q) = \frac{N}{f} \cdot \prod_{i=1}^{d} (s_{1,i} + q_i) \qquad (8.4)$$

where

$$s_{1,i} = (f/N)^{1/fd}, \ \forall i = 1, \ldots, d$$

and f is the average capacity (fanout) of the R-tree nodes.

In [62], the Hausdorff fractal dimension (FD_0) is used to estimate the cost of a range query. In [20], the correlation fractal dimension (FD_2) is used to make selectivity estimation. In both cases, the accuracy of the estimations is very high, a fact that illustrated how surprisingly often real (point) datasets behave like fractals. Reference [20, 62] are also the first attempts to support analytically non-uniform distributions of data (with uniform distribution being a special case) superseding [65] analysis that assumes uniformity. However the models proposed are applicable to point datasets only.

In order to overcome this disadvantage, Acharya et al. [2] proposed a binary space partitioning technique, called the Min-Skew Partitioning, which can be used to estimate the selectivity of point and rectangular datasets. Defining the spatial density of a point to be the number of rectangles (spatial objects) containing that point, and the spatial skew of a bucket to be the statistical variance of all points in the bucket, they introduced an algorithm that minimizes the spatial skew. The algorithm decomposes the space in buckets containing points, which have minimal variance in the value of their spatial density, resulting into buckets with near-uniform distribution. Experimental results showed the selectivity estimation error to be low, varying from 25% to 5% depending on the number of buckets and the query size.

Proietti and Faloutsos [193] study the node distribution of R-tree storing real spatial region data (islands, lakes, etc.). Having discovered that the area distribution of such datasets obeys a hyperbolic power law, called REGAL (REGion Area Low), they extended it and showed that for an R-tree storing region data obeying this low, the MBRs inside it should also obey the same law. Then the low validity propagates toward further aggregation levels (e.g., buckets of MBRs, MBRs in higher tree levels, obey the same law). More precisely, the REGAL low states that the number $C(\alpha)$ of regions having area at least α is:

$$C(\alpha) = k \cdot \alpha^{-P_e} \tag{8.5}$$

where k, P_e are constants greater than zero and $\alpha \geq 0$.

Based on the previous, [193] provided an accurate estimation on the I/O complexity for range queries posed on real region datasets stored inside R-trees:

$$
\begin{aligned}
C_W(T, q) = {} & \sum_{j=1}^{h} \alpha_j \cdot \frac{\frac{N}{f^{j-1}} - 1}{1 - \frac{1}{P_e}} \\
+ {} & \left(q_x \cdot \sqrt{\frac{1}{\rho}} + q_y \cdot \sqrt{\rho} \right) \cdot \sum_{j=0}^{h} \alpha_j \cdot \frac{\frac{N}{f^{j-1}}^{1-1/2P_e} - 1}{1 - \frac{1}{2P_e}} \\
+ {} & q_x \cdot q_y \cdot n
\end{aligned}
\tag{8.6}
$$

where N is the cardinality of the dataset, n is the total number of nodes in the tree, α_j is the area of the largest rectangle in the j-th level of the R-tree, q_x and q_y are the query extents, ρ is the fixed aspect ratio of MBRs between width and height (computed as an average of all aspect ratios of MBRs) and P_e is the patchiness exponent. Results from this work showed that the relative error of the model ranges from 22% to 32% and is significantly better than a model assuming dataset uniformity.

In a different line, [234] used another property of the dataset, called *density surface*. The density Den of a set of N (hyper-)rectangles with average extent $s = (s_1, \ldots, s_d)$ is the average number of rectangles that contain a given point in n-dimensional space. Equivalently, Den can be expressed as the ratio of the global data area over the work space area. If we consider a unit workspace $[0,1)^d$ then the density $Den(N, s)$ is given by the following formula:

$$Den(N, s) = \sum_N \prod_{i=1}^{d} s_i = N \cdot \prod_{i=1}^{d} s_i \qquad (8.7)$$

Using the framework proposed in [167] and based on the investigations that:

- the expected number of node accesses $C_W(T, q)$ for a query window q is equal to the expected number of intersected nodes at each level,
- the average number of intersected nodes is equal to the density Den of the node rectangles inflated by q_i at each direction,
- the average number of nodes n_j at level j is $n_j = N/f^j$, where N is the cardinality of the dataset and f is the fanout, and
- the density Den_j of node rectangles at each level j can be expressed as a function of the density of the dataset,

the authors of [234] proposed the following formula:

$$C_W(T, q) = \sum_{j=1}^{1+\log_f \frac{N}{f}} \left\{ \frac{N}{f^j} \cdot \prod_{i=1}^{d} \left((Den_j \cdot \frac{f^j}{N})^{1/d} + q_i \right) \right\} \qquad (8.8)$$

To reach this formula, the authors assumed square node rectangles and argue that this is a reasonable simplification and a nice property for an efficient R-tree (the same is also argued in [104]). They also assumed a uniform distribution for both data and node rectangles. Under these assumptions, Equation 8.8 estimates the number of node accesses by only using the dataset properties N and Den, the typical R-tree parameter f and the extents of query window q.

The authors of [234] also provided a formula for the selectivity σ of a range query specified by a query window q, i.e., the ratio of the expected number of hits in the dataset over the total number N of entries. Since, σ is equal to the ratio of the number of intersected rectangles among the N rectangles of the input dataset over N, the formula proposed for the selectivity is the following:

$$\sigma = \prod_{i=1}^{d} \left((\frac{Den}{N})^{1/d} + q_i \right) \qquad (8.9)$$

However, as already mentioned, Equations 8.8 and 8.9 assume uniformity of data (in particular, in order to express the density of parent nodes at a level $j+1$ as a function of the density of child nodes at level j). This assumption is restrictive, therefore, to overcome it, the authors proposed the evolution of density from a single number Den to a varying parameter (graphically, a surface in 2-dimensional space) showing deviations, if projected in different points of the work space, with respect to the average value Den. For example,

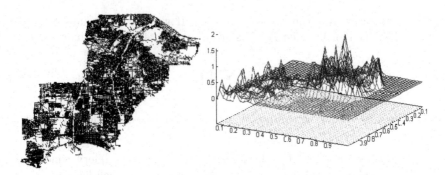

Fig. 8.1. A real dataset (LB county TIGER dataset) and its density surface.

a real dataset [239] is illustrated in Figure 8.1, together with its density surface, which is actually a 2D histogram (illustrations come from [234]).

Using the introduced density surface, [234] showed that non-uniform distributions of data could be supported as well, after the following modifications performed over Equations 8.8 and 8.9:

- the average density Den_0 of the dataset is replaced by the actual density Den'_0 of the dataset within the area of the query window q, and
- the cardinality N of the dataset is replaced by a transformation of it, called N', computed as follows: $N' = \frac{Den'_0}{Den_0} \cdot N$.

In [234], it is also noted that for the previous formulae to be usable for point datasets also, the average density of a dataset is considered to be always $Den_0 > 0$, even for point datasets, because zero density corresponds to a zero-populated work area. A comparison of the analytical estimates with experimental results using R*-trees on synthetic and real datasets showed that the estimates were accurate enough, with the relative error being below 10% (20%) for C_W on uniform (non-uniform) data and below 5% (10%, respectively) for S.

A similar idea is found in [8, 99], where a density file is proposed to be maintained in addition to the R-tree. In particular, the *density file* proposed in [99] is an auxiliary data structure that contains the number of points (assuming a point dataset) falling within a specific Hilbert range. In case of rectangular data items, a cumulative density scheme was proposed, gridding spatial extents and keeping four values for each Hilbert cell about the number of rectangles whose lower-left, lower-right, upper-left, and upper-right corner, respectively, lies in the cell. Based on this density file, models for estimating the selectivity as well as the cost of a range query were proposed with their accuracy shown to be high (usually less than 5% error for uniform to skewed datasets using the packed R-tree [104] as a case-study).

However, previous work on R-tree cost models assumed that the extent of the data objects inserted in the tree is uniformly distributed along each dimension. Though this may be true for several spatial objects, there are numerous applications such as temporal, spatiotemporal, and multimedia databases where dimensions behave differently from each other. For example, in spatiotemporal applications indexed by the widely used 3D R-tree [238], which simply treats time as an extra spatial dimension, object trajectories tend to be 3D shapes elongated in the time dimension, thus resulting in elongated (in time dimension) 3D R-tree leaf nodes.

To resolve this problem, Tao and Papadias [225] have thoroughly examined the R*-tree split algorithm and proposed an extent regression function (ERF), which computes the node extents as a function of the number of node splits. In particular, using each level and axis length distribution function (which, in the leaf level, derives from the actual data), they calculate the introduced extent regression function $ERF_i(t)$ for each tree level in the i-th dimension having as parameter t the total number of splits performed along the i-th dimension in this tree level.

The average extent $s_{i,j}$ of a level-i node along the j-th dimension is calculated using the computed ERFs and adopting a technique that under constraints, estimates the number of splits performed along the j-th dimension in the i-th tree level by minimizing an objective function. Finally, having been estimated offline, without accessing the tree, the average values of $s_{j,i}$ in each tree level, the following formula:

$$C_W(T, q) = \sum_{j=1}^{1 + \log_f (N/f)} \left\{ \frac{N}{f^j} \cdot \prod_{i=1}^{d} (s_{i,j} + q_i) \right\} \tag{8.10}$$

that generalizes Equation 8.8 can be used to determine the total number of node accesses. The authors also suggest that the (demanding) computation of average $s_{j,i}$ for all levels and dimensions can be precomputed off-line, thus reducing the time to produce a cost estimate for a range query to the cost of evaluating Equation 8.8.

Experimental evaluation presented in [225] shows that the proposed model provides accurate estimations in all settings, including ones where other tested cost models (such as [234]) completely fail. However, contrary to previously presented cost models, the one presented in [225] cannot be generally used to indices belonging in the R-tree family because the calculation of the extent regression function is based on and fits in the R*-tree splitting algorithm.

All the previous models can provide cost estimations measured in number of R-tree nodes accessed, which is an upper bound for the number of actual disk accesses. The latter may turn out to be significantly lower than the former with the existence of a buffering scheme, which is always the case in real life systems. The effect of the buffering on the R-tree performance for selection queries is studied in [136]. In particular, Leutenegger and Lopez [136] modify Equation 8.2, by introducing the size of a buffer following the LRU replacement policy. The authors also discuss the appropriate number of R-tree levels to be pinned and argue that pinning may mostly benefit point queries and, even then, only under special conditions. For example, for point queries, it is argued that pinning R-tree levels is advantageous, but only when the total number of nodes pinned is within a factor of two of the buffer size, while for range queries the benefit is even more modest. Practically, if the buffer is shared among many applications, reference [136] suggests that pinning R-trees should be done only when the rest of the applications do not need the full buffer capacity.

8.1.2 Formulae for Nearest-Neighbor Queries

Exploiting the branch-and-bound algorithm for nearest-neighbor query processing proposed in [197], Papadopoulos and Manolopoulos [177] derived lower and upper bounds for its performance (number of disk accesses to R-tree leaf pages). In particular, they first prove two propositions for the expected number of R-tree leaf pages accessed to find the nearest neighbor of a point P: the minimum (maximum) number of leaf pages touched is the number of leaf pages intersected by a circle C_1 (C_2) with center q and radius $dist_{nn}$ ($dist_m$), where $dist_{nn}$ is the actual distance between q and its nearest neighbor (not known in advance) and $dist_m$ is the MINMAXDIST between q and the first touched leaf page (cf. Section 4.3 for a definition and discussion of MINMAXDIST metric). Then, extending Equation 8.4 proposed in [62] for range queries on uniform datasets, [177] came up with the following pair of formulae for lower and upper bounds:

$$C_{NN}(T, q)_{lower} = \frac{N - 1}{f} \cdot (s + 2 \cdot dist_{nn})^{FD_2} \tag{8.11}$$

$$C_{NN}(T, q)^{upper} = \frac{N - 1}{f} \cdot (s + 2 \cdot dist_m)^{FD_2} \tag{8.12}$$

The experimental results presented in [177] showed that the actual cost is well bounded by the two proposed bounds and, in general, the measured cost is closer to the lower than to the upper bound.

The previous analysis is restricted to estimating the cost for the first nearest neighbor, and its extension to support k-NN queries is not straightforward. In [116], closed-form formulae for k-NN queries, for arbitrary k are proposed. Moreover, the formulae proposed by Korn et al. in [116] for estimating the cost of k-NN queries can be simplified, and thus lead to fundamental observations that deflate the dimensionality curse. In particular, these formulae involve two measures of the intrinsic dataset dimensionality, the Hausdorff fractal dimension FD_0, and the correlation fractal dimension FD_2, also used in [62] and [20], respectively. They show, both analytically and experimentally, that it is the fractal dimensionality rather than the address-space dimensionality that determines the search performance of a k-NN query in a multi-dimensional space.

However, the preceding analysis is valid only for uniform data distribution because this technique can provide only a single estimation representing the average cost of all queries but used for the optimization of a single query. In general, cost models trying to accommodate the non-uniform distribution of data by computing the fractal dimension of the input dataset disregard the fact that queries at various locations usually have different characteristics (e.g., they lead to different value of $dist_k$) [231].

In [22], Berchtold et al. presented a cost model for query processing in high-dimensional data spaces. They provide accurate estimations for nearest-neighbor queries and range queries using the Euclidean distance, and assumptions of independence are implicit in the formulae. This paper introduced the concept of the Minkowski sum to determine the access probability of a rectangular page for spherical queries (i.e., range queries and nearest-neighbor queries). The Minkowski sum can be used to determine the index selectivity of distance-based join operations. The authors in [23] extended their previous work and proposed an analytical cost model for NN query processing in high dimensional space. They present closed formula for the cost of NN queries depending on the space dimensionality the block size and the database size. Contrary to their previous work, where the Minkowski sum needed to be computed numerically, the formula provided can be used to optimize the block size. The model can also be used to determine the dimensionality above which the sequential scan will surpass R-tree-based searching, as a side effect of the curse of dimensionality.

Boehm [29] and Tao et al. [226] tackled the problem of estimating the average $dist_k$ distance between q and its k-th nearest neighbor. The model proposed in [29] involves integrals in the computation of $dist_k$, which can be solved only numerically, thus making it not easily applicable for query optimization purposes. On the other hand, [226] proposed the following closed formula:

$$dist_k = \frac{2}{C_V} \cdot \left\{ 1 - \sqrt{1 - (k/N)^{1/d}} \right\} \tag{8.13}$$

where

$$C_V = \frac{\sqrt{\pi}}{\Gamma(d/2 + 1)^{1/d}}$$

and

$$\Gamma(x + 1) = x \cdot \Gamma(x), \Gamma(1) = 1, \Gamma(1/2) = \pi^{1/2}$$

A side effect of this analysis is also the estimation of the smallest value for k for which sequential scan would surpass R-tree-based searches. According to the authors' experiments, the threshold value decreases dramatically with the dimensionality, a conclusion consistent with related work (e.g. [243]).

Recently, a cost model for k-NN queries was proposed in [231] for low and medium dimensionalities, using a new technique based on the concept of vicinity rectangles and Minkowski rectangles (instead of the traditional vicinity circles and Minkowski regions, respectively), which simplifies the resulting equations with minimal computational overhead. Particularly, [231] proposes the calculation of the number of node accesses for a k-NN query $C_{kNN}(T, q)$ based on the following formulae:

$$C_{kNN}(T, q) = \sum_{i=0}^{\log_f(N/f)} \left[\frac{N}{f^{i+1}} \cdot \frac{L_i - (L_i/2 + s_i/2)^2}{1 - s_i} \right] \tag{8.14}$$

where:

$$L_i = \left[\sum_{i=0}^{d} \binom{d}{i} \cdot s_i^{d-i} \cdot \frac{\sqrt{\pi^i}}{\Gamma(i/2 + 1)} \cdot dist_k^i \right]$$

and the average extend of a level-i node, s_i, is calculated by:

$$s_i = \left(1 - \frac{1}{f} \right) \cdot min \left(\frac{f^{i+1}}{N}, 1 \right)^{1/d}$$

and $dist_k$ comes from Equation 8.11.

The work in [231] confirmed the accuracy of the model through extensive experiments using the R*-tree as the underlying spatial access method (with uniform and real datasets) and demonstrated its applicability and effectiveness by incorporating it in various query-optimization problems related to nearest-neighbor search. The proposed model has a great advantage in comparison to previous methods because it permits the application of conventional multidimensional histograms to support non-uniformly distributed datasets. However, its applicability is limited by the number of dimensions, because after ten dimensions, the experimental results have shown that it is inaccurate. Moreover, it can be used only in point datasets and its employment in other kinds of data (e.g., rectangles) is not straightforward.

8.2 Selectivity and Cost Models for Join Queries

Spatial join requires high processing cost due to the high complexity and large volume of spatial data. Therefore, the accurate selectivity estimation and cost of spatial join queries have a great influence on the query optimizer. Unlike range queries, the number of input datasets in join queries is variable, thus we distinguish between models proposed for pair-wise joins and those proposed for multiway joins.

8.2.1 Formulae for Pair-Wise Joins

The first work on predicting the selectivity of join queries was by Aref and Samet [13]. In this paper, the authors propose analytical formulae for the number of hits, based on uniformity assumption and the R-tree analysis provided in [104]. The motivating idea was the consideration of a join query as a set of selection queries (with the first R-tree playing the role of the target index and the second R-tree assumed to be the source of query windows). Demonstrated experimental results showed the accuracy of the proposed selectivity estimation formula.

Also assuming uniform distribution of data, Huang et al. [91] propose a cost model for R-tree-based spatial joins distinguishing two cases: either lack or existence of a buffering mechanism. Two corresponding formulae are proposed, one estimating the cost assuming no buffering and one estimating the actual cost taking into account the probability of a page not to be (re-)visited due to buffering mechanism, Equations 8.15 and 8.16, respectively:

$$C_{SJ}(T_1, T_2) = 2 \cdot \sum_{l=1}^{h-1} \sum_{i=1}^{N_1^l} \sum_{j=1}^{N_2^l} \prod_{k=1}^{d} (s_{T_1,k} + s_{T_2,k}) \tag{8.15}$$

and

$$C_{SJ}(T_1, T_2)^{actual} = n + m + (C_{SJ}(T_1, T_2) - n - m) \cdot \mathrm{Prob}(x \geq b) \tag{8.16}$$

The triple sum in Equation 8.15 denotes the pairs of considered node MBRs, one for each tree, for all levels. Thus, to find the cost this number is counted twice (once for each tree). Also, in Equation 8.16, the first two terms $(n + m)$ represent the total number of first accesses for all tree pages traversed during the join (every node will be traversed at least once), while the term $C_{SJ}(T_1, T_2) - n - m$ represents the expected number of non-first accesses with the probability of one such access causing a page fault. The accuracy of the two formulae was also demonstrated after a comparison with experimental results for varying buffer size (with the relative error being around 10% to 20%).

Theodoridis et al. [236, 237] also considered the depth-first approach for a join query between two R-trees T_1 and T_2 as a series of query windows, where, e.g., the node rectangles of T_1 at a level l could play the role of query windows on a dataset consisting of the node rectangles of T_2 at a corresponding level. Under this consideration, Equation 8.8, originally proposed in [234] for range queries, is modified to calculate the cost of a join query. In particular, the cost for each R-tree at level l is the sum of costs of $N_{T_2,l+1}$ different window queries on T_1:

$$C_W(T_1^l, T_2^l) = C_W(T_2^l, T_1^l) = N_{T_2,l+1} \cdot N_{T_1,l+1} \cdot (|s_{T_1,l+1}| + |s_{T_2,l+1}|)^d \tag{8.17}$$

for $0 \leq l \leq h - 2$.

Hence, for R-trees with equal height h, the total cost of a spatial join between T_1 and T_2 is the sum of node accesses at each level:

$$
\begin{aligned}
C_{SJ}(T_1, T_2) &= \sum_{l=0}^{h-2} \left\{ C_W(T_1^l, T_2^l) + C_W(T_2^l, T_1^l) \right\} \\
&= 2 \cdot \sum_{l=1}^{h-1} \left\{ N_{T_2,l} \cdot N_{T_1,l} \cdot (|s_{T_1,l}| + |s_{T_2,l}|)^d \right\} \tag{8.18}
\end{aligned}
$$

Evidently, the cost shown in Equation 8.18 is an upper bound without taking buffering into consideration, and every node access in T_i corresponds to a node access in T_j. The work in [237] provided a detailed description of cost formulae for R-tree-based join queries, including the case of R-trees with different heights. As in [234], all the involved parameters are expressed as functions of dataset properties, namely cardinality N and density Den. Experimental results suggested that the cost model is accurate for uniform data (where the density remains almost invariant through the workspace), and reasonably good for non-uniform data distributions, where the density surface is used (similar results were shown in [142]).

In reference [30], an analytical model and a performance study of the similarity join operation on indexes are presented. In this context, the optimization conflict between CPU and I/O optimization is studied. To solve this conflict, a complex index architecture called Multipage Index (MuX) and a join algorithm (MuX-join), which allows a separate optimization of the CPU time and the I/O time, are proposed. This architecture, which is based on R-trees (for a fast index construction, the bottom-up algorithm for X-tree construction [24] was adopted), utilizes large primary pages, which are subject to I/O processing and optimized for this purpose. The primary pages accommodate a secondary search structure to reduce the computational effort. The experimental evaluation using the join algorithm (MuX-join) over the index architecture (MuX) showed good performance.

8.2.2 Formulae for Multiway Joins

As already discussed in Section 5.3, multiway spatial join queries between n R-trees $T_1, \ldots, T_n$, can be represented by a graph Q where Q_{ij} denotes the join condition between T_i and T_j. Papadias et al. [171, 172] provided formulae for the selectivity (i.e., the number of solutions among all possible n-tuples in the Cartesian product) and the cost (in terms of node accesses) of some special cases of multiway queries. In particular, taking into consideration the general idea that the total number of solutions is given by the following formula:

$$
\begin{aligned}
\#\text{solutions} \quad = \quad & \#(\text{all possible } n-\text{tuples}) \\
& \cdot \quad \text{Prob(an } n-\text{tuple constitutes a solution)} \quad (8.19)
\end{aligned}
$$

and the fact that the pairwise probabilities are independent in case of acyclic graphs, the selectivity of an acyclic join graph is:

$$
\text{Prob(an } n-\text{tuple is a solution)} \quad = \prod_{\forall i,j: Q(i,j)=TRUE} \left(|s_{T_i}| + |s_{T_j}| \right)^d \quad (8.20)
$$

and the total number of solutions at tree level l is:

$$
\#\text{solutions}(Q, l) \quad = \quad \prod_{i=1}^{n} N_{T_i, l} \cdot \prod_{\forall i,j: Q(i,j)=TRUE} \left(|s_{T_i, l}| + |s_{T_j, l}| \right)^d \quad (8.21)
$$

However, in case of cycles, the assignments are not independent anymore and Equation 8.19 does not accurately estimate the probability that a random tuple constitutes a solution. For the special case of cliques, reference [172] provides a formula for selectivity, based on the fact that if a set of rectangles mutually overlap, then they must share a common area (the proof is extensive and can be found in [172]):

$$\#\text{solutions}(Q, l) = \prod_{i=1}^{n} N_{T_i,l} \cdot \left(\sum_{i=1}^{n} \prod_{j=1, j \neq i}^{n} |s_{T_j,l}| \right)^{d} \tag{8.22}$$

In order to provide cost formulae for multiway joins, [172] decomposed the query graph Q into a set of legal subgraphs $Q_{x,y}$ (legal means connected graph), which could be processed, e.g., by applying Synchronous Traversal (cf. ST algorithm in Figure 5.8). Since, according to the ST algorithm, the x R-trees roots must be accessed to find root level solutions and, in turn, each solution will lead to x accesses at the next (lower) level, in its generalization at level l, there will be $x \cdot \#\text{solutions}(Q_{x,y}, l + 1)$ node accesses and the total cost for processing $Q_{x,y}$ using ST would be:

$$C_{mSJ}(T_1, T_2, \ldots, T_n, Q_{x,y}) = x + \sum_{l=0}^{h-2} x \cdot \#\text{solutions}(Q_{x,y}, l + 1) \tag{8.23}$$

Again, this formula is useful for query optimization purposes only when an accurate estimation of the number of solutions is possible, i.e., in the cases of acyclic graphs and cliques only. Experimental results on those types of query graphs and uniform distributions of data demonstrated the accuracy of Equations 8.19 to 8.22, with the relative error being below 10% on the average and below 25% on the worst case. The extension of the cost models to support arbitrary query graphs and non-uniform data distribution was left as an open issue.

Extending [171], Park and Chung [183] analyzed the time and temporary space complexity of the formulae for tree and clique multiway joins and showed that the complexity for the former type is much higher than that for the latter type.

In a different line, Mamoulis and Papadias [145] addressed the problem of complex query processing, in which an n-way join follows n independent selection queries on the original (R-tree-indexed) spatial datasets. Assuming that the original datasets share a common workspace, the authors anticipated that the spatial selections would affect not only the number of objects that would participate in the succeeding join, but also their spatial distribution, adding a dependency overhead. Two selectivity formulae, one for acyclic and one for clique joins, have been proposed. The experimental results provided in [145] showed that the formulae were accurate enough, especially for pair-wise joins (the relative error was 8% for $n = 2$, rising to 38% for n=4). Although the above analysis assumed uniformity, the model is also extendable to work for arbitrary data distributions, taking into account the density surface concept [234, 236]. However, in that case the accuracy of the estimation is decreased.

8.2.3 Formulae for Distance-Join Queries

In reference [52], an I/O cost model for the k closest-pairs query (k-CPQ) [50] and buffer query (BQ) [40] has been proposed. The development of the cost model for k-CPQ is based on previous analytical results for k-NN [116] and spatial intersect join queries [237], which can be considered a generalization of them. The unrealistic assumptions of uniformity and independence are avoided. On the contrary, the formulae correspond to real data and depend mainly on the correlation exponent (ρ) and number of pairs in the final result (k). This analysis assumes a typical (non-uniform) workload where *queries are more probable in high-density areas of the address space*. Moreover, the authors successfully extended the cost model to the analytical study by including buffering (LRU buffer model [26]) for these kinds of distance-join queries using R-trees [136].

First of all, the k-CPQ *index selectivity* ($\sigma(k)$) must be calculated, and it can be obtained (as for k-NN query and spatial join) by using the concept of Minkowski sum [22, 29]. The Minkowski can be applied for real data (non-uniform and independent data distributions) to determine $\sigma(k)$, assuming the pairs distribution is smooth (in this case, smoothness means that the density of pairs (number of pairs inside a given volume) does not vary severely inside the Minkowski enlargement of page pairs). The volume of the Minkowski sum of two MBRs of two levels l_1 and l_2 R-tree nodes ($0 \leq l_i \leq h_{T_i}1$) from two R-trees T_1 and T_2 with heights $h_{R_2} \leq h_{R_1}$ and one sphere of radius $dist_{cp}(k)$, divided by the data space volume (the volume of the n-dimensional unit space $[0,1]^n$, which is equal to 1), expresses the access probability (k-CPQ index selectivity, $\sigma(k)$) of the corresponding nodes and is given by the following binomial formula (note that T_i contains N_{T_i,l_i} nodes of average side lengths s_{T_i,l_i} with minimum distance between them smaller than or equal to $dist_{cp}(k)$):

$$\sigma(k) = \left(\sum_{k=0}^{d} \left\{ \binom{d}{k} \cdot (s_{T_1,l_1} + s_{T_2,l_2})^{(d-k)} \cdot \frac{\pi^{k/2} \cdot (dist_{op}(k))^k}{\Gamma(k/2+1)} \right\} \right)^{\rho/n}$$

where:

$$l_2 = \begin{cases} l_1 & 0 \leq l_1 \leq h_{T_2} - 1 \\ h_{T_2} - 1 & h_{T_2} \leq l_1 \leq h_{T_1} - 1 \end{cases}$$

and ρ is the *correlation exponent*. The estimation of the distance of the k-th closest pair ($dist_{cp}(k)$) is computed as follows:

$$dist_{cp}(k) = \frac{(\Gamma((n/2)+1))^{1/n}}{\sqrt{\pi}} \cdot \left(\frac{k}{N_{T_1} \cdot N_{T_2}} \right)^{1/\rho}$$

The estimation of the correlation exponent (ρ) is based on the *pair-count law* [64], which governs the distribution of pair-wise distance between two real, n-dimensional point datasets. The exponent of the pair count law, the so-called *pair-count exponent* ρ (correlation exponent), can be calculated by using a box-counting algorithm based on the concept of *box occupancy product sum (BOPS)* [64]. The algorithm of computing BOPS is an interesting extension of the algorithm proposed in [21] for computing the *generalized fractal dimension*.

Finally, the overall estimation of the total I/O cost in terms of R-tree node accesses for k-CPQ is given by the following formula (without loss of generality, it is assumed that $h_{T_2} \leq h_{T_1}$). Where the multiplier (i.e., the factor 2) corresponds to the cost of two R-trees (T_1 and T_2), $N_{T_1,l_1} \cdot N_{T_2,l_2}$ is the R-tree node pairs density of the R-trees T_1 and T_2 at levels l_1 and l_2, and $\sigma(k)$ represents the percentage of pairs of R-tree nodes that are accessed at these levels for the k-CPQ algorithm.

$$C_{CPQ}(T_1, T_2, k) = 2 \cdot \sum_{l_1=0}^{h_{T_1}-1} N_{T_1,l_1} \cdot N_{T_2,l_2} \cdot \sigma(k)$$

where:

$$l_2 = \begin{cases} l_1 & 0 \leq l_1 \leq h_{T_2} - 1 \\ h_{T_2} - 1 & h_{T_2} \leq l_1 \leq h_{T_1} - 1 \end{cases}$$

A simple derivation of the I/O cost model for k-CPQ (previous formulae for $\sigma(k)$ and $C_{CPQ}(T_1, T_2, k)$) can estimate the number of node accesses for buffer queries (where points are indexed by R-trees). It consists of replacing $dist_{cp}(k)$ by δ (distance threshold) in the formula of $\sigma(k)$, giving rise to $\sigma(\delta)$ and $C_{CPQ}(T_1, T_2, \delta)$. Remember that the answer of a buffer query is a set of pairs of spatial objects (in this case, pairs of points) from the two input datasets (indexed by two R-trees) that are within distance d from each other [40].

In reference [52], experimental results on both synthetic (uniform) and real datasets showed that the proposed analytical model was very accurate (varying several parameters as cardinality of the query result (k), distance threshold (δ), maximum branching factor, different dataset cardinalities and data distributions, etc.), with the relative error being usually around 0% to 6% (k-CPQ) and 0% to 14% (for buffer queries) when the estimated results are compared to the measured costs using R*-trees. These error values are within an acceptable confidence level of cost prediction for distance-join queries, demonstrating that the proposed cost model can be considered an effective mechanism in the cost estimations of R-tree distance joins during the distance-join query optimization step.

8.3 Spatiotemporal Query Optimization

Although the domain of spatiotemporal databases has been the center of research interest for several years, developing novel indexing schemes mainly based on the R-tree, the work conducted for cost models and selectivity estimation for such indexing schemes is very limited.

As already discussed in Chapter 6, spatiotemporal indexing schemes are divided into two categories: those treating time as an extra dimension, thus incorporating phenomena that involve continuous changes in object position and extent, and those that assume objects remain unchanged between timestamps. The second category includes indexes based on the R-tree, the HR-tree [158], which is an overlapping version of the R-tree, and the MV3R-tree [223] (a multi version R-tree). For such structures, Tao et al. [229] provide a framework for reducing their performance analysis to that of the corresponding ephemeral structures. The proposed framework can be applied to any multi-version or overlapping structure; the authors experimentally show its applicability on R-trees (in particular, in HR-trees [158] and Bitemporal R-trees [125]). The developed models capture the behavior of those structures very well, yielding errors of 5% and 15% for uniform and non-uniform data, respectively.

Preliminary work in the domain of cost models for R-tree-based indexes supporting continuous object changes (e.g., moving objects) includes the selectivity estimation for spatiotemporal queries over moving objects presented in [46]. In this paper, Choi and Chung calculated the selectivity estimation for moving objects stored in an index, indexing their future positions (like the TPR-tree [202]). In particular, they utilized a spatiotemporal histogram, which consists of disjoint buckets like other existing spatial histograms. Additionally, they adopted a TPR-tree-like [202] strategy over the buckets, storing, along with the number of objects contained inside each bucket, a velocity-bounding rectangle, which bounds the velocities of objects in the cell. The histogram is re-constructed in every time unit, updating approximately the 1% of the moving objects. The data used to reconstruct the histogram are selected with a simple round-ribbon scheme. Experimental results showed that such a methodology to construct and maintain a spatiotemporal histogram is possible due to the relatively small computational overhead introduced by it (almost 0.15 second to reconstruct the whole histogram). (It was also shown that the model proposed was efficient because the spatiotemporal selectivity estimation has an average error between 9% and 23%.)

Hadjieleftheriou et al. [82] also studied the problem of selectivity estimation in spatiotemporal databases and proposed two alternative solutions for calculating the selectivity of point objects. The first uses the duality transform introduced in [112], transforming each moving object's trajectory into a point in the 4D dual space straightforwardly, leading to the utilization of any multidimensional histogram, as in [2]. Then, each query is also transformed into the same dual space, and using the histogram, the method predicts the number of objects inside the original query region. The other utilizes the extents of the leaf nodes of an existing index (such as an R-tree) as the histogram buckets.

The analysis presented in [46] is only a special case of the work presented in [230], where Tao et el. estimated the selectivity of several spatiotemporal queries including moving range queries over moving points and moving regions, spatiotemporal joins, and the estimation of the k-NN distance. The methodology proposed decreases the problem's complexities, transforming the moving objects to static, using their relative query window speed. The proposed solutions involve integrals that need numerical evaluation. While the method supports uniformly distributed spatiotemporal data, the authors extend it to non-uniform data developing spatiotemporal histograms. They utilize a simple spatial histogram as in [2], treating each n-dimensional point along with its velocity as a point in the $2n$-dimensional space. The approach is similar to [82] and generalizes the latter by maintaining the histogram incrementally.

Regarding the cost models for estimating the number of node accesses, the only one that can be applied in the case of spatiotemporal data is the one presented in [225] for the R∗-tree and demonstrated in Section 8.1. Although the model has not been specifically developed for spatiotemporal data, it is capable of predicting the performance of a 3D R*-tree storing spatiotemporal objects because it supports tree nodes being elongated in any of their dimensions (in the case of moving objects in the temporal dimension).

8.4 Sampling and Histogram-Based Techniques

In a line different from cost-based estimation, selectivity estimation can be based on samples of the two (or n, in general) spatial datasets involved. An et al. [10] propose the following three-step methodology:

1. pick samples from input datasets, either exploiting their R-tree indices or not;
2. construct an R-tree for each of the samples; and
3. perform an R-tree join on the constructed R-trees.

This process is evaluated in comparison with the alternative of joining one sample with the entire other dataset. The conclusions drawn from the experimentation were clearly in favor of the proposed methodology.

In [129], Lang and Singh present a sampling-based cost model, which predicts the NN query performance of an R-tree in high-dimensional space (in their case study they used the VAMSplit R-tree [244] but other R-tree variants can utilize the same model). The technique simply uses the same construction algorithm as the underlying structure applied in a subset of the data, therefore constructing a miniature of the original index. The nodes of the resulting mini-index have a fanout reduced by the factor of the sample ratio (e.g., if the sample ratio is 0.10, the fanout of the mini-index is 0.10 of the fanout of the original structure). This approach requires that a part of the mini-index will be stored in the disk and therefore not be applicable for query optimization. However, since it is very accurate (typical error below 5%), it can be used in high-dimensional spaces to tune the index structure (determine the page size) without building the index.

Recently, a significant research effort has also focused on selectivity estimation based on histograms. In particular, [10] and [221] introduce novel types of histograms for estimating the selectivity of spatial selections and spatial joins, respectively, while [1] address the issue of accuracy in estimations of related work due to the ignorance of the cost of the refinement step and propose new types of histograms that capture the complexity, size, and location of the spatial objects. We do not provide further details about these works because they are not directly related to R-tree-based query optimization. The interested reader can find more in the cited papers.

8.5 Summary

Query optimization plays a very important role to more efficient query processing. The estimation of query cost helps the query optimizer select a promising query execution plan. For disk-resident implementations, the cost of a query usually corresponds to the number of disk accesses required. Another important measure is the selectivity of a query, which measures the number of objects that satisfy the query. The estimation of the cost and the selectivity of a query require a solid mathematical background to model both the distribution of the data objects and the distribution of the queries. Some approaches use specific characteristics of the data (distribution, density, fractal dimension), whereas others are based on histograms that hold summary information for specific parts of the dataspace. In many cases the developed cost models are accurate, enabling the determination of an appropriate execution plan. Since more complex query types are continuously proposed in the literature, there is room for further research in the area, aim at novel or more accurate estimations of the selectivity and query cost.

9. Implementation Issues

The implementation of an access method in a commercial DBMS or a research prototype raises many issues that must be considered to provide effective and efficient access to the underlying data. An access method is useless unless it can be efficiently implemented in real-life data intensive applications. Making the access method part of a larger (usually multiuser) system is not an easy task. The access method must be adjusted to the underlying system architecture and therefore issues like concurrency control and parallelism must be handled carefully. In this chapter, we discuss implementation issues regarding the R-tree access method. More specifically, we investigate the following topics:

- the adjustment of the R-tree to parallel architectures,
- the management of concurrent accesses, and
- R-tree implementations in research prototypes and commercial systems.

9.1 Parallel Systems

One of the primary goals in database research is the investigation of innovative techniques to provide more efficient query processing. This goal becomes much more important considering that modern applications are more resource demanding and are usually based on multiuser systems. A database research direction that has been widely accepted by developers is the exploitation of multiple resources (processors and disks) to more efficient processing.

The design of algorithms for parallel database machines is not an easy task. Although in some cases the parallel version of a serial algorithm is straightforward, one must look carefully at three fundamental performance measures:

- *speed-up*: shows the capability of the algorithm when the number of processors is increased and the input size is constant. The perfect speed-up is the linear speed-up, meaning that if T seconds are required to perform the operation with one processor, then $T/2$ seconds are required to perform the same operation using two processors.
- *size-up*: shows the behavior of the algorithm when the input size is increased and the number of processors remains constant.
- *scale-up*: shows the performance of the algorithm when both the input size and the number of processors are increased.

There are three basic parallel architectures that have been used in research and development fields [57]:

- *shared everything*: all processors share the same resources (memory and disks) and the communication among processors is performed by means of the global memory.
- *shared disk*: all processors share the disks but each has its own memory.
- *shared nothing*: the processors use different disks and different memory units and the communication among processors is performed using message-passing mechanisms.

In addition to these basic parallel architectures, several hybrid schemes have been proposed, to combine the advantages and avoid the disadvantages of each. For example, the *shared virtual memory* [36, 215] scheme combines the shared nothing and the shared memory scheme to provide a global address space.

Parallelism can also be categorized in:

- *CPU parallelism*, where a task is partitioned to several processors for execution, or
- *I/O parallelism*, where the data are partitioned to several secondary storage units (disks or CD-ROMs) to achieve better I/O performance.

9.1.1 Multidisk Systems

Using more than one disk device leads to increased system throughput, because the workload is balanced among the participating disks and many operations can be processed in parallel [43, 44]. RAID systems have been introduced in [187] as an inexpensive solution to the I/O bottleneck.

Given a disk array, one faces the problem of partitioning the data and the associated access information, to take advantage of the I/O parallelism. The way data are partitioned reflects the performance of read/write operations. The declustering problem attracted many researchers, and a lot of work has been performed to take advantage of the I/O parallelism, to support data-intensive applications. Techniques for B^+-tree declustering have been reported in [209]. In [251] the authors study effective declustering schemes for the grid file structure. The challenge is to decluster an R-tree structure among the available disks, in order to:

- distribute the workload during query processing as evenly as possible among the disks, and
- activate as few disks as possible.

There are several alternative designs that could be followed to take advantage of the multiple disk architecture. These alternatives have been studied in [103].

Independent R-trees. The data are partitioned among the available disks, and an R-tree is built for each disk (Figure 9.1). The performance depends on how the data distribution is performed:

Data Distribution. The data objects are assigned to different disks in a round-robin manner or by using a hash function. This method guarantees that each disk will host approximately the same number of objects. However, even for small queries, all disks are likely to be activated to answer the query.

Space Distribution. The space is divided to d partitions, where d is the number of available disks. The drawback of this approach is that due to the non-uniformity of real-life datasets, some disks may host more objects than the others, and therefore may become a bottleneck. Moreover, for large queries (large query regions), this method fails to balance the load equally among all the disks.

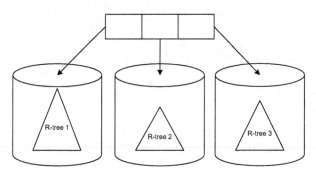

Fig. 9.1. Independent R-trees.

R-tree with Supernodes. This alternative uses only one R-tree (Figure 9.2). The exploitation of the multiple disks is obtained by expanding each tree node. More specifically, the logical tree node size becomes d times larger, and therefore each node is partitioned to all d disks (disk stripping). Although the load is equally balanced during query processing, all disks are activated in each query. This happens because there is no total order of the MBRs that are hosted in a tree node, so each node must be reconstructed by accessing all the disks (each node is partitioned among all disks).

Multiplexed (MX) R-trees. This alternative uses a single R-tree with its nodes distributed among the disks. The main difference with an ordinary R-tree is that inter-disk pointers are used to formulate the tree structure. Each node pointer is a pair of the form $< diskID, pageID >$, where $diskID$ is the disk identifier that contains the page $pageID$. An example of an MX R-tree with ten nodes distributed in three disks is given in Figure 9.3. It is assumed that the R-tree root is memory resident.

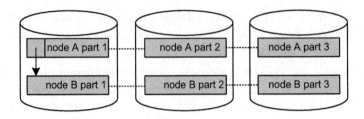

Fig. 9.2. R-tree with supernodes.

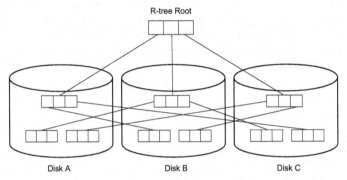

Fig. 9.3. MX R-tree example.

The main issue that must be explained is the node-to-disk assignment policy. The insertion of new objects will cause some nodes to split. The problem is to which disk the newly created node N_n will be assigned, whereas the target is to minimize the query response time. In order to obtain the best result, we could examine all nodes that lie in the same tree level. However, this operation is very costly because it results in many I/O operations. Instead, only the sibling nodes are examined, i.e., the nodes that have the same parent with N_n. Moreover, it is not necessary to fetch the sibling nodes, because the information that we require (MBRs) resides in the parent node (which has been fetched already in memory to insert the new object). There are several criteria that could be used to perform the placement of the new node N_n:

Data balance. In the best case, all disks must host the same number of tree nodes. If a disk contains more nodes than the others, it may become a bottleneck during query processing.

Area balance. The area covered by each disk plays a very important role when we answer range queries. A disk that covers a large area, will be accessed with higher probability than the others, and therefore it may become a bottleneck.

Proximity. If two nodes are near in space, the probability that they will be accessed together is high. Therefore, proximal nodes should be stored to different disks to maximize parallelism.

Although it is very difficult to satisfy all criteria simultaneously, some heuristics have been proposed to attack the problem:

Round-robin. The new node is assigned to a disk using the round-robin algorithm.

Minimum area. This heuristic assigned the new node to the disk that covers the smallest area.

Minimum intersection. This heuristic assigned the new node to a disk to minimize the overlap between the new node and the nodes that are already stored in this disk.

Proximity index. This heuristic is based on the proximity measure, which compares two rectangles and calculates the probability that they will be accessed together by the same query. Therefore, rectangles (which correspond to tree nodes) with high proximity must be stored in different disks.

Several experimental results have been reported in [103]. The main conclusion is that the MXR-tree with the proximity index method for node-to-disk assignment outperforms the other methods for range query processing. The performance evaluation has been conducted using uniformly distributed spatial objects and uniformly distributed range queries. The proposed method manages to activate few disks for small range queries and to activate all disks for large queries, achieving good load balancing, and therefore can be used as an efficient method for parallelizing the R-tree structure. It would be interesting to investigate the performance of the method for non-uniform distributions.

Parallel Query Processing. The parallel version of the R-tree answers the same type of queries as the original R-tree structure much more efficiently. Although [103] focuses on range queries, parallel algorithms exist for other types of queries. In [179] parallel algorithms for NN queries on a multidisk system have been studied. Three possible similarity search techniques are presented and studied in detail: Branch-and-Bound (BBSS), Full-parallel (FPSS), and Candidate Reduction (CRSS). Moreover, an optimal approach (WOPTSS) is defined, which assumes that the distance $dist_k$ from the query point to the k-th NN is known in advance, and therefore only the relevant nodes are inspected. Evidently, this algorithm is hypothetical, because the distance $dist_k$ is generally not known. However, useful lower bounds are derived by studying the behavior of the optimal method. All methods are studied under extensive experimentation through simulation. Among the studied algorithms, the proposed one (CRSS), which is based on a careful inspection of the R*-tree nodes and leads to an effective candidate reduction, shows the best performance. However, the performance difference between CRSS and WOPTSS suggests that further research is required to approach the lower bound as much as possible.

9.1.2 Multiprocessor Systems

The exploitation of multiprocessor systems for spatial query processing has been used to achieve better performance of spatial data-intensive applications. The ability to execute several operations in parallel may have a dramatic impact on the efficiency of the database system. While in multidisk systems the main target is to achieve I/O parallelism, in multiprocessor systems I/O and processing parallelism may be achieved (each processor may control one or many disks).

Although the use of parallelism seems extremely attractive to query performance efficiency, several factors must be taken into consideration to provide a viable solution. Parallel query execution plans must be constructed in order to exploit the multiple processors. Therefore, careful decomposition of the query must be performed to achieve good load balancing among the processors. Otherwise a processor to whom the largest task has been assigned will become a bottleneck. Moreover, if the processors communicate by means of a local area network (LAN), communication costs for interprocessor data exchange must be taken into account. These costs must also be included during query optimization and query cost estimation. Although the proposed techniques are applied in the case where processors communicate by means of a local area network (loosely coupled architecture), they can be applied as well in the case where processors are hosted in the same computer (tightly coupled architecture).

Independent R-trees. Some of the methods used for multidisk R-tree declustering can be used in the multiprocessor case. For example, the spatial data could be partitioned, allowing each processor to manipulate its own local R-tree structure (independent R-trees). If such a scheme is used, the following disadvantages are observed:

- If the majority of the queries refer to a subset of the data that most of them are hosted to a single processor, this processor may become a bottleneck, and therefore parallelism is not being exploited to a sufficient degree.
- In the case where the spatial data are partitioned with respect to a partitioning scheme based on a non-spatial attribute, all processors must be activated to answer a single query, even if a processor contains irrelevant data with respect to the query's spatial attributes.

Leaf-based Declustering. In [123] a parallel version of the R-tree has been proposed to exploit parallelism in a multicomputer system, such as a network of workstations. The system architecture is composed of a master processor (primary site) and a number of slave processors (secondary sites). All sites communicate via an ethernet network. The allocation of pages to sites is carefully performed, in order to achieve efficiency in range query processing. The leaves and the corresponding data objects are stored in the secondary sites, whereas the upper tree levels are maintained in the primary site. More specifically, the leaf level stored at the master contains entries of the form (MBR, serverID, pageID). Since the upper tree levels occupy relatively little space, they can be maintained in the main memory of the primary processor.

Given that the dataset is known in advance, Koudas and Faloutsos [123] suggest sorting the data with respect to the Hilbert value of the object's MBR centroid. Then, the leaf tree level is formed, and the assignment of leaves to sites is performed in a round-robin manner. This method guarantees that leaves that contain objects close in the address space will be assigned to different sites (processors), thus increasing the parallelism during range query processing. In Figure 9.4 we present a way to decluster an R-tree in four processors, one primary and three secondary. For simplicity it is assumed that each processor controls only one disk.

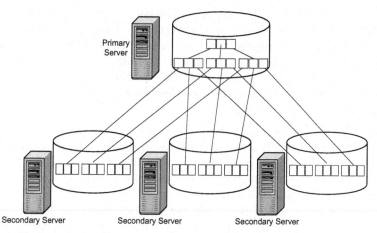

Fig. 9.4. Declustering an R-tree over three sites.

The parallel version of this R-tree can be implemented easily in a multicomputer system (e.g., network of workstations). The main drawback of this approach is that the processor, which contains the upper levels of the R-tree, may become a bottleneck during intensive demands.

GPR-tree. The GPR-tree proposed in [68] utilizes a global index structure shared by a number of processors in a multicomputer system. Each processor maintains in memory a fraction of the GPR-tree, having its nodes partitioned into two groups:

– local, when the corresponding page resides in the local disk, and
– remote, when the corresponding page is managed by another processor.

Master-Client R-trees. This technique was proposed in [207], and as in the leaf-based declustering approach it uses a master-slave architecture. The master holds the upper levels of the R-tree. Unlike the previous approach, the leaf level of the master contains entries of the form (MBR, serverID). Each client maintains its own local R-tree that is used to index the portion of the data that has been assigned to it. A potential problem with this method is that the master may become a hot spot.

Upgraded Parallel R-trees. In [128] an upgraded parallel R-tree structure has been proposed. A partition function is used to partition the area into several subareas. The partition function is determined according to the distribution of the underlying data. Each subarea is indexed by an R-tree structure. The whole structure is composed of:

- a number of subtrees,
- data partitioning functions,
- a primary mapping category, and
- a secondary mapping category.

Each item in the primary mapping category is of the form (processorID, number of objects). Each item in the secondary mapping category is of the form (subtree pointer, number of objects). In order to reduce communication costs, each processor hosts the complete structure, although only a fraction of the database is stored locally. In [128] experimental results are offered to demonstrate the performance of the method. However, a comparison with previous approaches is not provided.

Parallel Query Processing. Several methods have been proposed for parallel query processing using R-trees. In [89] a performance evaluation has been performed by comparing the parallel equivalents of R-trees and PMR Quadtrees in a shared memory architecture. Experimental results have been reported for range queries and spatial join queries.

Brinkhoff et al. in [36] study efficient parallel algorithms for parallel spatial join processing using R-trees. In their work the *shared virtual memory* architecture has been used (a special implementation of shared-nothing with a global address space, [215]) to implement the access methods and the proposed algorithms.

Parallel range query processing using R-trees with leaf-based declustering has been studied in [123]. The authors also provide cost estimates, taking into consideration the communication costs incurred due to message passing among processors.

Parallel NN query processing techniques are provided in [176, 178], which are based on the multicomputer architecture of [123] described previously. The main motivation is that although the branch-and-bound NN algorithm proposed in [197] can be directly applied in a parallel R-trees structure, intraquery parallelism is not being exploited due to the serial nature of the algorithm. Several parallel algorithms have been proposed, implemented, and evaluated using synthetic and real-life spatial datasets.

In [9] the authors discuss R-tree implementation issues in a multicomputer architecture. The performance of parallel R-trees has been evaluated using insertions, range queries with large query windows, and range queries with small query windows. Uniform and non-uniform datasets have been used for the performance evaluation. Two metrics have been used: query response time and system throughput when multiple queries are executed concurrently. It has been shown that parallel implementation of R-trees on a cluster of workstations comprising eight Sun Ultra-Sparc processors give significant improvement in response time and throughput.

Parallel range query processing in distributed shared virtual memory architecture has been reported in [242]. A range query is decomposed to a number of subqueries, and each subquery is assigned to a processor. Two phases are identified:

- in the *workload phase*, a number of internal tree nodes are determined, and
- in the *search phase* the corresponding subqueries are executed in parallel.

Performance results based on query response time and speed-up are provided in [242].

A very important issue in parallel and distributed query processing is the migration of data from one disk to another or from one server to another, according to the access patterns used to access the data. In [137] the authors study migration issues for R-trees. Finally, in [180] the authors study the problem of parallel bulk loading an R-tree in a multicomputer architecture by performing redistribution of the objects' MBRs.

9.2 Concurrency Control

The management of concurrent operations in access methods is considered very important because it is strongly related to system performance, data consistency, and data integrity. When index updates interfere with access operations, a synchronization mechanism must exist to guarantee that the result of each operation is correct. Moreover, this synchronization must be efficient, preventing exclusive index locking for long time periods. In [200] two main categories for scheduling operations have been identified:

top-down approaches, where an update operation locks its scope to prevent other updates. Read operations might not be allowed in the scope of an update operation until the latter commits, or they may be allowed during the search phase or the restructuring phase of the update.

bottom-up approaches, where an update operation behaves like a read operation on the way to the leaf level of the index and then moves up the tree, locking only a few nodes simultaneously and making the necessary changes.

Since the B-tree is implemented in many commercial systems, concurrency control issues in B-trees have been extensively studied [101, 151, 200, 214]. As concurrent operations can improve the efficiency of B-trees, they can also improve R-tree efficiency. However, due to the different nature of the tree structure, the B-tree cannot be applied directly. Moreover, although some straightforward modifications could be applied, the results are not efficient enough.

9.2.1 R-link Method

Ng and Kameda in [160] discuss methods for concurrency control in spatial access methods, particularly in R-trees. The first method that we discuss is similar to the B-link method for the case of B-trees. The R-link method has been proposed by Ng and Kameda in [161] and almost simultaneously by Kornacker and Banks in [119] as a solution for the concurrency control problem in R-tree-based access methods. The R-link is an R-tree variant, where each tree node contains a number of pointers, one for each child node, and an additional link pointer used for concurrency control. All nodes that reside at a specific level of the tree are linked together. The main purpose of the link pointers is to be able to decompose operations into smaller atomic actions.

Two types of locks are used. An R-lock is used for shared reading, and an X-lock is used as an exclusive lock. As in the case of a B-link, when a search takes place, a concurrent insertion or deletions might split or merge a node, respectively. As a result, link pointers should be followed to check for cases where the split has not yet been propagated to the parent node.

Search operations start at the root and descend the tree using R-locks. Upon visiting a tree node an R-lock is applied to the node. The R-lock is released when the child nodes that must be visited have been determined. The problem is that some insertions may not have been committed, which means that some split nodes may not have been recorded in their parent nodes but have only been recorded as link pointers to their siblings. Therefore, we have to examine all nodes emanating from horizontal pointers. If the MBRs of these nodes overlap with the query region, we check if their parent node is valid. If it is valid, the corresponding search path would be examined from the parent node according to the R-tree search algorithm. Otherwise, we include in the search path the subtree emanating from the corresponding split node, because it contains relevant data that their existence has not yet been recorded in the parent node.

Insertion operations start at the root and descend the tree until the appropriate leaf node is detected. If the leaf cannot hold more entries, a split operation is performed. Changes must be propagated upward. Only MBRs that need enlargement are going to change. In order to avoid conflicts with other operations, the MBR enlargement is deferred. During tree descent the expanded MBR is stored in a list of pending updates. This list is used in the second phase, where MBR enlargement takes place. Subsequent operations must examine this list. During the first phase of descending the tree, the corresponding MBRs are enlarged and parent nodes are updated with the new split nodes that only existed as linked nodes until now.

In the case of deletions, multiple paths are examined during tree descend, and in every node we execute the pending updates that have been registered by previously executed insertions, deletions, or splits. If a node becomes empty, it is marked as *deleted* and it is not yet removed because other operations may be using it. A garbage collection algorithm is executed periodically to delete all marked nodes. If a node underflows, it is appended to a list, and when the size of the list reaches a threshold a condense algorithm is executed.

A slightly different approach has been followed in [119], where a more sophisticated technique is used to provide ordering of sibling nodes. Logical sequence numbers (LSN) are assigned to the nodes. These numbers are similar to timestamps because they monotonically increase over time. The LSN numbers are used during search and insert operations to make correct decisions about tree traversal. During tree descent no lock-coupling is needed, and therefore only one node is locked at any given time. The comparison of the method with lock-coupling concurrency control mechanisms in R-trees has shown that R-link trees maintain high throughput and low response times as the load increases.

9.2.2 Top-down Approaches

Although the B-link is widely recognized as a structure of theoretical and practical importance, this is not the case for the R-link. Commercial systems are using the classical R-tree structure or the R*-tree. In [41] concurrency control techniques have been proposed, using different methods from the R-link structure. Three types of locks are used: R-locks, W-locks and X-locks. Lock-coupling and breadth-first search are used to locate the set of objects that satisfy the query. A node that is examined remains locked until the search operation commits.

A search operation starts at the root and descends the tree by inserting each visited node into a queue. An element of the queue is extracted and examined to determine which of its children's MBR overlap with the query region. If the examined node is not a leaf, the children that are relevant to the query region are R-locked and inserted into the queue from left to right. On the other hand, if the examined node is a leaf, the corresponding children are data objects and must be examined further (refinement step) to check if they satisfy the query. The search operation terminates when the queue is empty. Since all nodes in the queue are R-locked, update operations cannot be applied to these nodes.

Insertions are performed in two phases. During the first phase, lock coupling is used to the path from the root to the corresponding leaf node that will host the new object. At each node the appropriate path is selected and followed. The MBRs of the nodes are adjusted properly. In the second phase the new object is placed into the corresponding leaf node. If the leaf node is full, a split operation must be applied. To avoid interference of other update operations, the leaf and its parent are W-locked before the execution of the split. The same is applied to other ascendants if they are full. Therefore, all full nodes from the leaf to the root are W-locked. The set of these nodes is the scope of the current operation. During reconstruction of the tree the W-lock of a node must be converted to an X-lock before modification. After the split operations, the MBRs of the parent nodes are adjusted accordingly to cover the MBRs of their children.

Deletions are applied in a similar manner and are also characterized by two phases. During the first phase an appropriate leaf is found and the corresponding path from the root to the leaf is W-locked. We note that several paths may qualify, because many MBRs may totally cover the deleted object. In order to guarantee that the deleted object will not be missed, all paths must be examined in a breadth-first search manner. In the second phase the corresponding object is deleted. Appropriate actions must take place to deal with node underutilization. Changes are propagated upwards and the appropriate MBRs are adjusted accordingly. In general, there are three techniques that can be used in underutilized nodes:

- *reinsertion*, where objects in the underutilized node are reinserted in the tree,
- *merge-at-half*, where the node is merged, and
- *free-at-empty*, where the node is deleted when it is completely empty.

The proposed algorithm used the last technique because it is the most efficient according to [101]. A study of granular locking in R-trees can be found in [39].

9.3 Issues in Relational Implementations

The R-tree structure has been implemented in many commercial RDBMSs, like Oracle and Informix [94, 120, 196]. In these implementations, the R-tree is built on top of relational tables. The spatial column of these tables contains the spatial attributes, from which MBRs are extracted and stored in the R-tree. The nodes of the R-tree correspond to tuples of an *index table*, and their entries are organized within these tuples. In addition, metadata for the R-tree (e.g., root address, number of nodes, etc.) are stored as a row in a separate *metadata table*. Therefore, R-trees in relational implementations operate on the storage space that is allocated for relations, using the block-oriented management provided by the RDMBS for these relations, not on dedicated disk blocks. The advantage of this approach is that it allows for concurrency control and recovery mechanisms, which are offered by the kernel of the RDBMS. In the remainder of this section, we describe two issues that can be considered in relational R-tree implementations.

9.3.1 Stochastic Driven Relational R-trees

The use of relations to store the R-trees allows for new possibilities, because we do not have to pay attention to the physical level and to the physical blocks that will actually accommodate the tree's nodes. Kriegel et al. [124] are motivated by this fact and observe that it is not necessary to restrain the structure of the R-tree by factors like the minimum and maximum allowed number of entries within a node, because these factors are influenced only by the consideration of the physical disk blocks. In contrast, by allowing variable fanouts in each node, better decisions can be made about when to split a node or where to insert a new entry.

The aforementioned decisions can be guided by measuring the quality of the nodes and not by factors like the maximum/minimum fanouts. The advantage in the case that quality is considered can be exemplified as follows. Assume a node, which when considering only the maximum fanout criterion (i.e., the case of normal R-tree), will have to be split. If this node contains MBRs that have a high degree of overlap, then by splitting the node, we will have as a result two highly overlapping nodes. These nodes will be probably invoked together during query processing, a fact that increases query execution time. However, if we detect, through a quality measure, that splitting will not yield to improvement, we can avoid it (the node will be overflowed in terms of the maximum-fanout criterion, but we do not consider it any more, so this node is legitimate).

The basic quality measures that are considered in [124] are all based on calculating the joint probability of two (or more) rectangles R and S to be invoked by the same query, which is denoted $P(R, S)$. By starting from the Insertion algorithm of the R*-tree, Kriegel et al. [124] propose modifications based on the consideration of quality measures, which lead to the definition of the RR-tree (Relational R-tree). The modifications are for the following parts of insertion:

- **ChooseLeaf**: while inserting a new rectangle R, if we have currently visited node RN, we select the entry E of RN, which maximizes the probability $P(R, E)$. The intuition behind this is that the subtree rooted at E is suitable to store R, because they will tend to be invoked together during query processing. This way, the RR-tree tries to minimize overlapping.
- **Splitting**: during an insertion, a split occurs only when its entries are relatively dissimilar. In particular, if $E.mbr$ is the MBR of the node and $E_i.mbr$, $1 \leq i \leq f_E$ are the MBRs of its children, then a split is performed when $P(E_1.mbr, \ldots, E_{f_E}.mbr | E.mbr)$ is below a certain threshold. That is, when the children's MBRs will tend not to be invoked during a query that invoked $E.mbr$ (note that it is a conditional probability). Nevertheless, to prevent having a high number of nodes with very few entries, the RR-tree examines the aforementioned splitting criterion only for nodes whose number of entries exceeds a prespecified threshold.
- **Assignment of entries during splitting**: when a split occurs, the R*-tree first chooses the split axis. Each dimension is examined separately, and the intervals I_i and I_j (projections of MBRs on a dimension) that have the maximum distance in this dimension, are found. I_i and I_j are assigned as the first entries of the newly created nodes RN_1 and RN_2, respectively. Next, the R*-tree proceeds by assigning to RN_1 and RN_2 all the remaining entries, according to their distance. The RR-tree follows a different approach. For each of the remaining entries, it finds the interval I that corresponds to its projection on the dimension of the split axis. Then it calculates two

probabilities: $x_1 = P(I|I_i)$ and $x_2 = P(I|I_j)$. If $x_1 - x_2 > \tau$, where τ is a threshold, then the entry is assigned to RN_1, otherwise to RN_2. This procedure is repeated for a predetermined number of iterations, and finally the partitioning that minimizes the overlap is selected. Evidently, the approach of the RR-tree may not result in nodes that have a number of entries larger than a minimum allowed value. As in previous cases, this is not a problem, because this issue is not considered in the RR-tree.

Experimental results in [124], mainly for two-dimensional data, show an improvement of RR-trees against R*-trees for queries with high selectivity. Also, the RR-tree is faster during the insertion of new entries.

9.3.2 Lazy Deletion Methods

With the original R-tree, the underflow of a node that results during a deletion operation is handled at the moment it occurs, and it is treated dynamically by deleting the node and reinserting its remaining entries. This guarantees the minimum utilization in each node, but it may lead to significant overhead due to the high cost of reinsertions.

Moreover, due to the high cost of the reinsertion operation, in some of the current relational implementations of the R-tree [196], this operation is avoided. Although reinsertion is optional for insertion (in the case of the R*-tree), the same does not apply for the original deletion algorithm because the underflow is handled only with reinsertion. Also, avoiding reinsertions can significantly simplify the procedure of recovery. For instance, in the Informix database, the R-tree secondary access method creates its own logical records (logging) so as to recover from deletion operations from the leaf nodes [94] (for deletions from internal nodes an extensible log manager is used). Evidently, the design of a roll-back operation is much more complex when taking into account the reinsertion of entries for almost every deletion, because this can yield to roll-backs from numerous insertions. Analogous reasoning can be followed for the simplification of concurrency control, when reinsertion is avoided.

From the aforementioned issues, it follows that there is a need for alternative deletion algorithms, which will not use reinsertion and will advocate the implementations of R-trees in relational systems in the case where reinsertion is avoided. A simple approach to handle deletions is to allow tree nodes to be deleted only during a reorganize operation [196]. Following such a policy, when a node underflows, it continues to remain underflowing. Periodically, a criterion is tested, and if it is fulfilled, a global reorganization is applied that eliminates all underflowing nodes and reinserts all the orphan entries. Therefore, this approach treats deletions in a lazy way.

Nanopoulos et al. [156] describe two general categories that can be considered for lazy deletion methods in R-trees:

- **Local.** The methods in this category are restricted in each single node, trying to postpone the reinsertion of its contents, when it underflows.

– **Global.** The methods in this category have a global perspective, maintaining statistics for the tree nodes, on which they postpone the reinsertion of the contents of all underflowing nodes.

Regarding local methods, the most direct way of avoiding reinsertion is to allow nodes to become entirely empty (without any nodes), and then be removed by deleting the respective entries from the parent nodes. It has to be noted that the latter procedure may need to be applied recursively, up to the root. This scheme has been also applied to other structures, like the B-tree, and is called the free-at-empty (FE) technique. With FE, the average node utilization is expected to decrease, and both the space cost and query performance may be impacted. However, FE opts to a small degradation of query performance and a significant improvement of the deletion cost.

With global lazy deletion methods, underflowing nodes remain intact in the tree. The contents of these nodes are collected and reinserted all together, during a global reorganization operation (the empty nodes are simply removed from the tree). The reorganization procedure is required to maintain the quality of the tree, because the existence of underflowing nodes affects space overhead and query performance. There is a tradeoff between the frequency with which the reorganization procedure is invoked (due to its cost) and the tree quality, which may decrease substantially if reorganization is not performed. What is required are criteria to determine if (and when) reorganization should be applied. In [156] reorganization is applied when a substantial fraction of the tree nodes are underflowing. The resulting deletion method is called Global-reorganization (GL). GL maintains a counter of the underflowing nodes, which is updated during the deletion and insertion operations.

The experimental comparison in [156] compares the original deletion algorithm (which uses reinsertions), FE, and GL. The results indicate that FE represents the one extreme point that reduces the cost of deletions but leads to the worst query performance. The original deletion algorithm represents the other extreme point that achieves the best query performance, but it requires the largest cost for deletions due to the large number of reinsertions. GL represents a medium ground between these two points, trying to reduce the cost of deletions without severely impacting query performance.

9.3.3 R-trees in Research Prototypes

By studying the literature on SAMs it is evident that the R-tree structure and its variants attracted a lot of attention. The simplicity of the structure and its ability to handle spatial objects efficiently are two very tempting reasons to incorporate the structure in research prototypes and commercial database systems. It is well known that it is not sufficient to support spatial objects in a database system. Efficient methods to access these data are of great importance taking into consideration the requirements of modern demanding applications [213].

There are several implementations of the R-tree access method and its variants that are offered by researchers all over the world.[1] Most of these implementations have been performed to conduct experiments and performance comparisons with other structures, to investigate the performance of a proposed algorithm, or to provide modifications and enhancements to the structure to improve its efficiency. However, these implementations have been performed for research purposes and, therefore issues like concurrency control, recovery, buffering issues, and other implementation details have generally been neglected. Moreover, the majority of these implementations are stand-alone, meaning that they only serve the needs of the experimental evaluation rather than being an integral part of a platform. In the sequel we briefly describe efforts for R-tree implementations in research prototypes and commercial database systems.

BASIS. The BASIS prototype system (Benchmarking Approach for Spatial Index Structures) has been proposed in [80] to provide a platform for experimental evaluation of access methods and query processing algorithms. An outline of the architecture is depicted in Fig.9.5. The platform has been implemented in C++ and runs on top of UNIX or Windows. The platform is organized in three modules:

- the *storage manager:* provides I/O and caching services,
- the *SAM toolkit:* a set of commonly used SAMs that defines some design patterns, which support an easy development of new structures, and
- the *query processor:* a library of algorithms whose design follows the general framework of the iterator model [75].

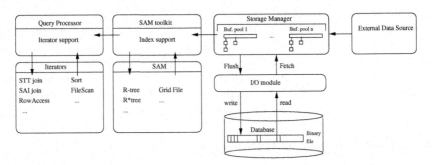

Fig. 9.5. The BASIS architecture.

The storage manager is essentially in charge of managing a database. A database is a set of binary files that store either datasets (i.e., sequential collection of records) or SAMs. A SAM or index refers to records in an indexed data file through record identifiers.

---

[1] A collection of several implementations can be found at the R-tree portal, http://www.rtreeportal.org

The buffer manager handles one or several buffer pools. A data file or index (SAM) is assigned to one buffer pool, but a buffer pool can handle several indices. This allows much flexibility, when assigning memory to the different parts of a query execution plan. The buffer pool is a constant-size cache with LRU or FIFO replacement policy (LRU by default). Pages can be pinned in memory. A pinned page is never flushed until it is unpinned.

There are two main types of files that are handled by the storage manager:

1. *data files* are sequential collections of formatted pages storing *records* of the same type. Records in a data file can either be accessed sequentially or by their address.
2. *SAMs* are structured collections of index entries. An index entry is a built-in record type with two attributes: the key and a record address. The key is the geometric key, usually the MBR. The currently implemented SAMs are a grid file, an R-tree, an R*-tree, and several R-tree variants based on bulk-loading techniques.

The BASIS architecture allows easy customization and extension. Depending on the query processing experiment, each level is easily extendable: the designer may add a new SAM, add a new spatial operator or algorithm at the query processor level, or decide to implement his/her own query processing module on top of the buffer management (I/O) module, which implements adequate functionality. As an example, a performance evaluation of spatial join processing algorithms implemented in BASIS has been reported in [181]. Generally, the BASIS prototype system can be used for experimental evaluation of SAMs and spatial query processing algorithms, by allowing the designer to create various query execution plans according to the needs of the experimentation. Moreover, the platform offers a fair comparison among the competing methods because the same storage and buffer management policies are used. Some issues, however, have not been taken into consideration, like concurrency control and recovery.

Generalized Search Trees (GiST). Extensibility of data types and queries is very important to allow database systems to support new non-traditional applications. GiST (Generalized Search Trees) is an index structure that supports an extensible set of data types and queries. GiST is a balanced tree (all leaf nodes are at the same tree level) that provides template algorithms for searching and modifying the tree structure [84, 118]. In leaf node pairs of $(key, recordID)$ are stored, whereas in internal nodes the GiST stores $(predicate, treePTR)$ pairs. GiST supports the standard search, insert and delete operations. However, in order for these operations to work properly, external functions must be provided. Therefore, the combination of the generic functionality of GiST and the functionality provided by the designer results in a fully functional access method.

An overview of the GiST architecture is presented in Figure 9.6. External functions are called by the GiST core in order to provide the required functionality. These external functions, which comprise the GiST interface, are briefly described below [84]:

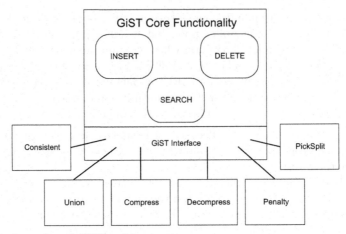

Fig. 9.6. Overview of GiST architecture.

- *Consistent*(E, q): given an entry $E = (p, ptr)$ and a query predicate q, the function returns true if and only if the p matches q.
- *Union*$(\mathcal{P})$: given a set $\mathcal{P}$ of entries $(p_1, ptr_1), \ldots, (p_n, ptr_n)$ the function returns the union of $p_1, \ldots, p_n$.
- *Compress*(E): given an entry $E = (p, ptr)$, the function returns the entry $E' = (p', ptr)$, where p' is a compressed representation of p.
- *Decompress*(E): Returns a decompressed representation of E.
- *Penalty*(E_1, E_2): given two entries $E_1 = (p_1, ptr_1)$ and $E_2 = (p_2, ptr_2)$ returns a domain-specific penalty for inserting E_2 in the subtree rooted at E_1. This function is used for insertion and splitting purposes, where criteria for selecting a subtree and splitting a node must be specified.
- *PickSplit*$(\mathcal{P})$: given a set $\mathcal{P}$ of $RN+1$ entries, the function divides $\mathcal{P}$ into two subsets $\mathcal{P}_1$ and $\mathcal{P}_2$. The function is used for splitting purposes, where criteria for node splitting must be defined.

By providing implementations for these functions, all R-tree variants, except the R$^+$-tree, can be supported by GiST. This is due to the fact that the R$^+$-tree performs object splitting allowing pieces of an object to be stored in several leaf nodes. This functionality is not supported by GiST, which assumes that the tree is a hierarchical partitioning of data. In [84] support for B$^+$-trees, R-trees, and RD-trees [85] is provided, and several performance and implementation issues are discussed.

The SHORE Project. SHORE integrates concepts and services from file systems and object-oriented databases. The main objective of the SHORE project [37] is to provide a persistent object system to serve the needs of modern demanding applications such as CAD systems, persistent programming languages, geographic information systems (GIS), satellite data repositories, and multimedia applications. SHORE extends the EXODUS storage manager, providing more features and support for typed objects and multiple programming languages. The SHORE architecture is based on the following layers:

- *SHORE Storage Manager (SSM)*: a persistent object storage engine that supports creation of persistent files of records. The storage manager offers concurrency control and recovery, supporting two-phase locking and write-ahead logging.
- *SHORE Value-Added Server (SVAS)*: based on the functionality of SSM to provide support for types objects, UNIX-like naming, access control mechanisms and client-server capabilities.
- *SHORE Data Language (SDL)*: based on ODMG ODL, supports object-oriented data types independently of the programming language used.

Paradise [58] is a parallel geographic information system, based on SHORE, with many capabilities in handling large geographic datasets. Paradise applies object-oriented and parallel database features to provide efficiency in storing and querying large amounts of spatial data. The Paradise server is implemented as a SHORE value-added server on top of the SHORE storage manager. Paradise adds extra functionality to the basic SHORE server: catalog manager, extend manager, tuple manager, query optimizer, query execution engine, and support for spatial abstract data types (points, polylines, polygons and raster). Efficient access of the stored spatial objects is enhanced by the use of R*-trees. The R*-tree has been implemented in the SHORE storage manager relatively easily, because a lot of B^+-tree code (already supported by SHORE) was reused. In addition, Paradise supports bulk-loaded R-trees. The packing algorithm used in Paradise is similar to the packing algorithm used in [104], which is based on the Hilbert curve.

9.3.4 R-trees in Commercial Database Systems

The support of complex data types (non-alphanumeric) and access methods is a key issue in the modern database industry, because it allows the DBMS to extend its functionality beyond pure relational data handling. A simple approach for complex data handling is to use BLOBs (binary large objects) to store the complex data. The limitation of this approach is that the DBMS is not aware of what is stored in the BLOB, and therefore the management of the BLOB contents must be performed by the user application. The operations and algorithms to manipulate the contents of the BLOB are not available to the query processor. Another approach is to allow the DBMS to provide the needed functionality for complex data types (e.g., polygons, line segments) and access methods. These data types are supported by the DBMS just like the ordinary alphanumeric data types. The problem is that it is not possible for each DBMS vendor to implement all the data types and access methods that any application demands (or will require in the future). A more revolutionary approach is to allow the user to define additional data types and access methods for data handling according to application needs (extendible DBMS). In the sequel we briefly describe efforts from database vendors for spatial query processing using R-trees:

PostgreSQL: PostgreSQL provides support for B-trees, R-trees, GiST, and Hashing. Therefore, a user can rely on the provided R-tree implementation or can implement other R-tree variants using the GiST approach. The R-tree supported is based on the original proposal by Guttman and based on the quadratic split policy. To create an R-tree index using SQL, one should issue the command:

CREATE INDEX *myindex* ON *mytable* USING RTREE (*mycolumn*)

Details regarding PostgreSQL features can be found in [190].

Mapinfo SpatialWare: SpatialWare extends an Informix, Microsoft SQL Server, IBM DB2, or Oracle database to handle spatial data such as points, lines, and polygons. It extends database capabilities avoiding a middleware architecture. All functionality is contained directly in the DBMS environment. SpatialWare is implemented in the following ways:
 − in Informix as a datablade,
 − in SQL Server using the Extended Stored Procedure mechanism,
 − in IBM DB2 as an extender, and
 − in Oracle as a Spatial Server.
SpatialWare provides R-tree support for spatial data indexing purposes [148, 150].

Oracle Locator and Oracle Spatial: Oracle Locator, which is a feature of Oracle Intermedia, provides support for location-based queries in Oracle 9i DBMS. Geographic and location data are integrated in the Oracle 9i server, just like ordinary data types like CHAR and INTEGER. Oracle Spatial provides location-based facilities allowing the extension of Oracle-based applications. It provides data manipulation tools for accessing location information such as road networks, wireless service boundaries, and geocoded customer addresses. Both Oracle Locator and Oracle Spatial provide support for linear Quadtrees and R-trees for spatial data indexing purposes [120, 165].

IBM Informix and DB2: In Informix, the R-tree is built-in to the database kernel and works directly with the extended spatial data types. The Informix R-tree implementation supports full transaction management, concurrency control, recovery, and parallelism. A detailed description of the Informix R-tree implementation can be found in [94]. A description of spatial data handling in a DB2 database can be found in [3].

Other Vendors: Apart from large database vendors, the R-tree has been adopted by other application vendors. Examples include the EzGIS and EzCAD applications that exploit the R-tree to index spatial objects [59].

9.4 Summary

Taking into consideration that R-trees were proposed in 1984 and the fact that only recently have they been incorporated in commercial systems, we understand that there are serious implementation issues that must be solved before a new access method can be adopted by the industry. An access method is useless unless it can be efficiently implemented in real-life data-intensive applications. Making the access method part of a larger (usually multiuser) system is not an easy task.

Some of these implementation issues were touched on in this chapter. More specifically, we discussed parallelism and concurrency control, and we examined the use of the structure in research prototypes and commercial systems. The methods used resemble the ones used for the B-tree access method (adapted accordingly), which is a strong argument for the incorporation of R-trees in modern database systems. In the future, we anticipate that the R-tree will play a very important role in several application domains, that require the representation and processing of non-traditional data types.

Epilogue

Although "trees have grown everywhere" [212] because of their simplicity and their satisfactory average performance, up until now only a small subset of them have been successfully used by researchers and developers in prototype and commercial database systems. The R-tree is the most influential SAM and has been adopted as the index of choice in many research works regarding spatial and multidimensional query processing. Taking into consideration the work performed so far, we can state that the R-tree is for the spatial databases what the B-tree is for alphanumeric data types. In fact, a serious reason for its acceptance is exactly the resemblance to the B-tree.

Considering the rich work performed on R-trees we realize that it contains almost all aspects concerning a database system: query processing, query optimization, cost models, parallelism, concurrency control, and recovery. This is the main reason why gradually database vendors adopted the R-tree and implemented it in their products for spatial data management purposes.

In this book we have presented research performed during the last 20 years, after the introduction of the R-tree access method by Guttman 1984 [81]. We have described several modifications to the original structure that improve its query processing performance during searches, inserts, deletes, and updates. These modifications range from structural modifications to algorithmic enhancements in a number of settings, such as for static or dynamic environments, for point or non-point data, and for static or moving objects. Also, query processing algorithms have been described in detail, which enable the structure to answer range searches, nearest-neighbor finding, spatial joins, closest-pair finding and other more complex query types. Several cost models estimating the output size and the number of node accesses have been presented, according to the query type used. These cost estimates, along with sampling and histogram-based techniques, are invaluable for query optimizers. Finally, implementation issues were covered, regarding concurrency control, recovery, and parallel processing, along with a presentation of R-tree implementations by several database vendors.

Conclusively, over the last two decades we have witnessed that the R-tree family is of great theoretical interest from several points of view as explained herein. However, it has to be emphasized that R-trees are not only of theoretical importance. On the contrary, in view of the advent of the new emerging technologies and the new "killer" applications, the R-tree is a sine-qua-non structure. For example, consider flash memory storage systems that are an alternative media for hard disks in many applications. Flash memories cannot be updated (overwritten) unless they are first erased. Therefore, their operation in a dynamic environment with inserts, deletes, and updates has to be more close studied. On the other hand, geographical applications often run over hand-held devices that rely on flash memory storage. In this respect, the adaptation of all the well-known R-tree operations need to be studied afresh [247].

It is also worth noting that new textbooks and monographs that have appeared recently are focusing on this perspective. For instance, the book by Schiller and Voisard [205] covers the area of Location Based Services (LBS), a challenging new concept integrating the geographic location of a user with the general notion of services, such as finding the closest gasoline station or using a car navigation system. Applications integrating spatial data management and mobile communications are representatives of a new era in our "brave new world".

Finally, the recent book by Kothuri, Godfrind and Beinat entitled "Pro Oracle Spatial: an Essential Guide to Developing Spatially-Enabled Business Applications" [121], verifies the industrial interest in the general area of spatial databases, and in particular in our object of study: the ubiquitous R-tree.

Taking into consideration the significant research performed on R-trees during the last 20 years, one could think that there is no more room for improvements or variations. However, current research in the area proves exactly the opposite. There are new and exciting application domains that require efficient representation and processing of objects that can be handled by R-tree-based access methods. Modern areas of increasing importance, such as P2P systems, data streams, and bioinformatics, are making use of R-trees as a powerful data management mechanism. Thus, it is sound to anticipate that in the future, R-trees will be granted an exalted position in modern systems and future applications.

References

1. A. Abulnaga and J.F. Naughton: "Accurate Estimation of the Cost of Spatial Selections", *Proceedings 16th IEEE International Conference on Data Engineering (ICDE'00)*, pp.123-134, San Diego, CA, 2000.
2. S. Acharya, V. Poosala and S. Ramaswamy: "Selectivity Estimation in Spatial Databases", *Proceedings ACM SIGMOD Conference on Management of Data*, pp.13-24, Philadelphia, PA, 1999.
3. D.W. Adler: "IBM DB2 Spatial Extender - Spatial Data within the DBMS", *Proceedings 27th International Conference on Very Large Data Bases (VLDB'01)*, pp.687-690, Rome, Italy, 2001.
4. P.K. Agarwal, M. deBerg, J. Gudmundsson, M. Hammar and H.J. Haverkort: "Box-trees and R-trees with Near Optimal Query Time", *Proceedings Symposium on Computational Geometry*, pp.124-133, Medford, MA, 2001.
5. C. Aggarwal, J. Wolf, P. Wu and M. Epelman: "The S-tree - an Efficient Index for Multidimensional Objects", *Proceedings 5th International Symposium on Spatial Databases (SSD'97)*, pp.350-373, Berlin, Germany, 1997.
6. R. Agrawal, C. Faloutsos and A. Swami. "Efficient Similarity Search in Sequence Databases", *Proceedings 4th International Conference of Foundations of Data Organization and Algorithms (FODO'93)*, pp.69-84, Chicago, IL, 1993.
7. V.T. Almeida and R.H. Guting: "Indexing the Trajectories of Moving Objects in Networks", *Proceedings 16th International Conference on Scientific and Statistical Database Management (SSDBM'04)*, pp.115-118, Santorini Island, Greece, 2004.
8. N. An, J. Jin and A. Sivasubramaniam: "Toward an Accurate Analysis of Range Queries on Spatial Data", *IEEE Transactions on Knowledge and Data Engineering*, Vol.15, No.2, pp,305-323, 2003.
9. N. An, L. Qian, A. Sivasubramaniam and T. Keefe: "Evaluating Parallel R-tree Implementations on a Network of Workstations", *Proceedings 6th ACM International Symposium on Advances in Geographic Information Systems (GIS'98)*, pp.159-160, Washington, DC, 1998.
10. N. An, Z.-Y. Yang and A. Sivasubramanian: "Selectivity Estimation for Spatial Joins", *Proceedings 17th IEEE International Conference on Data Engineering (ICDE'01)*, pp.368-375, Heidelberg, Germany, 2001.
11. C.H. Ang and T.C. Tan: "New Linear Node Splitting Algorithm for R-trees", *Proceedings 5th International Symposium on Spatial Databases (SSD'97)*, pp.339-349, Berlin, Germany, 1997.
12. C.H. Ang and T.C. Tan: "Bitmap R-trees", *Informatica*, Vol.24, No.2, 2000.
13. W.G. Aref and H. Samet: "A Cost Model for Query Optimization Using R-trees", *Proceedings 2nd ACM International Symposium on Advances in Geographic Information Systems (GIS'94)*, Gaithersburg, MD, 1994.
14. L. Arge: "The Buffer Tree: a New Technique for Optimal I/O Algorithms", *Proceedings 4th International Workshop on Algorithms and Data Structures (WADS'95)*, pp.334-345, Kingston, Canada, 1995.

15. L. Arge, M. deBerg, H.J. Haverkort and K. Yi: "The Priority R-Tree: a Practically Efficient and Worst-Case Optimal R-Tree", *Proceedings ACM SIGMOD Conference on Management of Data*, pp.347-358, Paris, France, 2004.

16. L. Arge, K. Hinrichs, J. Vahrenhold and J.S. Vitter: "Efficient Bulk Operations on Dynamic R-trees", *Algorithmica*, Vol.33, No.1, pp.104-128, 2002.

17. L. Arge, O. Procopiuc, S. Ramaswamy, T. Suel, J. Vahrenhold and J.S. Vitter: "A Unified Approach for Indexed and Non-Indexed Spatial Joins", *Proceedings 8th International Conference on Extending Database Technology (EDBT'00)*, pp.413-429, Konstanz, Germany, 2000.

18. B. Becker, S. Gschwind, T. Ohler, B. Seeger and P. Widmayer: "An Asymptotically Optimal Multi-Version B-tree", *The VLDB Journal*, Vol.5, No.4, pp.264-275, 1996.

19. N. Beckmann, H.P. Kriegel, R. Schneider and B. Seeger: "The R*-tree: an Efficient and Robust Method for Points and Rectangles", *Proceedings ACM SIGMOD Conference on Management of Data*, pp.322-331, Atlantic City, NJ, 1990.

20. A. Belussi and C. Faloutsos: "Estimating the Selectivity of Spatial Queries Using the 'Correlation' Fractal Dimension", *Proceedings 21st International Conference on Very Large Data Bases (VLDB'95)*, pp.299-310, Zurich, Switzerland, 1995.

21. A. Belussi and C. Faloutsos: "Self-Spatial Join Selectivity Estimation Using Fractal Concepts", *ACM Transactions on Information Systems*, Vol.16, No.2, pp.161-201, 1998.

22. S. Berchtold, C. Boehm, D.A. Keim and H.-P. Kriegel. "A Cost Model for Nearest Neighbor Search in High-Dimensional Data Space", *Proceedings 16th ACM Symposium on Principles of Database Systems (PODS'97)*, pp.78-86, Tucson, AZ, 1997.

23. S. Berchtold, C. Boehm, D.A. Keim, F. Krebs and H.P. Kriegel: "On Optimizing Nearest Neighbor Queries in High-Dimensional Data Spaces", *Proceedings 8th International Conference on Database Theory (ICDT'01)*, pp.435-449, London, UK, 2001.

24. S. Berchtold, D.A. Keim and H.P. Kriegel: "The X-tree - an Index Structure for High-Dimensional Data", *Proceedings 22nd International Conference on Very Large Data Bases (VLDB'96)*, pp.28-39, Bombay, India, 1996.

25. E. Bertino, B. Catania and L. Chiesa: "Definition and Analysis of Index Organizations for Object-oriented Database Systems", *Information Systems*, Vol.23, No.2, pp.65-108, 1998.

26. A.K. Bhide, A. Dan and D.M. Dias: "A Simple Analysis of the LRU Buffer Policy and its Relationship to Buffer Warm-up Transient", *Proceedings 9th IEEE International Conference on Data Engineering (ICDE'93)*, pp.125-133, Vienna, Austria, 1993.

27. R. Bliujute, C.S. Jensen, S. Saltenis and G. Slivinskas: "R-tree Based Indexing of Now-Relative Bitemporal Data", *Proceedings 24th International Conference on Very Large Data Bases (VLDB'98)*, pp.345-356, New York, NY, 1998.

28. R. Bliujute, C.S. Jensen, S. Saltenis and G. Slivinskas: "Light-Weight Indexing of Bitemporal Data", *Proceedings 12th International Conference on Scientific and Statistical Database Management (SSDBM'00)*, pp.125-138, Berlin, Germany, 2000.

29. C.A. Boehm: "A Cost Model for Query Processing in High-Dimensional Spaces", *ACM Transactions on Database Systems*, Vol.25, No.2, pp.129-178, 2000.

30. C. Bohm and H.P. Kriegel: "A Cost Model and Index Architecture for the Similarity Join", *Proceedings 17th IEEE International Conference on Data Engineering (ICDE'01)*, pp. 411-420. Heidelberg, Kriegel, 2001.

31. P. Bozanis, A. Nanopoulos and Y. Manolopoulos: "LR-tree - a Logarithmic Decomposable Spatial Index Method", *The Computer Journal*, Vol.46, No.3, pp.319-331, 2003.

32. S. Brakatsoulas, D. Pfoser and Y. Theodoridis: "Revisiting R-tree Construction Principles", *Proceedings 6th East European Conference on Advances in Databases and Information Systems (ADBIS'02)*, pp.149-162, Bratislava, Slovakia, 2002.

33. T. Brinkhoff, H. Horn, H.-P. Kriegel and R. Schneider. "A Storage and Access Architecture for Efficient Query Processing in Spatial Database Systems", *Proceedings 3rd International Symposium on Spatial Databases (SSD'93)*, pp.357-376, Singapore, 1993.

34. T. Brinkhoff, H.-P. Kriegel, R. Schneider and B. Seeger. "Multi-Step Processing of Spatial Joins", *Proceedings ACM SIGMOD Conference on Management of Data*, pp.197-208, Minneapolis, MN, 1994.

35. T. Brinkhoff, H.-P. Kriegel and B. Seeger: "Efficient Processing of Spatial Joins Using R-trees", *Proceedings ACM SIGMOD Conference on Management of Data*, pp.237-246, Washington, DC, 1993.

36. T. Brinkhoff, H.-P.Kriegel and B. Seeger: "Parallel Processing of Spatial Joins Using R-trees", *Proceedings 12th IEEE International Conference on Data Engineering (ICDE'96)*, pp.258-265, New Orleans, LA, 1996.

37. M.J. Carey, D.J. DeWitt, M.J. Franklin, N.E. Hall, M.L. McAuliffe, J.F. Naughton, D.T. Schuh, M.H. Solomon, C.K. Tan, O.G. Tsatalos, S.J. White and M.J. Zwilling: "Shoring Up Persistent Applications", *Proceedings ACM SIGMOD Conference on Management of Data*, pp.383-394, Minneapolis, MN, 1994.

38. V.P. Chakka, A. Everspaugh and J. Patel: "Indexing Large Trajectory Data Sets with SETI", *Proceedings 1st Biennial Conference on Innovative Data Systems Research (CIDR'03)*, Asilomar, CA, 2003.

39. K. Chakrabarti and S. Mehrotra: "Dynamic Granular Locking Approach to Phantom Protection in R-trees", *Proceedings 14th IEEE International Conference on Data Engineering (ICDE'98)*, pp.446-454, Orlando, FL, 1998.

40. E.P.F. Chan: "Buffer Queries", *IEEE Transactions on Knowledge and Data Engineering*, Vol.15, No.4, pp.895-910, 2003.

41. J.K. Chen, Y.F. Huang and Y.H. Chin: "A Study of Concurrent Operations on R-trees", *Information Sciences*, Vol.98, No.1-4, pp.263-300, 1997.

42. L. Chen, R. Choubey and E.A. Rundensteiner: "Bulk-Insertions into R-trees Using the Small-Tree-Large-Tree Approach", *Proceedings 6th ACM International Symposium on Advances in Geographic Information Systems (GIS'98)*, pp.161-162, Washington, DC, 1998.

43. P.M. Chen, E.K. Lee, G.A. Gibson, R.H. Katz and D.A. Patterson: "RAID, High-Performance, Reliable Secondary Storage", *ACM Computing Surveys*, Vol.26, No.2, pp.145-185, 1994.

44. S. Chen and D. Towsley: "A Performance Evaluation of RAID Architectures", *IEEE Transactions on Computers*, Vol.45, No.10, pp.1116-1130, 1996.

45. K.L. Cheung and A. Fu: "Enhanced Nearest Neighbor Search on the R-tree", *ACM SIGMOD Record*, Vol.27, No.3, pp.16-21, 1998.

46. Y. Choi, and C. Chung: "Selectivity Estimation for Spatio-Temporal Queries to Moving Objects", *Proceedings ACM SIGMOD Conference on Management of Data*, pp.440-451, Madison, WI, 2002.

47. R. Choubey, L. Chen and E. Rundensteiner: "GBI - a Generalized R-tree Bulk-Insertion Strategy", *Proceedings 6th International Symposium on Spatial Databases (SSD'99)*, pp.91-108, Hong-Kong, China, 1999.

48. J. Clifford, C.E. Dyresom, T. Isakowitz, C.S. Jensen and R.T. Snodgrass: "On the Semantics of 'now'", *ACM Transactions on Database Systems*, Vol.22, No.2, pp.171-214, 1997.

49. D. Comer: "The Ubiquitous B-tree", *ACM Computing Surveys*, Vol.11, No.2, pp.121-137, 1979.

50. A. Corral, Y. Manolopoulos, Y. Theodoridis and M. Vassilakopoulos: "Closest Pair Queries in Spatial Databases", *Proceedings ACM SIGMOD Conference on Management of Data*, pp.189-200, Dallas, TX, 2000.

51. A. Corral, Y. Manolopoulos, Y. Theodoridis and M. Vassilakopoulos: "Multiway Distance Join Queries in Spatial Databases", *GeoInformatica*, Vol.8, No.4, pp.373-402, 2004.

52. A. Corral, Y. Manolopoulos, Y. Theodoridis and M. Vassilakopoulos: "Cost Models for Distance Join Queries Using R-trees", accepted, 2005.

53. A. Corral and M. Vassilakopoulos: "An Approximate Algorithms for Distance-Based Queries Using R-Trees, *The Computer Journal*, Vol.48, No.2, pp.220-238, 2005.

54. A. Corral, M. Vassilakopoulos and Y. Manolopoulos. "Algorithms for Joining R-Trees and Linear Region Quadtrees", *Proceedings 6th International Symposium on Spatial Databases (SSD'99)*, pp.251-269, Hong-Kong, China, 1999.

55. A. Corral, M. Vassilakopoulos and Y. Manolopoulos: "The Impact of Buffering on Closest Pairs Queries Using R-trees", *Proceedings 5th East European Conference on Advances in Databases and Information Systems (ADBIS'01)*, pp.41-54, Vilnius, Lithuania, 2001.

56. M. deBerg, M. Hammar, M.H. Overmars and J. Gudmundsson: "On R-trees with Low Stabbing Number", *Computational Geometry - Theory and Applications*, Vol.24, No.3, pp.179-195, 2002.

57. D. DeWitt and J. Gray: "Parallel Database Systems, the Future of High Performance Database Systems", *Communications of the ACM*, Vol.35, No.6, pp.85-98, 1992.

58. D.J. DeWitt, N. Kabra, J. Luo, J.M. Patel and J.-B. Yu: "Client-Server Paradise", *Proceedings 20th International Conference on Very Large Data Bases (VLDB'94)*, pp.558-569, Santiago, Chile, 1994.

59. EzSoft Engineering Website: http://www.ezgis.com

60. C. Faloutsos, *Searching Multimedia Databases by Content*, Kluwer Academic Press, 1996.

61. C. Faloutsos, R. Barber, M. Flickner, J. Hafner, W. Niblack, D. Petkovic and W. Equitz. "Efficient and Effective Querying by Image Content". *Journal of Intelligent Information Systems*, Vol.3, No.3/4, 231-262, 1994.

62. C. Faloutsos and I. Kamel: "Beyond Uniformity and Independence: Analysis of R-trees Using the Concept of Fractal Dimension", *Proceedings 13th ACM Symposium on Principles of Database Systems (PODS'94)*, pp.4-13, Minneapolis, MN, 1994.

63. C. Faloutsos, M. Ranganathan and Y. Manolopoulos. "Fast Subsequence Matching in Time-Series Databases". *Proceedings ACM SIGMOD Conference on Management of Data*, pp.419-429, Minneapolis, MN, 1994.

64. C. Faloutsos, B. Seeger, A. Traina and C. Traina: "Spatial Join Selectivity Using Power Law", *Proceedings ACM SIGMOD Conference on Management of Data*, pp.177-188, Dallas, TX, 2000.

65. C. Faloutsos, T. Sellis and N. Roussopoulos: "Analysis of Object-Oriented Spatial Access Methods", *Proceedings ACM SIGMOD Conference on Management of Data*, pp.426-439, San Francisco, CA, 1987.

66. H. Ferhatosmanoglu, I. Stanoi, D. Agrawal and A. Abbadi: "Constrained Nearest Neighbor Queries", *Proceedings 7th International Symposium on Spatial and Temporal Databases (SSTD'01)*, pp.257-278, Redondo Beach, CA, 2001.

67. E. Frentzos: "Indexing Objects Moving on Fixed Networks", *Proceedings 8th International Symposium on Spatial and Temporal Databases (SSTD'03)*, pp.289-305, Santorini Island, Greece, 2003.

68. X. Fu, D. Wang and W. Zheng: "GPR-tree, a Global Parallel Index Structure for Multiattribute Declustering on Cluster of Workstations", *Proceedings Conference on Advances in parallel and Distributed Computing (APDC'97)*, pp.300-306, Shanghai, China, 1997.

69. V. Gaede and O. Guenther: "Multidimensional Access Methods", *ACM Computing Surveys*, Vol.30, No.2, pp.170-231, 1998.

70. Y. Garcia, M. Lopez and S. Leutenegger: "A Greedy Algorithm for Bulk Loading R-trees", *Proceedings 6th ACM International Symposium on Advances in Geographic Information Systems (GIS'98)*, pp.163-164, Washington, DC, 1998.

71. Y. Garcia, M. Lopez and S. Leutenegger: "On Optimal Node Splitting for R-trees", *Proceedings 24th International Conference on Very Large Data Bases (VLDB'98)*, pp.334-344, New York, NY, 1998.

72. Y. Garcia, M. Lopez and S. Leutenegger: "Post-Optimization and Incremental Refinement of R-trees", *Proceedings 7th ACM International Symposium on Advances in Geographic Information Systems (GIS'99)*, pp.91-96, Kansas City, MO, 1999.

73. M. Gorawski and R. Malczok: "Aggregation and Analysis of Spatial Data by Means of Materialized Aggregation Tree", *Proceedings 3rd International Conference on Advances in Information Systems (ADVIS'04)*, pp.24-33, Izmir, Turkey, 2004.

74. M. Gorawski and R. Malczok: "Distributed Spatial Data Warehouse Indexed with Virtual Memory Aggregation Tree", *Proceedings 2nd International Workshop on Spatio-Temporal Database Management (STDBM'04)*, pp.25-32, Toronto, Canada, 2004

75. G. Graefe: "Query Evaluation Techniques for Large Databases", *ACM Computing Surveys*, Vol.25, No.2, pp.73-170, 1993.

76. J. Gray, A. Bosworth, A. Layman and H. Pirahesh. "Data Cube: a Relational Aggregation Operator Generalizing Group-By, Cross-Tab, and Sub-Totals", *Proceedings 12th IEEE International Conference on Data Engineering (ICDE'96)*, pp.152-159, New Orleans, LA, 1996.

77. O. Guenther: "The Cell Tree - an Object Oriented Index Structure for Geometric Databases", *Proceedings 5th IEEE International Conference on Data Engineering (ICDE'89)*, pp.598-605, Los Angeles, CA, 1989.

78. O. Guenther and V. Gaede: "Oversize Shelves - a Storage Management Technique for Large Spatial Data Objects", *International Journal of Geographical Information Science*, Vol.11, No.1, pp.5-32, 1997.

79. O. Guenther and H. Noltemeier: "Spatial Database Indices for Large Extended Objects", *Proceedings 7th IEEE International Conference on Data Engineering (ICDE'91)*, pp.520-526, Kobe, Japan, 1991.

80. C. Gurret, Y. Manolopoulos, A. Papadopoulos and P. Rigaux, "The BASIS System: a Benchmarking Approach for Spatial Index Structures", *Proceedings 1st International Workshop on Spatiotemporal Databases Management (STDBM'99)*, pp.152-170, Edinburgh, Scotland, 1999.

81. A. Guttman: "R-trees: a Dynamic Index Structure for Spatial Searching", *Proceedings ACM SIGMOD Conference on Management of Data*, pp.47-57, Boston, MA, 1984.

82. M. Hadjieleftheriou, G. Kollios and V. Tsotras: "Performance Evaluation of Spatio-Temporal Selectivity Estimation Techniques", *Proceedings 15th International Conference on Scientific and Statistical Database Management (SSDBM'03)*, pp.202-211, Cambridge, MA, 2003.

83. J. Han, K. Koperski and N. Stefanovic: "GeoMiner: a System Prototype for Spatial Data Mining", *Proceedings ACM SIGMOD Conference on Management of Data*, pp.553-556, Tucson, AZ, 1997.

84. J. Hellerstein, J. Naughton and A. Pfeffer: "Generalized Search Trees for Database Systems", *Proceedings 21st International Conference on Very Large Data Bases (VLDB'95)*, pp.562-573, Zurich, Switzerland, 1995.

85. J.M. Hellerstein and A. Pfeffer: "The RD-tree: an Index Structure for Sets", Technical Report No. 1252, University of California, Berkeley, 1994.

86. G. Hjaltason and H. Samet. "Ranking in Spatial Databases", *Proceedings 4th International Symposium on Spatial Databases (SSD'95)*, pp.83-95, Portland, ME, 1995.

87. G. Hjaltason and H. Samet: "Incremental Distance Join Algorithms for Spatial Databases", *Proceedings ACM SIGMOD Conference on Management of Data*, pp.237-248, Seattle, WA, 1998.

88. G. Hjaltason and H. Samet: "Distance Browsing in Spatial Databases", *ACM Transactions on Database Systems*, Vol.24, No.2, pp.265-318, 1999.

89. E.G. Hoel and H. Samet: "Performance of Data-Parallel Spatial Operations", *Proceedings 20th International Conference on Very Large Data Bases (VLDB'94)*, pp.156-167, Santiago, Chile, 1994.

90. E.G. Hoel and H. Samet: "Benchmarking Spatial Join Operations with Spatial Output", *Proceedings 21st International Conference on Very Large Data Bases (VLDB'95)*, pp.606-618, Zurich, Switzerland, 1995.

91. Y.-W. Huang, N. Jing and E. Rundensteiner: "A Cost Model for Estimating the Performance of Spatial Joins Using R-trees", *Proceedings 9th International Conference on Scientific and Statistical Database Management (SSDBM'97)*, pp.30-38, Olympia, WA, 1997.

92. Y.-W. Huang, N. Jing and E. Rundensteiner. "Spatial Joins Using R-trees: Breadth-First Traversal with Global Optimizations", *Proceedings 23rd International Conference on Very Large Data Bases (VLDB'97)*, pp.396-405, Athens, Greece, 1997.

93. P.W. Huang, P.L. Lin and H.Y. Lin: "Optimizing Storage Utilization in R-tree Dynamic Index Structure for Spatial Databases", *Journal of Systems and Software*, Vol.55, No.3, pp.291-299, 2001.

94. Informix Corporation: "The Informix R-tree Index User's Guide", Informix Press, 2001.

95. Y. Ioannidis and Y. Kang: "Randomized Algorithms for Optimizing Large Join Queries", *Proceedings ACM SIGMOD Conference on Management of Data*, pp.312-321, Atlantic City, NJ, 1990.

96. H.V. Jagadish: "Spatial Search with Polyhedra", *Proceedings 6th IEEE International Conference on Data Engineering (ICDE'90)*, pp.311-319, Orlando, FL, 1990.

97. H.V. Jagadish: "Analysis of the Hilbert Curve for Representing Two-Dimensional Space", *Information Processing Letters*, Vol.62, No.1, pp.17-22, 1997.

98. C.S. Jensen and R. Snodgrass: "Semantics of Time-Varying Information", *Information Systems*, Vol.21, No.4, pp.311-352, 1996.

99. J. Jin, N. An and A. Sivasubramanian: "Analyzing Range Queries on Spatial Data", *Proceedings 16th IEEE International Conference on Data Engineering (ICDE'00)*, pp.525-534, San Diego, CA, 2000.

100. H. Jin and H.V. Jagadish: "Indexing Hidden Markov Models for Music Retrieval", *Proceedings 3rd International Symposium on Music Information Retrieval (ISMIR'02)*, Paris, France, 2002.

101. T. Johnson and D. Shasha: "The Performance of Concurrent B-tree Algorithms", *ACM Transactions on Database Systems*, Vol.18, No.1, pp.51-101, 1993.

102. M. Juergens and H. Lenz: "The Ra*-tree - an Improved R-tree with Material-ized Data for Supporting Range Queries on OLAP Data", *Proceedings 9th International Workshop on Database and Expert Systems Applications (DEXA'98)*, pp.186-191, Vienna, Austria, 1998.

103. I. Kamel and C. Faloutsos: "Parallel R-trees", *Proceedings ACM SIGMOD Conference on Management of Data*, pp.195-204, San Diego, CA, 1992.

104. I. Kamel and C. Faloutsos: "On Packing R-trees", *Proceedings 2nd ACM International Conference on Information and Knowledge Management (CIKM'93)*, pp.490-499, Washington, DC, 1993.

105. I. Kamel and C. Faloutsos: "Hilbert R-tree - an Improved R-tree Using Fractals", *Proceedings 20th International Conference on Very Large Data Bases (VLDB'94)*, pp.500-509, Santiago, Chile, 1994.

106. I. Karydis, A. Nanopoulos, A. Papadopoulos and Y. Manolopoulos: "Audio Indexing for Efficient Music Information Retrieval". *Proceedings 11th International Multimedia Modeling Conference (MMM'05)*, Melbourne, Australia, 2005.

107. I. Karydis, A. Nanopoulos, A. Papadopoulos and Y. Manolopoulos: "Musical Retrieval in P2P Networks under the Warping Distance", *Proceedings 8th International Conference on Enterprise Information Systems (ICEIS'05)*, Miami, FL, 2005.

108. N. Katayama and S. Satoh: "The SR-tree - an Index Structure for High-Dimensional Nearest Neighbor Queries", *Proceedings ACM SIGMOD Conference on Management of Data*, pp.369-380, Tucson, AZ, 1997.

109. L. Kaufman and P. Rousseeuw: *Finding Groups in Data: an Introduction to Cluster Analysis*, Wiley, 1990.

110. K. Kim, S. Cha and K. Kwon: "Optimizing Multidimensional Index Trees for Main Memory Access", *Proceedings ACM SIGMOD Conference on Management of Data*, pp.139-150, Santa Barbara, CA, 2001

111. D. Knuth: *The Art of Computer Programming: Sorting and Searching*, Vol.3, Addison-Wesley, 1967.

112. G. Kollios, D. Gunopoulos and V. Tsotras: "On Indexing Mobile Objects", *Proceedings 18th ACM Symposium on Principles of Database Systems (PODS'99)*, pp.261-272, Philadelphia, PA, 1999.

113. G. Kollios, V.J. Tsotras, D. Gunopoulos, A. Delis and M. Hadjieleftheriou: "Indexing Animated Objects Using Spatiotemporal Access Methods", *IEEE Transactions on Knowledge and Data Engineering*, Vol.13, No.5, pp.758-777, 2001.

114. K. Koperski and J. Han: "Discovery of Spatial Association Rules in Geographic Information Databases", *Proceedings 4th International Symposium on Spatial Databases (SSD'95)*, pp.47-66, Portland, ME, 1995.

115. F. Korn and S. Muthujrishnan: "Influence Sets Based on Reverse Neighbor Queries", Technical Report, AT&T Labs Research, 1999.

116. F. Korn, B.U. Pagel and C. Faloutsos: "On the 'Dimensionality Curse' and the 'Self-Similarity Blessing'", *IEEE Transactions on Knowledge and Data Engineering*, Vol.13, No.1, pp.96-111, 2001.

117. F. Korn, N. Sidiropoulos, C. Faloutsos, E. Siegel and Z. Protopapas: "Fast Nearest Neighbor Search in Medical Image Databases", *Proceedings 22nd International Conference on Very Large Databases*, pp.215-226, Mumbai, India, 1996.

118. M. Kornacker: "High-Performance Extensible Indexing", *Proceedings 25th International Conference on Very Large Data Bases (VLDB'99)*, pp.699-708, Edinburgh, Scotland, 1999.

119. M. Kornacker and D. Banks: "High-Concurrency Locking in R-trees", *Proceedings 21st International Conference on Very Large Data Bases (VLDB'95)*, pp.134-145, Zurich, Switzerland, 1995.

120. R.K.V. Kothuri, S. Ravada and D. Abugov: "Quadtree and R-tree Indexes in Oracle Spatial: a Comparison Using GIS Data", *Proceedings ACM SIGMOD Conference on Management of Data*, pp.546-557, Madison, WI, 2002.

121. R.K.V. Kothuri, A. Godfrind and Beinat: *Pro Oracle Spatial: an Essential Guide to Developing Spatially-Enabled Business Applications*, Apress, 2004.

122. Y. Kotidis and N. Roussopoulos, "An Alternative Storage Organization for ROLAP Aggregate Views Based on Cubetrees", *Proceedings ACM SIGMOD Conference on Management of Data*, pp.249-258, Seattle, WA, 1998.

123. N. Koudas, C. Faloutsos and I. Kamel: "Declustering Spatial Databases on a Multi-computer Architecture", *Proceedings 6th International Conference on Extending Database Technology (EDBT'96)*, pp.592-614, Avignon, France, 1996.

124. H.-P. Kriegel, P. Kunath, M. Pfeifle, M. Potke, M. Renz and P.-M. Strauss: "Stochastic Driven Relational R-Tree", *Proceedings Brazilian Symposium on Geoinformatics (GEOINFO)*, Campos do Jordao (SP), Brazil, 2003.

125. A. Kumar, V.J. Tsotras and C. Faloutsos: "Designing Access Methods for Bitemporal Databases", *IEEE Transactions on Knowledge and Data Engineering*, Vol.10, No.1, pp.1-20, 1998.

126. R. Kurniawati, J.S. Jin and J.A. Shepard: "SS⁺-tree: an Improved Index Structure for Similarity Searches in a High-Dimensional Feature Space", *Proceedings 5th Conference on Storage and Retrieval for Image and Video Databases (SPIE'97*, pp.110-120, San Jose, CA, 1997.

127. D. Kwon, S.J. Lee and S. Lee: "Indexing the Current Positions of Moving Objects Using the Lazy Update R-tree", *Proceedings 3rd International Conference on Mobile Data Management (MDM'02)*, pp.113-120, Singapore, 2002.

128. S. Lai, F. Zhu and Y. Sun: "A Design of Parallel R-tree on Cluster of Workstations", *Proceedings 1st International Workshop Databases in Networked Information Systems (DNIS'00)*, pp.119-133, Aizu, Japan, 2000.

129. C. Lang and A. Singh: "Modeling High Dimensional Index Structures Using Sampling", *Proceedings ACM SIGMOD Conference on Management of Data*, pp.389-400, Santa Barbara, CA, 2001.

130. R. Laurini and D. Thomson: *Fundamentals of Spatial Information Systems*, Academic Press, London, 1992.

131. T. Lee and S. Lee: "OMT - Overlap Minimizing Top-down Bulk Loading Algorithm for R-tree", *Proceedings of Short Papers at 15th Conference on Advanced Information Systems Engineering (CAiSE'03)*, Klagenfurt, Austria, 2003.

132. T. Lee, B. Moon and S. Lee: "Bulk Insertion for R-tree by Seeded Clustering", *Proceedings 14th International Conference on Database and Expert Systems Applications (DEXA'03)*, pp.129-138, Prague, Czech Republic, 2003.

133. Y.J. Lee and C.W. Chung: "The DR-tree - a Main Memory Data Structure for Complex Multidimensional Objects", *Geoinformatica*, Vol.5, No.2, pp.181-207, 2001.

134. S. Leutenegger, J.M. Edgington and M.A. Lopez: "STR - a Simple and Efficient Algorithm for R-tree Packing", *Proceedings 13th IEEE International Conference on Data Engineering (ICDE'97)*, pp.497-506, Birmingham, England, 1997.

135. S. Leutenegger and M. Lopez: "A Buffer Model for Evaluating the Performance of R-tree Packing Algorithms", *Proceedings ACM International Conference on Measurements and Modeling of Computer Systems (SIGMETRICS)*, pp.264-265, Philadelphia, PA, 1996.

136. S. Leutenegger and M. Lopez: "The Effect of Buffering on the Performance of R-trees", *IEEE Transactions on Knowledge and Data Engineering*, Vol.12, No.1, pp.33-44, 2000.

137. S. Leutenegger, R. Sheykhet and M. Lopez: "A Mechanism to Detect Changing Access Patterns and Automatically Migrate Distributed R-tree Indexed Multidimensional Data", *Proceedings 8th ACM International Symposium on Ad-*

vances in Geographic Information Systems (GIS'00), pp.147-152, Washington, DC, 2000.

138. K.-I. Lin, H. V. Jagadish and C. Faloutsos: "The TV-Tree: an Index Structure for High-Dimensional Data", *The VLDB Journal*, Vol.3, No.4, pp.517-542, 1994.

139. M.-L. Lo and C. Ravishankar: "Spatial Joins Using Seeded Trees", *Proceedings ACM SIGMOD Conference on Management of Data*, pp.209-220, Minneapolis, MN, 1994.

140. M.-L. Lo and C.V. Ravishankar: "Spatial Hash-Joins", *Proceedings ACM SIGMOD Conference on Management of Data*, pp.247-258, Montreal, Canada, 1996.

141. G. Lu: "*Multimedia Database Management Systems*", Artech House, 1999.

142. N. Mamoulis and D. Papadias: "Integration of Spatial Join Algorithms for Processing Multiple Inputs", *Proceedings ACM SIGMOD Conference on Management of Data*, pp.1-12, Philadelphia, PA, 1999.

143. N. Mamoulis and D. Papadias: "Selectivity Estimation of Complex Spatial Queries", *Proceedings 7th International Symposium on Spatial and Temporal Databases (SSTD'01)*, pp.155-174, Redondo Beach, CA, 2001.

144. N. Mamoulis and D. Papadias: "Multiway Spatial Joins", *ACM Transactions on Database Systems*, Vol.26, No.4, pp.424-475, 2001.

145. N. Mamoulis and D. Papadias: "Slot Index Spatial Join", *IEEE Transactions on Knowledge and Data Engineering*, Vol.15, No.1, pp.211-231, 2003.

146. Y. Manolopoulos, E. Nardelli, A. N. Papadopoulos, and G. Proietti: "QR-tree: a Hybrid Spatial Data Structure", *Proceedings 1st International Conference on Geographic Information Systems in Urban, Regional and Environmental Planning*, pp.247-262, Samos Island, Greece, 1996.

147. Y. Manolopoulos, Y. Theodoridis and V. Tsotras: "*Advanced Database Indexing*", Kluwer Academic Publishers, 1999.

148. Mapinfo Website: http://www.mapinfo.com

149. M. Martynov. "Spatial Joins and R-trees", *Proceedings 2nd International Workshop on Advances in Databases and Information Systems (ADBIS'95)*, pp.295-304, Moscow, Russia, 1995.

150. C. Mina: "Mapinfo SpatialWare: a Spatial Information Server for RDBMS", *Proceedings 24th International Conference on Very Large Data Bases (VLDB'98)*, p.704, New York, NY, 1998.

151. Y. Mond and Y. Raz: "Concurrency Control in B$^+$-trees Databases Using Preparatory Operations", *Proceedings 11th International Conference on Very Large Data Bases (VLDB'85)*, pp.331-334, Stockholm, Sweden, 1985.

152. B. Moon, H.V. Jagadish, C. Faloutsos and J.H. Saltz: "Analysis of the Clustering Properties of the Hilbert Space-Filling Curve", *IEEE Transactions on Knowledge and Data Engineering*, Vol.13, No.1, pp.124-141, 2001.

153. A. Nanopoulos and P. Bozanis: "Categorical Range Queries in Large Databases", *Proceedings International Symposium on Spatial and Temporal Databases (SSTD'03)*, pp.122-139, Santorini Island, 2003.

154. A. Nanopoulos, Y. Theodoridis and Y. Manolopoulos: "C^{2}P - Clustering with Closest Pairs", *Proceedings 27th International Conference on Very Large Data Bases (VLDB'01)*, pp.331-340, Rome, Italy, 2001.

155. A. Nanopoulos, Y. Theodoridis and Y. Manolopoulos: "An Efficient and Effective Algorithm for Density Biased Sampling", *Proceedings 11th ACM International Conference on Information and Knowledge Management (CIKM'02)*, pp.398-404, MacLean, VA, 2002.

156. A. Nanopoulos, M. Vassilakopoulos and Y. Manolopoulos: "Performance Evaluation of Lazy Deletion Methods in R-trees", *GeoInformatica*, Vol.7, No.4, pp.337-354, 2003.

157. B. Nam and A. Sussman: "A Comparative Study of Spatial Indexing Techniques for Multidimensional Scientific Datasets", *Proceedings 16th International Conference on Scientific and Statistical Database Management (SSDBM'04)*, pp.171-180, Santorini Island, Greece, 2004.

158. M.A. Nascimento and J.R.O. Silva: "Towards Historical R-trees", *Proceedings 13th ACM Symposium on Applied Computing (SAC'98)*, pp.235-240, Atlanta, GA, 1998.

159. M.A. Nascimento, J.R.O. Silva and Y. Theodoridis: "Evaluation of Access Structures for Discretely Moving Points", *Proceedings 1st International Symposium on Spatiotemporal Database Management (STDBM'99)*, pp.171-188, Edinburgh, Scotland, 1999.

160. V. Ng and T. Kameda: "Concurrent Access to R-trees", *Proceedings 3rd International Symposium on Spatial Databases (SSD'93)*, pp.142-161, Singapore, 1993.

161. V. Ng and T. Kameda: "The R-link Tree: a Recoverable Index Structure for Spatial Data", *Proceedings 5th International Workshop on Database and Expert Systems Applications (DEXA'94)*, pp.163-172, Athens, Greece, 1994.

162. K. S. Oh, Y. Feng, K. Kaneko and A. Makinouchi: "SOM Based R*-tree for Similarity Retrieval", *Proceedings 7th International Conference on Database Systems for Advanced Applications (DASFAA'01)*, pp.182-198, Hong Kong, China, 2001.

163. F. Olken and D. Rotem: "Sampling from Spatial Databases", *Proceedings 9th IEEE International Conference on Data Engineering (ICDE93)*, pp.199-208, Vienna, Austria, 1993.

164. P. Oosterom: "Reactive Data Structures for Geographic Information Systems", Ph.D. dissertation, University of Leiden, 1990.

165. Oracle WebSite: http://www.oracle.com.

166. B.-U. Pagel and H.-W. Six: "Are Window Queries Representative for Arbitrary Range Queries?", *Proceedings 15th ACM Symposium on Principles of Database Systems (PODS'96)*, pp.150-160, Montreal, Canada, 1996.

167. B.-U. Pagel, H.-W. Six, H. Toben and P. Widmayer: "Towards an Analysis of Range Query Performance", *Proceedings 12th ACM Symposium on Principles of Database Systems (PODS'93)*, pp.214-221, Washington, DC, 1993.

168. B.-U. Pagel, H.-W. Six and M. Winter: "Window Query-Optimal Clustering of Spatial Objects", *Proceedings 14th ACM Symposium on Principles of Database Systems (PODS'95)*, pp.86-94, San Jose, CA, 1995.

169. D. Papadias and D. Arkoumanis: "Approximate Processing of Multiway Spatial Joins in Very Large Databases", *Proceedings 8th International Conference on Extending Database Technology (EDBT'02)*, pp.179-196, Prague, Czech Republic, 2002.

170. D. Papadias, P. Kanlis, J. Zhang and Y. Tao: "Efficient OLAP Operations in Spatial Data Warehouses", *Proceedings 7th International Symposium on Spatial and temporal Databases (SSTD'01)*, pp.443-459, Redondo Beach, CA, 2001.

171. D. Papadias, N. Mamoulis and Y. Theodoridis. "Processing and Optimization of Multiway Spatial Joins Using R-trees", *Proceedings 18th ACM Symposium on Principles of Database Systems (PODS'99)*, pp.44-55, Philadelphia, PA, 1999.

172. D. Papadias, N. Mamoulis and Y. Theodoridis: "Constraint-based Processing of Multi-way Spatial Joins", *Algorithmica*, Vol.30, No.2, pp.188-215, 2001.

173. D. Papadias, Y. Tao, P. Kanlis and J. Zhang: "Indexing Spatio-Temporal Data Warehouses", *Proceedings 18th IEEE International Conference on Data Engineering (ICDE'02)*, pp.166-175, San Jose, CA, 2002.

174. D. Papadias, Y. Theodoridis and T. Sellis: "The Retrieval of Direction Relations Using R-trees", *Proceedings 5th International Workshop on Database and Expert Systems Applications (DEXA'94)*, pp.173-182, Athens, Greece, 1994.

175. D. Papadias, Y. Theodoridis, T. Sellis and M. Egenhofer: "Topological Relations in the World of Minimum Bounding Rectangles: a Study with R-trees", *Proceedings ACM SIGMOD Conference on Management of Data*, pp.92-103, San Jose, CA, 1995.

176. A.N. Papadopoulos and Y. Manolopoulos: "Parallel Processing of Nearest Neighbor Queries in Declustered Spatial Data", *Proceedings 4th ACM International Symposium on Advances in Geographic Information Systems (GIS'96)*, pp.37-43, Rockville, MD, 1996.

177. A.N. Papadopoulos and Y. Manolopoulos: "Performance of Nearest Neighbor Queries in R-trees", *Proceedings 6th International Conference on Database Theory (ICDT'97)*, pp.394-408, Delphi, Greece, 1997.

178. A.N. Papadopoulos and Y. Manolopoulos: "Nearest-Neighbor Queries in Shared-Nothing Environments", *Geoinformatica*, Vol.1, No.4, pp.369-392, 1997.

179. A.N. Papadopoulos and Y. Manolopoulos: "Similarity Query Processing Using Disk Arrays", *Proceedings ACM SIGMOD Conference on Management of Data*, pp.225-236, Seattle, WA, 1998.

180. A.N. Papadopoulos and Y. Manolopoulos: "Parallel Bulk-Loading of Spatial Data", *Parallel Computing*, Vol.29, No.10, pp.1419-1444, 2003.

181. A.N. Papadopoulos, P. Rigaux and M. Scholl: "A Performance Evaluation of Spatial Join Processing Strategies", *Proceedings 6th International Symposium on Spatial Databases (SSD'99)*, pp.286-307, Hong-Kong, China, 1999.

182. H.-H. Park, G.-H. Cha and C.-W. Chung. "Multi-way Spatial Joins Using R-trees: Methodology and Performance Evaluation", *Proceedings 6th International Symposium on Spatial Databases (SSD'99)*, pp.229-250, Hong-Kong, China, 1999.

183. H.-H. Park and C.-W. Chung: "Complexity of Estimating Multi-way Join Result Sizes for Area Skewed Spatial Data", *Information Processing Letters*, Vol.76, No.3, pp.121-129, 2000.

184. D.J. Park, S. Heu and H.J. Kim: "The RS-tree - an Efficient Data Structure for Distance Browsing Queries", *Information Processing Letters*, Vol.80, No.4, pp.195-203, 2001.

185. M. Park and S. Lee: "Optimizing Both Cache and Disk Performance of R-trees", *Proceedings 14th International Workshop on Database and Expert Systems Applications (DEXA'03)*, pp.139-147, Prague, Czech Republic, 2003.

186. J. Patel and D. DeWitt. "Partition Based Spatial-Merge Join", *Proceedings ACM SIGMOD Conference on Management of Data*, pp.259-270, Montreal, Canada, 1996.

187. D.A. Patterson, G. Gibson and R.H. Katz: "A Case for Redundant Arrays of Inexpensive Disks (RAID)", *Proceedings ACM SIGMOD Conference on Management of Data*, pp.109-116, Chicago, IL, 1988.

188. M. Pelanis, S. Saltenis, and C.S. Jensen: "Indexing the Past, Present and Anticipated Future Positions of Moving Objects", Technical Report TR-78, Time Center, 1999. Time Center Website: http://www.cs.auc.dk/TimeCenter/

189. D. Pfoser, C.S. Jensen and Y. Theodoridis: "Novel Approaches to the Indexing of Moving Object Trajectories", *Proceedings 26th International Conference on Very Large Data Bases (VLDB'00)*, pp.395-406, Cairo, Egypt, 2000.

190. PostgreSQL Website: http://www.postgresql.org

191. S. Prabhakar, Y. Xia, D.V. Kalashnikov, W.G. Aref and S.E. Hambrusch: "Query Indexing and Velocity Constrained Indexing: Scalable Techniques for Continuous Queries on Moving Objects", *IEEE Transactions on Computers*, Vol.51, No.10, pp.1124-1140, 2002.

192. C. Procopiuc, P. Agarwal and S. Har-Peled: "STAR-tree: an Efficient Self-adjusting Index for Moving Points", *Proceedings 3rd Workshop on Algorithm*

Engineering and Experiments (ALENEX'01), pp.178-193, San Francisco, CA, 2001.

193. G. Proietti and C. Faloutsos: "Analysis of Range Queries and Self-Spatial Join Queries on Real Region Datasets Stored Using an R-tree", *IEEE Transactions on Knowledge and Data Engineering*, Vol.12, No.5, pp.751-762, 2000.

194. K. Raptopoulou, Y. Manolopoulos and A.N. Papadopoulos: "Fast Nearest-Neighbor Search in Moving Object Databases", *International Journal on Advances of Computer Science for Geographical Information Systems (Geoinformatica)*, Vol.7, No.2, pp.113-137, 2003.

195. K. Raptopoulou, A.N. Papadopoulos and Y. Manolopoulos: "Incremental Nearest-Neighbor Search in Moving Objects", *Proceedings of IEEE International Conference on Pervasive Services (ICPS'05)*, Santorini Island, 2005.

196. S. Ravada and G. Sharma: "Oracle8i: Experiences with Extensible Databases", *Proceedings 6th International Symposium on Spatial Databases (SSD'99)*, pp.355-359, Hong Kong, China, 1999.

197. N. Roussopoulos, S. Kelley and F. Vincent. "Nearest Neighbor Queries", *Proceedings ACM SIGMOD Conference on Management of Data*, pp.71-79, San Jose, CA, 1995.

198. N. Roussopoulos and Y. Kotidis "Cubetree: Organization of and Bulk Updates on the Data Cube", *Proceedings ACM SIGMOD Conference on Management of Data*, pp.89-99, Tucson, AZ, 1997.

199. N. Roussopoulos and D. Leifker: "Direct Spatial Search on Pictorial Databases Using Packed R-trees", *Proceedings ACM SIGMOD Conference on Management of Data*, pp.17-31, Austin, TX, 1985.

200. Y. Sagiv: "Concurrent Operations on B-trees with Overtaking", *Proceedings 4th ACM Symposium on Principles of Database Systems (PODS'85)*, pp.28-37, Portland, OR, 1985.

201. S. Saltenis and C.S. Jensen: "R-tree based Indexing of General Spatiotemporal Data", Technical Report TR-45, Time Center, 1999. Time Center Website: http://www.cs.auc.dk/TimeCenter/

202. S. Saltenis, C.S. Jensen, S. Leutenegger and M. Lopez: "Indexing the Positions of Continuously Moving Objects", *Proceedings ACM SIGMOD Conference on Management of Data*, pp.331-342, Dallas, TX, 2000.

203. H. Samet: *The Design and Analysis of Spatial Data Structures*, Addison-Wesley, Reading MA, 1990.

204. H. Samet: *Applications of Spatial Data Structures*, Addison-Wesley, Reading MA, 1990.

205. J. Schiller and A. Voisard (eds.): *Location-based Services*, Morgan Kaufmann/Elsevier, San Francisco, CA, 2004.

206. M. Schiwietz: "Speicherung und Anfragebearbeitung Komplexer Geo-objekte", Ph.D. dissertation, Ludwig-Maximilians-Universitaet Muenchen, 1993.

207. B. Schnitzer and S. Leutenegger: "Master-Client R-trees - a New Parallel R-tree Architecture", *Proceedings 11th International Conference on Scientific and Statistical Database Management (SSDBM'99)*, pp.68-77, Cleveland, OH, 1999.

208. T. Schrek and Z. Chen: "Branch Grafting Method for R-tree Implementation", *Journal of Systems and Software*, Vol.53, No.1, pp.83-93, 2000.

209. B. Seeger and P.A. Larson: "Multi-disk B-trees", *Proceedings ACM SIGMOD Conference on Management of Data*, pp.436-445, Denver, Colorado, 1991.

210. T. Seidl and H.-P. Kriegel: "Optimal Multi-Step k-Nearest Neighbor Search", *Proceedings ACM SIGMOD Conference on Management of Data*, pp.154-165, Seattle, WA, 1998.

211. T. Sellis, N. Roussopoulos and C. Faloutsos: "The R^+-tree - a Dynamic Index for Multidimensional Objects", *Proceedings 13th International Conference on Very Large Data Bases (VLDB'87)*, pp.507-518, Brighton, England, 1987.

212. T. Sellis, N. Roussopoulos and C. Faloutsos: "Multidimensional Access Methods: Trees Have Grown Everywhere", *Proceedings 23rd International Conference on Very Large Data Bases (VLDB'97)*, pp.13-14, Athens, Greece, 1997.

213. J. Sharma: "Implementation of Spatial and Multimedia Extensions in Commercial Systems", tutorial during the 6th International Symposium on Spatial Databases (SSD'99), Hong-Kong, China, 1999.

214. D. Shasha and N. Goodman: "Concurrent Search Structure Algorithms", *ACM Transaction on Database Systems*, Vol.13, No.1, pp.53-90, 1988.

215. A. Shatdal and J.F. Naughton: "Using Shared Virtual Memory for Parallel Processing", *Proceedings ACM SIGMOD Conference on Management of Data*, pp.119-128, Washington, DC, 1993.

216. H. Shin, B. Moon and S. Lee: "Adaptive Multi-Stage Distance Join Processing", *Proceedings ACM SIGMOD Conference on Management of Data*, pp.343-354, Dallas, TX, 2000.

217. A.P. Sistla, O. OWolfson, S. Chamberlain and S. Dao: "Modeling and Querying Moving Objects", *Proceedings 13th IEEE International Conference on Data Engineering (ICDE'97)*, pp.422-432, Birmingham, UK, 1997.

218. R. Snodgrass and T. Ahn: "A Taxonomy of Time in Databases", *Proceedings ACM SIGMOD Conference on Management of Data*, pp.236-246, Austin, TX, 1985.

219. I. Stanoi, D. Agrawal and A. Abbadi. "Reverse Nearest Neighbor Queries for Dynamic Datasets", *Proceedings 5th ACM SIGMOD Workshop on Research Issues in Data Mining and Knowledge Discovery (DMKD'00)*, pp.44-53, Dallas, TX, 2000.

220. M. Stonebraker, T. Sellis and E. Hanson: "An Analysis of Rule Indexing Implementations in Data Base Systems", *Proceedings 1st Conference on Expert Database Systems*, pp.465-476, Charleston, SC, 1986.

221. C. Sun, D. Agrawal and A. El Abbadi: "Selectivity Estimation for Spatial Joins with Geometric Selections", *Proceedings 18th IEEE International Conference on Data Engineering (ICDE'02)*, pp.609-626, San Jose, CA, 2002.

222. Y. Tao and D. Papadias: "Efficient Historical R-trees", *Proceedings 13th International Conference on Scientific and Statistical Database Management (SSDBM'01)*, pp.223-232, Fairfax, VA, 2001.

223. Y. Tao and D. Papadias: "MV3R-tree - a Spatio-Temporal Access Method for Timestamp and Interval Queries", *Proceedings 27th International Conference on Very Large Data Bases (VLDB'01)*, pp.431- 440, Rome, Italy, 2001.

224. Y. Tao and D. Papadias: "Time-Parameterized Queries in Spatio-Temporal Databases", *Proceedings ACM SIGMOD Conference on Management of Data*, pp. 334-345, Madison WI, 2002.

225. Y. Tao and D. Papadias: "Performance Analysis of R*-trees with Arbitrary Node Extents", *IEEE Transactions on Knowledge and Data Engineering*, Vol.16, No.6, pp.653-668, 2004.

226. Y. Tao, D. Papadias, N. Mamoulis and J. Zhang: "An Efficient Cost Model for k-NN Search", Technical Report HKUST-CS01-13, 2001.

227. Y. Tao, D. Papadias and J. Sun: "The TPR∗-tree: an Optimized Spatiotemporal Access Method for Predictive Queries", *Proceedings 28th International Conference on Very Large Data Bases (VLDB'02)*, pp.790-801, Berlin, Germany, 2003.

228. Y. Tao, D. Papadias and J. Zhang: "Aggregate Processing of Planar Points", *Proceedings 8th International Conference on Extending Database Technology (EDBT'02)*, pp.682-700, Prague, Czech Republic, 2002.

229. Y. Tao, D. Papadias and J. Zhang: "Cost Models for Overlapping and Multiversion Structures", *ACM Transactions on Database Systems*, Vol.27, No.3, pp.299-342, 2002.

230. Y. Tao, J. Sun and D. Papadias: "Analysis of Predictive Spatio-Temporal Queries", *ACM Transactions on Database Systems*, Vol.28, No.4, pp.295-336, 2003.

231. Y. Tao, J. Zhang, D. Papadias and N. Mamoulis: "An Efficient Cost Model for Optimization of Nearest Neighbor Search in Low and Medium Dimensional Spaces", *IEEE Transactions on Knowledge and Data Engineering*, Vol.16, No.10, pp.1169-1184, 2004.

232. Y. Theodoridis: "Ten Benchmark Database Queries for Location-Based Services", *The Computer Journal*, Vol.46, No.6, pp.713-725, 2003.

233. Y. Theodoridis and T. Sellis: "Optimization Issues in R-tree Construction", *Proceedings International Workshop on Advanced Research in Geographic Information Systems (IGIS'94)*, pp.270-273, Ascona, Switzerland, 1994.

234. Y. Theodoridis and T. Sellis: "A Model for the Prediction of R-tree Performance", *Proceedings 15th ACM Symposium on Principles of Database Systems (PODS'96)*, pp.161-171, Montreal, Canada, 1996.

235. Y. Theodoridis, J.R.O. Silva and M.A. Nascimento: "On the Generation of Spatiotemporal Datasets", *Proceedings 6th International Symposium on Spatial Databases (SSD'99)*, pp.147-164, Hong Kong, China, 1999.

236. Y. Theodoridis, E. Stefanakis and T. Sellis: "Cost Models for Join Queries in Spatial Databases", *Proceedings 14th IEEE International Conference on Data Engineering (ICDE'98)*, pp.476-483, Orlando, FL, 1998.

237. Y. Theodoridis, E. Stefanakis and T. Sellis: "Efficient Cost Models for Spatial Queries Using R-trees", *IEEE Transactions on Knowledge and Data Engineering*, Vol.12, No.1, pp.19-32, 2000.

238. Y. Theodoridis, M. Vazirgiannis and T. Sellis: "Spatio-Temporal Indexing for Large Multimedia Applications", *Proceedings 3rd IEEE International Conference on Multimedia Computing and Systems (ICMCS'96)*, pp.441-448, Hiroshima, Japan, 1996.

239. TIGER/Line Files, 1994 Technical Documentation, Prepared by the Bureau of the Census, Washington, DC, 1994.

240. V. Vasaitis, A. Nanopoulos and P. Bozanis: "Merging R-trees". *Proceedings 16th International Conference on Scientific and Statistical Database Management (SSDBM'04)*, pp.41-150, Santorini Island, Greece, 2004.

241. M. Vazirgiannis, Y. Theodoridis and T. Sellis: "Spatio-Temporal Composition and Indexing in Large Multimedia Applications", *ACM Multimedia Systems*, Vol.6, No.4, pp.284-298, 1998.

242. B. Wang, H. Horinokuchi, K. Kaneko and A. Makinouchi: "Parallel R-tree Search Algorithm on DSVM", *Proceedings 6th International Conference on Database Systems for Advanced Applications (DASFAA'99)*, pp.237-245, Hsinchu, Taiwan, 1999.

243. R. Weber, H.J. Schek and S. Blott: "A Quantitative Analysis and Performance Study for Similarity-Search Methods in High-Dimensional Spaces", *Proceedings 24th International Conference on Very Large Data Bases (VLDB'98)*, pp.194-205, New York, NY, 1998.

244. D.A White and R. Jain: "Similarity Indexing: Algorithms and Performance", *Proceedings 4th International Conference on Storage and Retrieval for Image and Video Databases (SPIE'96)*, pp.62-73, San Diego, CA, 1996.

245. D.A. White and R. Jain: "Similarity Indexing with the SS-tree", *Proceedings 12th IEEE International Conference on Data Engineering (ICDE'96)*, pp.516-523, New Orleans, LA, 1996.

246. O. Wolfson, B. Xu, S. Chamberlain and L. Jiang: "Moving Objects Databases: Issues and Solutions", *Proceedings 10th International Conference on Scientific and Statistical Database Management (SSDBM'98)*, pp.111-122, Capri, Italy, 1998.

247. C.H. Wu, L.P. Chang and T.W. Kuo: "An Efficient R-tree Implemantation over Flash-memory Storage Systems", *Proceedings 11th ACM International Symposium on Advances in Geographical Information Systems (GIS'03)*, pp.17-24, New Orleans, LA, 2003.

248. Y. Xia and S. Prabhakar: "Q+R-tree: Efficient Indexing for Moving Object Databases", *Proceedings 8th International Conference on Database Systems for Advanced Applications (DASFAA'03)*, pp.175-182, Kyoto, Japan, 2003.

249. X. Xu, J. Han and W. Lu: "RT-tree: an Improved R-tree Index Structure for Spatiotemporal Databases", *Proceedings 4th International Symposium on Spatial Data Handling (SDH'90)*, pp.1040-1049, Zurich, Switzerland, 1990.

250. J. Zhang, N. Mamoulis, D. Papadias and Y. Tao: "All-Nearest-Neighbors Queries in Spatial Databases", *Proceedings 16th International Conference on Scientific and Statistical Database Management (SSDBM'04)*, pp.297-306, Santorini Island, Greece, 2004.

251. Y. Zhou, S. Shekhar and M. Coyle: "Disk Allocation Methods for Parallelizing Grid Files", *Proceedings 10th IEEE International Conference on Data Engineering (ICDE'94)*, pp.243-252, Houston, TX, 1994.

Index